D1615731

EZEKIEL
Prophecy of Hope

EZEKIEL
Prophecy of Hope

by
Andrew W. Blackwood, Jr.

BAKER BOOK HOUSE
Grand Rapids, Michigan
1965

EZEKIEL: Prophecy of Hope

Library of Congress Catalog Card Number: 65-18261
Copyright, 1965, by Baker Book House Company
Printed in the United States of America
First printing, June 1965

To
N.V.
with many thanks

Acknowledgments

The following publishers have graciously given permission to quote from copyright material:

The Abingdon Press, Nashville
    Herbert G. May and E. L. Allen, The Interpreter's Bible, *The Book of Ezekiel*, 1956.

T. & T. Clark, Edinburgh
    G. A. Cooke, The International Critical Commentary, *The Book of Ezekiel*, 1936.

Doubleday & Company, Inc., Garden City
    Theodore H. Gaster, *The Dead Sea Scriptures*.

Harper & Brothers, New York
    Julius A. Bewer, Harper's Annotated Bible, *The Book of Ezekiel*, 1954.

The Judson Press, Philadelphia
    I. G. Matthews, An American Commentary on the Old Testament, *Ezekiel*, 1939.

The Macmillan Company, New York
    Mary Ellen Chase, *The Bible and the Common Reader*, 1952.

Paternoster Press, London.
    H. L. Ellison, *Ezekiel, the Man and His Message*.

Princeton Alumni Weekly, Princeton.

Princeton University Press, Princeton
    J. Finegan, *Light from the Ancient Past*, 1946.
    J. B. Pritchard, *Ancient Near Eastern Texts*, 1950.

University of Chicago Press, Chicago
    William A. Irwin, *The Problem of Ezekiel*, 1943.

Viking Press, New York
    Millar Burrows, *The Dead Sea Scrolls*, 1956.
    Malcolm Cowley, *Writers at Work*, 1958.

The Westminster Press, Philadelphia
    G. Ernest Wright, *Biblical Archaeology*, 1957.
    Cyril C. Richardson, *Early Christian Fathers*, 1953.

Yale University Press, New Haven
    Charles G. Torrey, *Pseudo-Ezekiel and the Original Prophecy*, 1930.

The Bible text in this publication, unless otherwise indicated, is from the *Revised Standard Version of the Bible*, copyrighted 1946 and 1952 by the Division of Christian Education, National Council of Churches, and used by permission.

Selected Bibliography

Julius A. Bewer, Harper's Annotated Bible, *The Book of Ezekiel,* Harper & Brothers, New York, 1954.

G. A. Cooke, International Critical Commentary, *A Critical and Exegetical Commentary on the Book of Ezekiel,* T. and T. Clark, Edinburgh, 1937.

A. B. Davidson, Cambridge Bible, *The Book of Ezekiel the Prophet,* The University Press, Cambridge, 1906.

H. L. Ellison, *Ezekiel, the Man and His Message,* The Paternoster Press, London, 1956.

Rabbi Dr. S. Fisch, Soncino Books of the Bible. Hebrew Text and English Translation with an Introduction and Commentary, *Ezekiel,* The Soncino Press, London & Bournemouth, 1950.

W. F. Lofthouse, The Century Bible, *Ezekiel,* T. C. and E. C. Jack, Edinburgh.

I. G. Matthews, An American Commentary on the Old Testament, *Ezekiel,* The Judson Press, Philadelphia, 1939.

Herbert G. May and E. L. Allen, The Interpreter's Bible, *The Book of Ezekiel,* Abingdon Press, New York, 1956.

John Skinner, The Expositor's Bible, *The Book of Ezekiel,* Hodder & Stoughton, New York.

Quotations from the books in the selected bibliography are identified by the name of the author. The quotation in each case will be found by referring to the writer's commentary upon the particular verse or passage under discussion.

Abbreviations

AV   The Authorized or King James Version of the Holy Bible, 1611.

JPS   Jewish Publication Society, *The Holy Scriptures according to the Masoretic Text,* 1917.

LXX   *The Septuagint,* the Greek translation of the Old Testament.

MT   The Masoretic Text, the Hebrew Scripture as edited by the Masoretes, or Masters of Tradition.

NT   New Testament.

OT   Old Testament.

RSV   The Revised Standard Version of the Holy Bible, 1946 and 1952.

Contents

Foreword

Every Christian today needs Ezekiel's message of hope. Only a small number are receiving it. It is easy to understand why the prophecy is not widely read and appreciated, for the book is filled with material that is difficult to appreciate. But he who studies this grim prophecy begins to discern a haunting parallel with the events and attitudes of today. Different nations are involved, naturally, and men fight with different weapons, but the underlying issues are remarkably similar. When this becomes clear to the student, he finds that Ezekiel adds something almost completely missing from modern thought, the element of hope. The embattled prophet teaches us to open our eyes during the sandstorm and to see that the light of God still shines.

The student may expect to encounter three principal responses to the mention of Ezekiel. The theological illiterate grins and breaks into an alleged Negro spiritual, based more or less upon Chapter 37, "The toe-bone connected to the foot-bone, and the foot-bone connected to the heel-bone. . . ." Unless dissuaded, he may complete the entire anatomical assemblage. The theological sophisticate, almost without exception, asks, "What is your opinion about the problem of Ezekiel?" The general run of church members, who have looked briefly into Ezekiel and decided to do their Bible reading elsewhere, say "Ugh." The first thinks of Ezekiel as a joke, which is wrong. The second thinks of Ezekiel as a puzzle, which is scarcely less wrong. The third thinks of Ezekiel as unpleasant, which is true as far as it goes, but is not the full truth. All three attitudes existed while Ezekiel was living, and all three have persisted through the centuries. The widespread existence of the first and third has compelled me to write a book, with the prayer that it may help some to appreciate an important part of God's Word. The existence of the second compels me to write a foreword explaining why I am not trying to solve the problem of Ezekiel.

The problem of Ezekiel is thus summarized by an outstanding critic:

> The problem of Ezekiel is threefold. Is the book the work of the prophet Ezekiel, alleged to have lived and taught through the early part of the sixth century B.C., or is it pseudonymous? Is it of united authorship? If not, how is it to be analyzed? and, third, where was it written, specifically in Palestine or in Babylonia?[1]

The answers to the questions, offered by competent scholars, form a gigantic spectrum including every possibility. In 1891, S. R. Driver wrote:

> No critical question arises in connexion with the authorship of the book, the whole from beginning to end bearing unmistakably the stamp of a single mind.[2]

Later critics have roundly scolded Dr. Driver for his statement, because critical questions had been raised before 1891. Even so, the traditional view was widely held until it received a devastating examination by Gustav Hölscher, in his study: *Hesekiel, der Dichter, und das Buch.*[3] According to Dr. Hölscher, Ezekiel was essentially a poet who wrote only about 170 of the 1273 verses in the book that carries his name, while the main part of the book belongs to a redactor in the fifth century who adapted some of the prophet's oracles into the present form, to which others made comparatively small contributions.

The critical process was carried to the ultimate possible limit by Charles G. Torrey. Dr. Torrey holds, enthusiastically if not convincingly:

> The original Ezekiel . . . was a pseudepigraph purporting to come from the reign of Manasseh, but in fact composed many centuries later [about 230 B.C.]. It was converted into a prophecy of the so-called "Babylonian Golah" by an editor who accomplished his undertaking (in all probability) not many years after the original work had appeared. This redaction was not the result of any chance notion or caprice on the part of the man who effected the strange transformation; on the contrary, it was one of several

---

[1] William A. Irwin, *The Problem of Ezekiel*, University of Chicago Press, 1943, p. 3.

[2] *An Introduction to the Literature of the Old Testament*, Charles Scribner's Sons, p. 261.

[3] A. Töpelmann, Giessen, 1924.

features of a literary movement which seems to have originated in the middle of the third century B.C., having for its purpose the vindication of the tradition of Jerusalem.[4]

The Problem of Ezekiel by William A. Irwin, has been mentioned. This gives an exhaustive historical review of the problem, and an intensive examination of the material. Dr. Irwin concludes that there was a historical Ezekiel, who commenced his work in Jerusalem and completed it in Babylon, and who wrote, in whole or in part, 251 of the verses that appear in the present prophecy. In the course of his examination Dr. Irwin makes many sagacious comments that should be thoughtfully considered by all would-be Bible critics. He says:

> The radicalism or conservatism of any critical result is primarily a matter of complete indifference; the only important questions are what supporting facts have been adduced and how dependable is the process of reasoning that has yielded the result claimed.[5]

What has passed for conservative criticism has sometimes displayed more an emotional attachment to tradition than the incisive intellectual analysis implied in the very word "critic." Carl Gordon Howie has taken seriously his critical task in a brilliant monograph, all too short, *The Date and the Composition of Ezekiel.*[6] He uses the full intellectual armament of biblical criticism to examine the basic assumptions upon which the scholars mentioned above, and many, many others, have based their conclusions, and he finds that an imposing structure has been erected upon foundations that are, to put it charitably, shaky. He shakes the foundations, and the critical structure comes tumbling down. Essentially he reaffirms the traditional view that a flesh and blood prophet Ezekiel composed the greatest part of the book that bears his name. If Dr. Howie has not proved his case beyond the shadow of a doubt, he has at least made it clear that a person may with intellectual integrity hold to the traditional view about the writer of the prophecy.

Before leaving the question of authorship, I must at least

---

[4] *Pseudo-Ezekiel and the Original Prophecy,* Yale University Press, 1930, p. 2.
[5] *op. cit.* p. 12.
[6] Society of Biblical Literature, 1950.

14 *Ezekiel, Prophecy of Hope*

mention the oft-repeated statement from the Babylonian Talmud that "the men of the Great Synagogue wrote Ezekiel." It
might be advisable to examine the context in which the statement appears:

> Moses wrote his book and a portion of Bil'am [Numbers 22] and
> Job. Joshua wrote his book and the last eight verses of the Penta-
> teuch. . . . Samuel wrote his book, Judges, and Ruth. David wrote
> the Psalms with the assistance of ten elders . . . Jeremiah wrote his
> book, Kings, and Lamentations. King Hezekiah and his company
> wrote Isaiah, Proverbs, Songs, and Ecclesiastes. The men of the
> Great Synagogue wrote Ezekiel, the Twelve Prophets, Daniel, and
> the book of Esther.[7]

A conservative critic would reject many of the statements made,
a radical would reject many more of them. *Baba bathra* (The
Last Gate) is probably late fourth century. The statement is
evidence only that there was a tradition of multiple authorship
among the Hebrew people of the time.

My own belief is that there was a man named Ezekiel who
lived and worked in Babylon during the early years of the
exile. This man both repelled and attracted his fellow exiles
by his descriptions of visions he had seen and by his uncompromising conviction that Jerusalem must fall. When in historic
fact Jerusalem fell, this man continued unswervingly on the
course of faith. History swerved; he did not. He told the now
hopeless exiles that Jerusalem must rise. Some leader, with unspeakable power to stir thought, must have exercised such a
ministry among the exiles because, in historic fact, Jerusalem
rose again. I believe that this leader was Ezekiel, who wrote
the report of his visions and his dramatic parables.

Almost everything that Christians know about the other Son
of Man comes channelled through the life of Matthew, Mark,
Luke, or John. I believe that an unknown disciple performed
a similar work of love to bring to us Ezekiel's prophetic message by collecting his writings and assembling them into the
form we have today. Like Matthew and Mark and other chosen
servants of God, he left the imprint of his own personality upon
the completed work. I do not share the confidence of many
critics that they, or I, have the ability to discern precisely which

---

7 *Baba bathra*, 146, 152.

words the prophet wrote and which are the editor's. Studying
the conflicting theories about this matter has, if anything, decreased my confidence. By whatever earthly hand, I believe that
the Holy Spirit worked through a human agent to bring a
message that the world needs today.

My opinions about the prophet Ezekiel will emerge in the
ensuing pages. My opinion about the editor can briefly be
stated. He was almost the equal of the prophet in depth both of
passion and of thought. Some critics envision a long series of
editors, most of whom were blundering oafs. A completely
typical statement is that of I. G. Matthews:

> There is evidence that the scribes were not idle in the interpreta-
> tion of the Ezekiel text. The multiplicity of conventional phrases,
> such as, "son of man"—used a hundred times, "that you may know
> that I am Yahweh"—found sixty times, "thus says Yahweh," "oracle
> of Yahweh," and others—is so marked as to breed contempt rather
> than reverence. The perpetual recurrence of "the Lord Yahweh"
> borders on profanity. These and many similar phrases, all easy
> to repeat, testify to the scribe as well as to an original writer.[8]

From this I can but conclude that higher critics of the Bible
must lead sheltered lives. Any one who seriously believes that
a unified work was produced by many minds has been merci-
fully protected from committee meetings. The prophecy of
Ezekiel comes to us channelled through one mind, a mind that
shared the prophet's fire and depth, and placed truth far above
beauty.

The brief review above is intended only to sketch in the bewildering outlines of the task that confronts him who would
study the problem of Ezekiel. Anyone who shows the slightest
serious interest in the problem must read the books mentioned,
and in the course of his reading he will discover many more
that he must examine. He may also discover a few quiet, nag-
ging questions that have never been better expressed than by
William Irwin in 1942, a year of hellish tension and anxiety:

> In the end, it may be asked, who cares whether Ezekiel wrote all
> his book or none of it. It is as enticing as a jigsaw puzzle, and, it
> may appear, as worthless. Yet here again we must walk by
> faith. . . . The dull detail of critical results and the much more

---

[8] *Ezekiel*, The Judson Press, 1939, p. vii.

dull confusion of critical argumentation have been profoundly instrumental in the making of the "modern" world of the spirit. So one does not bring to completion a study of this sort with a guilty feeling of having fiddled while the world was falling in ruins, but rather with confidence that in a time of unparalleled human need he has done what he could.[9]

Thus half-apologetically Dr. Irwin presents to the world the result of many years of exhausting labor. He has made a brilliant contribution to the " 'modern' world of the spirit." As I minister to the results of this modern spirit day after day, I wonder increasingly if contemporary man is not being taught to ask the wrong question of faith and life.

The modern spirit is filled with good, chiefly the burning desire for truth, whatever the truth may be. This openmindedness, supposedly, is a traditional Christian virtue that many who call themselves orthodox Christians seem unwilling to apply. The modern spirit is questing, seeking always. And right here may be an essential weakness of our times. It has been said, I know not by whom, "The purpose of an open mind, like that of an open mouth, is to be closed upon something solid and digestible."

One analytic modern, a senior of the class of 1964, has said:

> The trouble with me is that I can't believe in anything. On some days I can, but most of the time I am smarter than that. I have been taught to question, not to believe, so I never know where to stop. . . . What I want is a cause; what I cannot have is a cause.[10]

No Christian, believing in the eternal God, would ask the young man to turn the clock backward, to seek intellectual embalming in ancient error, or to ignore the genuine contribution to human dignity that the spirit of our time has brought. The Christian seeks his standing ground not in the present, certainly not in the past, but in the Eternal where Ezekiel tells him to look. Ezekiel likewise dealt with people who longed for a cause and had none.

The higher criticism of the Bible is a completely legitimate function of those who have the necessary skills, the time, and the interest to engage in it. The antidote to false criticism is

---

[9] *op. cit.*, p. xiv.
[10] *Princeton Alumni Weekly*, June 7, 1963.

true criticism, not throwing stones at the critic with whom one disagrees. However, higher critics have been known to go beyond their search for fact and to engage in value judgments of dubious validity, and a great many Christians—may God forgive us—have accepted these judgments, as if serious investigation of the Bible's literary structure could affect its spiritual worth. I. G. Matthews, for example, has said:

> The message of Ezekiel is naturally limited to those writings that by virtue of their content and the canons of criticism, can with some degree of assurance be assigned to this Jerusalem prophet.[11]

If this value judgment is accepted, then Ezekiel has no message for us; for whose assurance shall we follow? Dr. Irwin allows 273 verses to Ezekiel, Dr. Hölscher concedes him 170, and Dr. Torrey none at all.

For those who care, the problem of Ezekiel offers a vast, absorbing field of inquiry. This is an area where angels fear to tread, yet there has been no dearth of enthusiasts who have rushed in with more good intentions than intellectual equipment. The problem of Ezekiel is important; for truth is always important. But the following pages are a discussion of something almost completely different and, I believe, a great deal more important. In them I am trying to examine the "something solid and digestible" that is contained in the prophecy, but sometimes well concealed.

Ezekiel is the name of a man and of a book. As I have indicated, scholarly opinion varies weirdly in the estimate of the relationship between the two. By all but a few the man is considered among the great prophets of old, and the book is considered a part of the Holy Bible, which many of us believe to be the written Word of God. If the book is God's Word, no amount of criticism can alter the fact. If it is not, no amount of spirited defense can make it so. And how can a person tell? The only test I can suggest is pragmatic. Read the book and see if God speaks to you through its pages.

Does the Book of Ezekiel have anything to say to us? If so, what? These are the questions I am asking. Thus I am approaching the book, not from a viewpoint of textual, gram-

---

11 *op. cit.*, p. xxiii.

matical, or historical study, but as the living Word of the living
God, whose thoughts are not always easily understood. The
answers to these questions are independent of the answer given
to the problem of Ezekiel.

William Faulkner, talking with a reporter from the Paris
Review, said something that might well be pondered by those
who would study Ezekiel:

Interviewer: How about yourself as a writer?
Mr. Faulkner: What is important is "Hamlet" and "Midsummer
                Night's Dream," not who wrote them, but that
                somebody did. The artist is of no importance.
                Only what he creates is important. . . .
Interviewer: . . . Isn't perhaps the individuality of the writer
                important?
Mr. Faulkner: Very important to himself. Everybody else should
                be too busy with the work to care about the
                individuality.[12]

Appreciation, literary or spiritual, depends on what is said
more than on who said it, where he said it, who edited it, and
when. If I accepted in full the conclusion of Charles Torrey
mentioned above, it would change little in the interpretation
that follows; for there may be truth in legend as well as in history. Legendary King Arthur, for example, is far more influential today than many historical British kings. Many passages in
Malory's *Morte d' Arthur* have profoundly influenced English
literature, art, tradition, and law. Does any one really care if
their historicity is debatable? The important matter about
Ezekiel is that God speaks through the prophecy today, and has
been speaking through the prophecy during the ages. If God
speaks to you through Ezekiel, all else is secondary. If He does
not, the rest matters only if you are an antiquarian.

One who attempts an essay in English Bible must be aware
of critical studies, but he ought not to debate questions that
can be intelligently discussed only by reference to the original
language. I have tried in the following pages to by-pass the
critical questions and to concentrate upon the spiritual, an
unusual procedure today, but one with some degree of merit.

It is commonplace to downgrade Ezekiel among the books of
the Bible. A typical comment is that of Mary Ellen Chase:

---

12 *Writers at Work*, Edited by Malcolm Cowley, Viking Press, 1958.

Ezekiel, whose rather dull and repetitious book lacks much of interest and meaning for us today, was apparently a sort of pastor to the exiled Jewish community in Babylon. . . . From his many trances, ecstasies, and visions, his denunciation of sin and his sense of doom, his intolerance toward non-Israelitish people, his air of complete seriousness and his seeming lack of any humour, he is in many ways an unattractive figure.[13]

Miss Chase concedes, however, that this crashing bore she has described:

stands forth as the most powerful figure during the years of Jewish captivity in Babylonia. . . . He kept alive in an alien land the faith which had made Israel.[14]

The downgrading of Ezekiel has a long history. In the Talmud we find:

Rabba said, All that Ezekiel saw [Ezekiel 1:4–3:27] Isaiah saw [Isaiah 6:1-9], but Ezekiel was like a villager who has seen the king for the first time [and therefore tells all that he has seen]. Isaiah, however, was like a townsman who has often seen the king [and therefore says little].[15]

Jerome compared the study of Ezekiel to walking through the catacombs where light seldom breaks through. John Calvin did not finish his commentary on Ezekiel. And most who study the prophecy today are willing to agree with Jerome and to sympathize with Calvin. But the matter goes deeper than recognizing difficulty and conceding that many passages in Ezekiel are downright offensive. Biblical students who normally are careful thinkers have totally misread the thorny prophecy. Even a great scholar like Bernhard Duhm has conceded to Ezekiel:

The merit of having transformed the ideals of the prophets into laws and dogmas, and destroyed spiritually free and moral religion.[16]

In the following pages I reveal a deeper sympathy with Ezekiel, the man and the book, than you will find in the

---

13 *The Bible and the Common Reader,* The Macmillan Company, 1958, pp. 49, 50.
14 *Ibid.,* p. 50.
15 *Hagiga,* 13b.
16 *Theologie der Propheten,* p. 263.

writings of most critics, either contemporary or ancient. I agree with most of their negative criticisms. I agree that other parts of the Bible are more uplifting and more accessible to our minds. I hope I do not find virtue in Ezekiel where there is none. The beautiful passages in his book are so few that I call attention to them. The repetitious passages are so many that I pass them by, more often than not. The ugly passages are so ugly that I comment only on the worst.

And yet, when all these things have been said, I find myself wearing the shoes that Ezekiel wore, attempting to do the work that he did: bringing a message of judgment to the fatuous, and a message of hope to the desperate. I find my task delineated in the prophecy of Ezekiel with a clarity and precision that I find nowhere else in the Holy Bible. I have been forced by the weight of circumstance (or the Hand of God) to take stands that must alienate me from people I love. I have been forced to speak truths that my hearers have rejected. I have walked where Ezekiel walked, and have found his companionship helpful.

I do not pretend that Ezekiel was a genial, gum-chewing Rotarian, nor do I deny that a psychologist could find evidence of unusual attitudes in his writing.[17] But I do find Ezekiel a thoughtful, sensitive, intelligent man of faith, who was given a task that he did not want, who discharged it as well as he could. After all, during the exile *someone* held the Hebrews together when they had no earthly reason for cohesion. *Someone* taught the exiles to open their eyes in the midst of the storm and to see that the light still shines. His name was Ezekiel. His book is difficult, obscure, tantalizing, and in places disgusting, but it contains a message that modern man needs just as much as the Hebrew exiles needed it.

The person who closes his eyes during a dust storm may not see the light, but likewise he misses a great deal of the darkness. Ezekiel will allow us to miss none of it. With painstaking attention he leads us to examine one horrible fact after another, until we are overwhelmed with the encircling gloom. Then something else happens. As another servant of God wrote:

> If I say surely the darkness shall cover me;
> even the night shall be light about me.

---

[17] See Edwin C. Broome, "Ezekiel's Abnormal Personality," *Journal of Biblical Literature, 1946*, pp. 277-292.

> Yea, the darkness hideth not from thee;
> but the night shineth as the day;
> the darkness and the light are both alike to thee.[18]

When the reader has this much understanding of Ezekiel's purpose (without which there is little spiritual benefit in studying his prophecy), he still is faced with a sizeable number of difficulties.

The first difficulty is one's basic understanding of the function of prophecy: is it a call back to first principles? or is it a compendium of tomorrow's headlines? I discuss this matter in connection with Chapters 18 and 26.

Secondly, the prophecy is expressed in symbols. Not only are some of the symbols almost unintelligible, but the whole method of symbolic teaching is uncongenial to our literal-minded culture. We want everything presented with the precision of an engineer's blueprint. The reader will discover, in Chapter 40f. that Ezekiel could draw a blueprint in words if it suited his purpose to do so. But reading more carefully, he will discover that the ground plan of the Temple is itself a vast symbol. The nature of symbolism is discussed in connection with Chapter 1.

A third basic difficulty is the large number of discrepancies between Ezekiel and other parts of the Bible. It is true, they concern matters that make no earthly difference to Christian faith, however they may have jarred the sensibilities of our Jewish forebears. There are twenty major discrepancies between Ezekiel and the Torah. Compare 46:6f. with Numbers 28:11, for example. Here are outright contradictions in the number of bullocks, lambs, and rams and the amount of flour to be used at the new moon offering ceremonies. I. G. Matthews dryly comments:

> How to make one equal two, six equal seven, and three-tenths equate with one was a problem for the discerning, but how to accept both of these and still adhere to the eternal unchangeableness of the Torah lay beyond human comprehension.[19]

Long ago the rabbis were driven to say that Elijah, when he came, would explain away the difficulties. They said likewise

---

18 Psalm 139:11f. (AV)
19 *op. cit.*, p. vi.

that the entire prophecy would have been excluded from the
canon were it not for the devoted labor of Rabbi Hanina ben
Hezekiah, a scholar in the first century A.D., who must have
written an extensive commentary on Ezekiel:

> Three hundred barrels of oil were provided for him [for light]
> and he sat in an upper chamber where he reconciled all discrep-
> ancies.[20]

It passes credulity that, if the good rabbi succeeded in his task,
his successors should so casually have let his work disappear.
One may take the three hundred barrels of oil as a good-hu-
mored way of saying that the critical problems are insoluble,
but a work of such depth as Ezekiel's prophecy, that brings a
message from God to troubled people, clearly belongs in the
Word of God, discrepancies or no.

A fourth difficulty is the uncertainty of the text. When the
original oracles left the editor's pen, they must have contained
all manner of obscurity. A scribe, copying the work, would be
tempted to make minor improvements here and there; so we
find different manuscripts that give divergent readings.

The Hebrew community developed a guild of scholars, the
Masoretes (masters of tradition), whose work was essentially
concluded in the tenth century A.D., with the labors of Rabbi
Aaron ben Asher. The works of Origen in the third century and
Jerome in the fourth show a text that is substantially the same
as Masoretic. However, LXX from the third century B.C. differs markedly from MT. There is an area of inquiry, almost as
complex and as interesting as the problem of Ezekiel, in the
differences between the two traditions and the reasons for those
differences. Christians forget sometimes that LXX was the
Bible of the early church, not MT. In MT are several words
of unknown meaning, retained despite a scribe's inclination to
write a familiar form. And there are many verses that can be
translated only by adopting a conjectural reading, or by turning to LXX and the other versions. I comment on some of these
obscurities where I think the matter will be of general interest.

The Italians have a saying, *Traduttori—traditore*, "A trans-
lator is a traitor." It is simply impossible to convey all of the

---

20 Babylonian Talmud, *Menahoth* 45a.

nuances of a complex expression from one language to another. In reading most of the Holy Bible for devotional purposes, I turn without hesitation to the majestic rhythms and the matchless beauty of AV. But in dealing with a book like Ezekiel, I turn to the careful, critical modern scholarship, expressed in relative clarity, of RSV. I would that the able scholars who labored on RSV had included one with Lancelot Andrewes' love for stately diction. (He might have been able to spare us "steadfast love.") But I cannot join with those who say that, because there are some things to criticize in RSV, therefore it must be thrown out entirely. It is a translation. So is AV, or J. B. Phillips', or James Moffatt's, or JPS, or the Vulgate, or LXX. Each has its strength. Each has its weakness.

In comparing AV and RSV, one finds that the translators in 1611 usually followed MT wherever it might lead, and sometimes it led into strange places. Ezekiel 32:20, for one example from many, is simply meaningless. The translators in the twentieth century accepted 51 conjectures, some of which give a clear meaning where otherwise there would be confusion. They likewise turned to LXX and the other versions. On occasion they followed alternative Hebrew readings, and sometimes they interpreted rather than translated. Where they have departed from the MT they have indicated their departure by a footnote. I may quarrel with this or that interpretation—and I do rather frequently—but when this is said, RSV remains the best translation of Ezekiel that I know, and so it has formed the basis for my study. Even Lancelot Andrewes could not make Ezekiel beautiful in English. The revisers at least make his book comparatively intelligible.

The purpose of this study is to seek light upon our present darkness, not Ezekiel's relevance to another era of history. Many others, whose help has been invaluable, have studied the prophecy with the same purpose in mind. Hebrew scholarship has been profound and sensitive to the meanings of Ezekiel. I have found much guidance in the rabbinic writings of the Mishnah and the Talmud. The Christian student, who may not be familiar with these works, should know that the rabbis had the valuable habit of examining an issue from every viewpoint; so any particular quotation must not be considered an authoritative expression of Jewish faith, but the opinion of one responsible thinker.

In more recent times, two Jewish commentators stand head and shoulders above all others; they are Rabbis Solomon Izhaqui (1040-1105), who is known as Rashi, and David Kimchi (*c* 1160-1235). Unfortunately their works are available only in Hebrew or Latin. The Christian, who believes that God has revealed Himself in the Messiah, Jesus of Nazareth, may receive much spiritual benefit from those who know the Messiah only in prospect, as Ezekiel knew Him. The difference between Christian and Jew lies, not in the interpretation of OT passages predicting the Christ, but in the question of historical fact, whether or not Jesus the Galilean carpenter is the Christ.

A selected bibliography is appended, comprising books that I have found helpful and believe will be helpful to the reader. These are written from many different theological perspectives. Of them all, I have found that by G. A. Cooke to be the most consistently valuable.

I have received invaluable help from groups of people with whom I have studied the prophecy. The Presbyterian ministers of Palm Beach County have valiantly struggled with the gloomy prophet, as have members of the Women's Association of the Church where I am privileged to serve. At several summer conferences classes have delved intensely into the prophecy, and taught me much, when I was supposed to be the teacher. To be sure, there have been moments when I might have qualified my enthusiasm, as when I asked what symbolic meaning one could find in the touching wingtips (1:9), and an earnest pursuer of truth said, "This emphasizes the importance of togetherness."

If I may employ, for the first and last time in these pages, the most overworked word in our decade, Ezekiel is an existentialist. He lives his truth. He knows God, not in abstraction from the tensions and heartaches of existence, but in the midst of the struggle. The reader who shows the slightest understanding of Ezekiel's message hears, across the centuries, a clear call to "engagement" with the struggle as it exists today.

While my concern is with the present relevance of the prophecy, I have not attempted to point out modern applications at every opportunity. In reading Chapter 13, for example, I hope the reader will need no reminder that the choice between true prophecy and false prophecy is always before him today. Chapter 16, which is not for the squeamish in heart, ought to remind any Christian citizen of the United States that our land has received lavish blessings from Almighty God, and it ought to raise a few questions about our acceptance of false deities. Chapter 27 concerns a commercial civilization. We are a commercial civilization. The dangers of success are just as dangerous today as they ever were. Chapter 29 considers the ruler over a powerful nation who is hostile to true faith. Such rulers exist in abundance today. And so one could go on for each of the forty-eight chapters.

For two reasons I have not often stopped to point out the parallels. First, this would double the size of a book that is already too bulky. Second, the shape of the storm cloud will be vastly changed even between the date of writing and the date of publication. But the eternal light will continue to shine.

Outline of Ezekiel

I. THE PROPHECY OF JUDGMENT, 1:1—24:27

  I. EZEKIEL'S VISION AND HIS COMMISSION, 1:1—3:27.
    A. The Superscription, 1:1-3.
    B. The Vision, 1:4-28.
    C. The Commission, 2:1—3:27.
      1. First Commission, 2:1-7.
      2. Second Commission—the Scroll, 2:8—3:3.
      3. Third Commission, 3:4-11.
      4. Time for Meditation, 3:12-15.
      5. Fourth Commission—the Watchman, 3:16-21.
      6. Fifth Commission—the Blight of Dumbness, 3:22-27.
  II. THE FIRST CYCLE OF WARNINGS, 4:1—7:27.
    A. Dramatic Parables, 4:1-5:17.
      1. The Siege of Jerusalem, 4:1-3.
      2. The Length of the Exile, 4:4-8.
      3. The Unclean Food, 4:9-17.
      4. The Doom of Jerusalem, 5:1-4.
      5. Explanation of the Parables, 5:5-17.
    B. Oracles against the Land and the People, 6:1-14.
      1. Oracle against the Mountains, 6:1-7.
      2. The Promise of a Remnant, 6:8-10.
      3. Renewed Warning to the People and the Mountains, 6:11-14.
    C. End of the First Cycle of Warnings, 7:1-27.
      1. The End Has Come, 7:1-4.
      2. Disaster after Disaster, 7:5-9.
      3. Behold the Day, 7:10-11.
      4. The Time Has Come, 7:12-13.
      5. Summary: Physical and Spiritual Collapse, 7:14-27.
  III. VISIONS OF JERUSALEM'S GUILT AND PUNISHMENT, 8:1—11:25.
    A. Jerusalem's Guilt, 8:1-18.
      1. The New Image of Jealousy, 8:1-6.
      2. The Hidden Idolatry of the Elders, 8:7-13.

    2. Lament for Tyre, 27:1-36.
       a. The Noble Ship, 27:1-9a.
       b. Tyre's Trade, 27:9b-25a.
       c. The Loss of the Ship, 27:25b-36.
    3. The Prince of Tyre, 28:1-19.
       a. The Prince's Sin, 28:1-5.
       b. The Prince's Judgment, 28:6-10.
       c. Lament for the Prince, 28:11-19.
    4. Oracle Against Sidon, 28:20-23.
    5. God's Mercy within His Judgment, 28:24-26.
  C. Against Egypt, 29:1—32:32.
    1. Pharaoh's Sin, 29:1-16.
    2. God's Judgment on Egypt, 29:17—30:19.
       a. Nebuchadrezzar, God's Agent of Judgment, 29:17-
          21.
       b. The Day of the Lord, 30:1-19.
       c. Pharaoh's Defeat, 30:20-26.
       d. The Allegory of the Cedar, 31:1-18.
    3. Lament for Pharaoh, 32:1-32.
       a. The Crocodile Slain, 32:1-8.
       b. Babylon the Destroyer, 32:9-16.
       c. Pharaoh's Descent into Sheol, 32:17-32.

II. PROPHECIES OF ISRAEL'S RESTORATION, 33:1— 37:28.

  A. From Judgment to Hope, 33:1-33.
    1. The Prophet's Responsibility, 33:1-9.
    2. The Hearer's Responsibility, 33:10-20.
    3. The Prophet Vindicated, 33:21-33.

  B. The Shepherds and the Flock, 34:1-31.
    1. The Evil Shepherds, 34:1-10.
    2. God, the True Shepherd, 34:11-22.
    3. The Ideal Shepherd to Come, 34:23-31.

  C. Israel's Restoration, 35:1—37:28.
    1. The Final Obstacle Removed, 35:1-15.
    2. Prophecy to the Mountains of Israel, 36:1-15.
    3. The Cleansing and the Increase of Israel, 36:16-38.
    4. The Return from Death to Life, 37:1-28.
       a. The Valley of Dry Bones, 37:1-14.
       b. The Reunion of the Two Kingdoms, 37:15-28.

I. THE PROPHECY OF JUDGMENT, 1:1–24:27

I. The Prophecy of Judgment, 1:1--24:27

I. EZEKIEL'S VISION AND HIS COMMISSION, 1:1—3:27.

A. The Superscription, 1:1-3.

1:1   The prophecy of Ezekiel opens with a phrase "in the thirtieth year" that has produced an insoluble puzzle. The thirtieth year of what? Every reasonable explanation has been advanced, and some that are less reasonable. It would seem quite simple to count back thirty years from the exact date (593 B.C.) in the following verse. This would give us the year 623, which is at least close to the time when, in the eighteenth year of King Josiah's reign, the Book of Law was discovered in the Temple (II Kings 22:3-20). According to tradition, the scroll of Law was opened at the verse, "The Lord will bring you, and your king whom you set over you, to a nation that neither you nor your fathers have known; and there you shall serve other gods, of wood and stone" (Deuteronomy 28:36). As far as we know, the discovery of the Law, with its poignant threat of impending tragedy, was not used for dating purposes. This suggestion was adopted by Jerome, but it is not widely accepted today.

  Another suggestion, proposed by Origen, and likewise not widely accepted today, is that the thirtieth year represents Ezekiel's age when the call of God came to him. In Numbers 4:3 we find that a Levite began his service at the age of thirty. Some have assumed that the same age held for the assumption of priestly duties. Since the dated prophecies cover a span of twenty-two years, they conjecture that Ezekiel's prophetic activity centered in the period of his life between the ages of thirty and fifty-two.

  Though scholars today usually dismiss the two interpretations proposed above, the alternatives are less than awe-inspiring. The principal ones are: an editor's reconciliation of the predicted forty years' exile with the seventy years mentioned in Jeremiah

25:12; a copyist's error for the third or the thirteenth year; the thirtieth year of Nabopolasser, the Babylonian monarch; the date when Ezekiel completed the written prophecy, three years after the last dated oracle (29:17); the thirtieth year of King Manasseh's reign (*c.* 663 B.C.). (This latter obviously involves a rough handling of the information.) Finally, and most widely accepted today, there were two systems of dating at the time. To avoid confusion, the editor helpfully slipped in a note to the effect that the fifth year was really the thirtieth year.

Thus it becomes evident in the first four words of the prophecy that we must make a choice. We can, if we will, easily become bogged down in the morass of endless speculation that has rendered many studies in Ezekiel utterly futile for the modern reader. Or we can, recognizing an insoluble problem, admit that it is insoluble and leave it there. The evidence is clear that in Ezekiel's own day his contemporaries did not understand much of what he said. Yet the people whom he puzzled so deeply retained his work. Why? Because it bewildered them? They retained the written prophecy and transmitted it to us, because, shining through the murk is the eternal light. Modern scholarship, by and large, concentrates upon the murk. Let us gratefully accept all the help that we can receive from those who have wrested with the riddles, while concentrating our attention upon the essential message that shines through the extravagant imagery, the obscure allusions to persons, places, and events unknown to us, and the badly mangled text. We must pin down the facts as accurately as we can; for Ezekiel's prophecy, more than any other prophecy, must be related to historical events. But we cannot enter deeply into the speculation that has added much confusion to the confusion with which Ezekiel is filled.

The events that gave rise to Ezekiel's first vision were filled with tragedy and horror. In 597 Nebuchadnezzar, King of 1:2 Babylon, besieged Jerusalem. King Jehoiachin (the Lord establishes), who had ascended the throne at the age of eighteen (or eight), and had reigned but three months and ten days, surrendered and was deported to Babylon with 10,000 (II Kings 24:14) or 3023 (Jeremiah 52:28) of the leading citizens. Mattaniah (gift of the Lord), the king's uncle, was placed on the throne as king-regent. Cuneiform tablets, found near the Ishtar Gate of Babylon, fill the gaps in the concise, tragic record of

II Kings 25:27-30. Some of these tablets dated 597-70 name Yaukin (Jehoiachin), King of Yahud. Others mention oil, barley
and other provisions for the skilled workers. Archaeologists
have likewise discovered three stamped jar handles in Palestine
that read, "Belonging to Eliakim, steward of Yaukin." Thus
one may conclude that, while Jehoiachin was exiled, his compatriots and even the Babylonians considered him the rightful
king.

The fifth year of the exile was 593 B.C. The fourth month was
Tammuz, a month of ill omen; for during Tammuz the first
breaches were made in the wall of Jerusalem. The fourth month,
in the Babylonian calendar, corresponded with the period from
mid-June to mid-July in our calendar. When the heavens
opened and Ezekiel saw visions from God, the lonely prophet
was standing by the river Chebar. Almost certainly this was a
gigantic irrigation canal, of which the present remains are
called *Shatt en Nil*. It started from the Euphrates above Babylon, flowed southeast through Nippur, and re-entered the
Euphrates near Erech. Recent excavations at Nippur have disclosed an extensive Jewish settlement in the neighborhood. Two
tablets have been found, dating from 443 and 424, that give the
Babylonian form of Ezekiel's words, *naru kabari,* the Great
Canal or River.

"The word of the Lord came to Ezekiel [God strengthens]"
by the Chebar. The "word of the Lord" includes what was seen
1:3 (in vision) as well as what was heard. Ezekiel's use foreshadows
that in John 1:1-14, where "word" has a far more inclusive
meaning than in contemporary English. Ezekiel was an exile,
whose king was exiled, in the land of the Chaldeans. (At this
stage of history "Chaldea" and "Babylon" were interchangeable
terms.) Ezekiel was the son of Buzi (descendant of Buz). We
know nothing else about Buzi. The Hebrew construction is
such that we cannot be sure whether Ezekiel or Buzi was the
priest.

Ezekiel's faith in God had been channelled through the
Temple, with its majestic ritual and its cleansing sacrifices. Yet
he was far from the Temple. Since the time of Moses, God had
not spoken to a prophet beyond the physical boundaries of
Palestine. Here it was, at the time and the place least expected,
that the "hand of the Lord was upon him." This phrase becomes almost a technical expression in the prophecy that fol-

lows. It expresses a condition of prophetic insight. Christians would describe the same reality by another figure of speech, the Spirit (or Breath) of God.

Ezekiel was an exile. This is the fact that gives such frightening—and encouraging—relevancy to his prophecy today. The outward, physical circumstances we know, and those Ezekiel knew, differ so markedly that comparison is almost impossible. But the inward, spiritual states of men today and in Ezekiel's day resemble each other almost to the point of identity.

Today the man of faith finds himself far from the country he wants to dwell in. He is surrounded by some who have given up their faith and have compromised with materialistic culture. Some retain the words and forms of faith, but deny its power. Some have decided that faith is a wistful dream out of the past. And many are quietly, stubbornly living their faith in the confidence that God still is almighty. Put this paragraph in the past tense, and it will describe the people among whom Ezekiel lived and prophesied. There is no part of the Old Testament that speaks more directly to our spiritual condition today than does the prophecy of Ezekiel. The central message filling the prophecy is that faith in God, confronting squarely every horror of the present darkness, still looks into the future with hope.

B. The Vision, 1:4-28.

To the lonely exile by the Chebar God sent a vision. Today a person who sees visions is generally assumed to have a deranged mind, and frequently the assumption is correct. We determine mental illness by examining a person's life. If one who sees visions shows by his daily conduct that he is out of touch with reality, we know that he needs medical care. But the fact that a person sees visions must be examined in the light of that person's total life before damaging—or laudatory—conclusions are drawn. Many insane people believe that they are rich. Few would conclude that all who think themselves rich are therefore insane. Some people really are rich. Likewise, some people really see visions from God. All manner of pathological explanations have been offered for Ezekiel's experience, but the record of the prophecy itself will refute any thought that he was deranged. History has proved that Ezekiel was bitterly right in his conviction of impending tragedy. Those who laughed at him and brought on the tragedy were wrong. Ezekiel was gloriously right in his conviction that God would salvage His people from the tragedy. Those who gave up in despair were wrong. History shows no other example of a nation in exile keeping its culture intact and returning from exile to the native land. Who brought about this statistically impossible result? Ezekiel, more than any other man, was the architect of the restoration. Ezekiel was surrounded by madmen, but he was triumphantly sane.

When we have rejected the idea that Ezekiel's was a sick mind, still we find that his prophecy opens with a vision that at first—or tenth—reading is simply baffling. Of course what we read is translation. The translators have struggled mightily to make intelligible the rugged grandeur of Ezekiel's Hebrew. But the Jewish people of old knew almost all the difficulty that we know. In the Mishnah (*Hagiga* 2,1), the teachers are told not to expound the mystery of creation in the presence of more than one person, and the mystery of Ezekiel's chariot-throne not even to the one, unless he be unusually wise and discreet.

In large measure, the study of Ezekiel is the study of symbolism. Centuries later another Teacher, like Ezekiel, called Himself the Son of Man and taught by means of symbolic devices. Jesus frequently used the parable as Ezekiel occasionally did. Jesus' symbols are more readily accessible to our minds than are Ezekiel's, yet He too used vivid oriental figures of speech that sometimes bewilder us prosaic westerners.

A symbol is the use of one thing to suggest another. The thing used as a symbol may be received through any one of the senses —a touch of the hand or a whiff of perfume may well communicate volumes of meaning. To communicate the idea of "cat" from my mind to yours, I could draw a picture. That would be a symbol. We could agree upon some kind of Indian sign language. That would be an acted symbol. The most readily available symbols are words, sounds made in my voice box impinging upon your ear. After first using spoken symbolism, our fathers learned to use the symbolism of writing. The marks on a piece of paper "c-a-t" can neither purr nor catch mice, but they suggest to your mind the mammal that does purr and catch mice. When I have spoken or written or acted or pictured the symbol, it is not necessary for me to produce an actual cat so that we can think about it. Ezekiel's symbols are usually word-pictures.

To receive a symbol intelligently you must remember that it
it supposed to be transparent. When I say "cat" you do not
dwell interminably upon the actual sound I make, or the long
history of the word, or any one of a thousand other important
matters, you "see" through the symbol to your mental image
of the animal in question. So when Ezekiel describes his vision,
we must look beyond the wheels within wheels. His eagerness to
enter into complex detail often makes it difficult for us to "see"
what he means. The description of a prophet's call in Isaiah
6:1-8 makes a deeper impact upon the reader than that in Ezekiel 1-3, in large part because of its brevity. We become so
absorbed with the mechanics of Ezekiel's symbol that we cannot
"see" the symbolized. Or can we?

The entire prophecy of Ezekiel is one vast symbol. If I could
sum up the meaning of this symbol in one sentence, it would
have been quite unnecessary for Ezekiel to write his book, or
for me to write mine. Yet anyone who reads the vast, overall
symbol will "see" hope in God when history offers only despair.
The individual parts of the prophecy, like details in a painter's
masterpiece, are themselves symbols making their individual
contribution to the completed work.

What is your first impression upon reading Ezekiel 1? Bewilderment? Yes. But likewise you have a sense that an irresistible power is at work, moving where He will. This power is
mystery unspeakable, but the mystery is light and life. If you
"see" this much in the report of Ezekiel's vision, it has served its
purpose. If you do not perceive this much, further analysis of
details is of little value.

Ezekiel, standing by the Chebar, saw a storm cloud approaching from the north. In all probability this was a literal, physi-
1:4   cal cyclonic storm cloud, of a kind that is frequent in tropical
regions. In or near desert country, such clouds often are highly
colored by the refraction of light against the dust particles.
One's natural inclination is to close the eyes during such a
storm. The farmer, hoeing cucumbers in the field near Ezekiel,
saw the cloud approaching and hid his face. Ezekiel opened his
eyes and faced the storm without shrinking, and he "saw" the
glory of God. And this is the burden of the following book. In
the midst of historic disaster, Ezekiel learned to keep his (spiritual) eyes open. He saw the glory of the Lord moving through

the swirling cross-currents of history, and thus he was able not only to retain his faith but to triumph over the disaster.

The storm blew down from the north. This may be a suggestion that the Chaldeans would descend upon Jerusalem from that direction (Jeremiah 1:14). If so, it is a solemn reminder that God is present when the eye of flesh can see nothing but destruction and grief.

Ezekiel does not dwell upon the blackness of the cloud. He emphasizes the light. Read through the chapter, marking the different terms for illumination. The exile was looking at an approaching dust storm, as far as optical vision is concerned. With the eyes of spiritual vision he sees "brightness," "fire flashing forth continually," (the Hebrew means, "a fire taking hold of itself"), "gleaming bronze," "burning coals of fire," "torches moving to and fro," "lightning," "gleaming chrysolite," "shining like crystal," "sapphire," "the bow that is in the cloud on the day of rain." The reader is reminded irresistibly of another occasion when a small group of people, who had no earthly reason for hope, heard a sound like the rushing of a mighty wind, and they saw tongues of fire (Acts 2:1-4). It is almost impossible to talk seriously about God without mentioning light.

Ezekiel's next impression is of life. In the midst of the fiery cloud he sees "the likeness of four living creatures." (The word 1:5 "likeness" or "like" recurs some fifteen times as Ezekiel depicts the vision. He is at least suggesting how utterly inadequate are concepts of sense experience, and words derived from them, to express the reality of God.) The four living creatures are not called cherubim on this occasion, though in Chapters 9 and 10 they are so named. In view of the following description, it is difficult to imagine how these living creatures had "the form of men." Difficult as it may be for our imaginations to recapture what Ezekiel saw, we can understand the symbol. At the heart of reality is personal being, with whom even exiles can have personal relationship.

The anatomy of the four living creatures is baffling. The symbolism—or most of it—is clear. The question must inevitably arise, "Where did these symbols come from?" The basic answer has already been given. They came from God. But God sent this particular vision to a man named Ezekiel, a man with a nervous system all his own, who lived in a particular culture, who had his own unique set of memories. As William James has said, "Religious language clothes itself in such poor symbols as our life affords" (*Varieties of Religious Experience,* p. 11).

It was natural for Ezekiel to associate winged beings with God; for in the Temple cherubim adorned the Ark of the Covenant (I Chronicles 28:18). They were usually represented with two wings (I Kings 6:27), though in Ezekiel's vision they had four. Among the Babylonians were innumerable winged mythological creatures. Even the idea of a chariot-throne was a familiar symbol for deity in ancient times. For example, the sarcophagus of King Hiram of Gebal from the tenth century bears such a representation. Thus, from boyhood memories of the Temple and from non-Hebrew sources, the prophet's imagination supplied physical details for the vision of Him who is unimaginable.

In the Temple of Solomon, the cherubim had two faces, as do those described in 41:18f. The living creatures in the first
1:6 vision had four. The confusion of detail should be sufficient warrant for the most devout that the cherubim described in the Bible are symbolic. They bear no physical resemblance to any creatures we are likely to meet in heaven. No carving representing a four-faced cherub has yet been discovered. Even in imagination such a figure is grotesque. But the four-faced living creature signifies something important. The representation associated with God sees in every direction. This was a message sorely needed among the exiles, who were tempted to think that God had forgotten them. As the depiction of the chariot-throne develops, Ezekiel keeps emphasizing and re-emphasizing the fourfold aspect: four living creatures, four faces, four wings, four hands, four sides, and four wheels that go in any of the four directions into all the world. The legs
1:7 were unjointed, and the feet sparkled as the living creatures brought close the vision of God.

The symbolism of hands, helping hands, is manifest to one who is in the valley of the shadow. Whenever men think about
1:8 God they express their thought in terms of wings, flight. In the
1:9 opening words of the Bible, "the Spirit of God was moving over the face of the waters" (Genesis 1:2), the verb suggests a hovering bird. The Baptist saw a dove descending upon our Lord, and believed that it represented the Holy Spirit (John 1:32). And near the end of the Bible, as the woman clothed with

the sun faces dangers she cannot overcome, she is given the wings of an eagle (Revelation 12:14). Wings are a metaphor, almost as inevitable as light, for the divine.

The description is not clear. Would one expect it to be? Apparently each of the four living creatures was at the center of a side of the throne-chariot, which was square. The wing tips were touching at the corners of the square, as, with his other wings, each creature veiled his body. Wings in a vision need not be aerodynamically functional. It is sufficient if they enable one's thoughts to soar. Since the throne-chariot had four pilots, it could travel in any direction without turning. The message of the throne-chariot is more important than the mechanical engineering. The message is that God works without deviation of purpose even amid the disasters of history.

1:10 Each of the living creatures had four faces. (According to Targum *Jonathan,* there were four faces on each side of each cherub; so each had a total of sixteen faces. This, perhaps, is carrying symbolism to extremes.) What Ezekiel was expressing has never been better interpreted than in the ancient Jewish comment:

> The king among living creatures is a lion, the king among domestic animals is an ox, the king among birds is an eagle, but man takes his place proudly above them, and the Holy One, blessed be He, takes His place proudly above them all, and above the whole world in its entirety. —Midrash, *Rabbah Shemoth*

Christians have used the four faces to symbolize the different evangelists. The man (reason) represents Matthew; the lion (majesty) Mark; the ox (strength) Luke; and the eagle (swiftness) John. Notice that the face of man is always to the fore. Faith is reasonable. God is not the sort of Being whom our minds can picture—Ezekiel is telling us this vividly—yet God is One with whom we can have personal, rational relationships. Wherever the throne-chariot goes, the viewer sees first the symbol of divine reason. Centuries later another seer began his meditation, "In the beginning was the Word" (John 1:1).

1:12 "Wherever the Spirit would go, they went." A common impulse animated the four living creatures. Ezekiel's words, thus far, have given an impression of terrifying diversity. He has stressed the manifold ways in which the mind of man apprehends the divine. But if God were many, then our faith, instead of pulling life together, would split it further apart. Of all the prophets, Ezekiel is the one who most heavily stresses the Spirit, the unifying power of faith. The Spirit is the vital impulse by which God acts. This impulse can be described only

1:13 in terms of fire, "torches moving to and fro among the living creatures." Christian thought about the Holy Spirit is the development and enrichment of such OT thought as Ezekiel's.

A new element enters the vision. Ezekiel sees wheels. To the Jewish mystics in ancient time these wheels were personified

1:15 as angelic beings. They stood beside the cherubim and seraphim in the presence of God (Enoch 61:10; 70:7). The twentieth century reader, who insists upon treating the vision as a problem in mechanical drawing, is just as far from the mark. A wheel is a transparent symbol. It moves. God moves. The exiles thought of God as enthroned above the cherubim in Jerusalem. At the outset of his prophetic ministry Ezekiel sees—perhaps dimly at first—that he must break the paralyzing effect of this thought upon the minds of his contemporaries. The ensuing prophecy shows a passionate concern for the Temple, the focal point of faith on earth. But it shows likewise that mere physical distance from this point does not mean separation from God, and that mere physical closeness to the Temple is no warrant of closeness to God. Down through the centuries the blazing symbol speaks to all who hold, more or less, a stagnant faith in a distant God. This faith is inherited from ancestors who believed devoutly in the flaming glory of the Lord. Our God is still a consuming fire. The fire still moves.

It is hard to determine whether the laughter of the impious or the solemn diagrams of the pious are more damaging to the

1:16 "wheel within a wheel" that Ezekiel saw. Wheels in a vision do not need axles. Possibly those Ezekiel saw intersected at right angles so that, wherever the Spirit might direct, the wheels

1:17 could move instantly in that direction. Wheels "turn" in two ways. First is revolution about the axle, second is turning in response to the steering mechanism. In the latter sense, the wheels in the vision did not turn as they went. The symbolism is evident, if the engineering is not. God has many purposes that in our eyes often seem to conflict with each other. But coursing through the quicksands, earthquakes and hurricanes of this world, unswerving, unaltering and unstoppable, is the

1:18 Spirit of the living God. Upon the rims of the wheels were eyes. Again, through grotesque imagery the symbol shines. Eyes see. God knows what is happening along the banks of the Chebar.

1:20 The wheels do not move independently, only in response to the Spirit. The thought is even more relevant today than it was in Ezekiel's time. We emphasize the forces of nature—gravity, electricity, geologic change, survival of the fittest—and study them in isolation. We forget, sometimes, that God created the forces of nature to express the divine will. A typhoon, for example, is a thing, a "wheel" on God's "chariot." It moves blind, unthinking, unfeeling, with irresistible force. But its force with every other force finally is under the control of God. We see the "wheels." Ezekiel teaches us to "see" the Spirit.

Spread out above the heads of the living creatures is a shining platform upon which the throne rests. When the throne
1:24 draws close, Ezekiel hears the sound of relentless power, the
1:25 throbbing beat of gigantic wings. But when God speaks from His throne, the sound of the wings is stilled.

As the dark cloud continues to clear before him, Ezekiel sees the likeness of a sapphire throne. The actual gem stone in
1:26 Ezekiel's mind was probably *lapis lazuli,* since our "sapphire" was almost unknown in his time. Consciously or not, Ezekiel is referring to the vision of Moses, who saw under God's feet "a pavement of sapphire stone, like the very heaven for clearness" (Exodus 24:10). There is at least a suggestion of the blue sky above, that God is enthroned not in some distant heaven but over the earth.

With reticence imposed by awe, Ezekiel does not attempt to describe the throne, the symbol of universal sovereignty. Far
1:28 less does he attempt to depict God. He is faced with a dilemma known to every one who has attempted to speak or write about God. The Almighty is indescribable, but how can one say anything about Him without using words that have down-to-earth meanings? How can a man say that God is One with whom man may have personal relationships unless he uses personal terms? It is dangerous to describe God in human language, as Ezekiel well knew. He sought to avoid the danger, as far as possible, by removing five steps from saying that the divine resembles a man. Since the charge is frequently hurled that Ezekiel gives a crude, anthropomorphic picture of God, we might notice that he does not profess to see God, but "the appearance of the likeness of

the glory of the Lord." As if these three removes were not
enough, one finds two more describing the climax of the vision,
"a likeness as the appearance of a man" (AV). Moses Maimon-
ides commented on this verse:

> *The glory of the Lord* is different from "the Lord" Himself. All
> the figures in this vision refer to the glory of the Lord, i.e. to the
> chariot, and not to Him who rides upon the chariot; for God
> cannot be compared to anything.   —*Guide, 3,7*

God is not a human personality inflated to unusually large
dimensions. Yet we can, by faith, enter into personal relationships with Him. This much Ezekiel's symbolism suggests.

What could Ezekiel do? What did Moses do when he saw the
burning bush, or the disciples when our Lord was transfigured
before them? He fell upon his face, and heard the voice of one
who spoke. After the vision, the duty.

The details of the vision are puzzling. Ezekiel intended them
to be. He is attempting to convey in words the *mysterium tre-
mendum,* not to draw a picture of God. He has seen the divine
creative force as gleaming bronze and fire surrounded by brightness. Fire both illuminates and destroys. Ezekiel's message for
the next seven years will be the coming destruction of Jerusalem. But in the vision he sees more than fire, he sees "the appearance of the bow that is in the cloud on the day of rain."
Possibly this alludes to God's covenant with Noah (Genesis
9:13), certainly it foretells peace after the storm.

C. The Commission, 2:1–3:27.

The record of Ezekiel's commission exposes a characteristic
of the prophecy that was becoming visible in the narration of
the vision. Ezekiel is a most repetitious book. Having said a
thing once, the writer says it again in a slightly different form.
This fact accounts, in large part, for the popular neglect of
Ezekiel today, when we need so desperately the message that he
states so clearly, and so often. In Chapters 2-3, Ezekiel recounts
his commission five times, with minor variations.

1. First Commission, 2:1-7.

While commissioning Ezekiel God calls him "Son of Man."
In the Hebrew idiom the term "son" denotes what we would
2:1 call membership in a class. Thus "Son of Man" means "a
member of the class of man," or "a mortal." Ezekiel's mortal

weakness contrasts with the vision of divine power that he has just witnessed. "Son of Man" occurs rarely in the rest of the OT, (e.g. Job 25:6; Psalm 8:4). But in Ezekiel God thus addresses the prophet eighty-seven times. Later Jews used the phrase messianically (see the Book of Enoch). In this sense, Jesus appropriated the title, while still retaining the original humble meaning.

God tells the Son of Man to stand upon his feet. "It is man erect, man in his manhood, with whom God will have fellowship and with whom He will speak" (A. B. Davidson).

Notice the four stages of the prophet's call, and compare them with the biblical record of the call to other strong men of God. First, Ezekiel was overwhelmed with awe (1:28). Second, he received clear, intellectual understanding of the duty implied in his knowledge of God (2:7—3:11). Third, he needed time to meditate (3:15f.). Fourth, he undertook the appointed task (4:1—48:35).

With a duty God gives the strength to perform it. The Spirit entered Ezekiel and set him upon his feet. In the prophecy the
2:2 doctrine of the Spirit is not developed to the extent that we find in the Acts of the Apostles and the letters of Paul, but the foundation for later development is firm. The word "spirit" recurs frequently, sometimes in the forms "Spirit of the Lord" or "Spirit of God." The OT concept of the Spirit reaches its thunderous climax in 37:7-10.

God commissions the Son of Man to go to the rebellious people of Israel. In 593 B.C., of course, the Kingdom of Israel,
2:3 as distinct from the Kingdom of Judah, had long ceased to be. The term "Israel" probably has no deeper significance than "the entire Hebrew community of faith, whether still in Jerusalem or exiled in Babylon." The Lord describes His people as "a nation of rebels" (literally "nations"). This is a difficult expression. The term "nations" applies to the heathen in contrast with Judah and Israel. The LXX and NT translation is "gentiles." The term is a forecast of the next twenty-two chapters. The Jewish people have become, for all spiritual purposes, "gentiles."

The idea of a "rebellious" people keeps recurring during the early stages of the prophecy. As will become clear, some foolhardy patriots were plotting a rebellion against Babylon. At the outset of his prophetic ministry Ezekiel must resist them—

vainly. He believed the Babylonian exile to be the will of God, and that hope for restoration lay in cooperating with Babylon, not rebellion.

To the impudent and stubborn people Ezekiel must bring a message: "Thus says the Lord God." The prophets were sent
2:4 to proclaim God's message, not their own transitory ideas. Ezekiel's term, "The Lord God," has occasioned much comment. The Hebrew is *Adonai YHWH. Adonai* means "my Lord." The name of God is *YHWH.* This word, in its written form, is called the Tetragram, or the Four Letters. Among the Hebrews the name is considered too sacred to be pronounced; so when the reader encounters it, he says, "my Lord," *Adonai.* The double term, *Adonai YHWH* is read "The Lord God." When vowels were added to the Hebrew text in the early Middle Ages, the scribes inserted the vowels for *Adonai* or *Elohim* (God) in the Tetragram, whence the pronunciation "Jehovah." Scholars today are universally agreed that this is not the correct pronunciation. Most agree that the name should be pronounced "Yahweh." Were this an ordinary word, their linguistic reasoning would be irrefutable. But this is a sacred word, left unpronounced for a millennium. It is better to leave it so. Some have found a special emphasis in Ezekiel's frequent use of the double term, as introducing or concluding an oracle. But there are sufficient exceptions to make it quite doubtful that Ezekiel intended any clear-cut distinction from his frequent use of *YHWH.*

In the initial commission the voice warns Ezekiel to expect rejection. He is to do his work, whether the people respond or
2:5 not. To the warning the voice adds a thought filled with strength, "They will know that there has been a prophet among them." This thought is repeated in 33:33. Hostile words and looks are likened to briars, thorns, and scorpions. The last
2:6 named are taken quite seriously by any who have lived in the tropics. But even with the image of scorpions before him, the prophet is admonished not to be fearful nor dismayed; for he is God's spokesman.

2. Second Commission—the Scroll, 2:8—3:3.

The second commission introduces an element that has caused much disagreement. Ezekiel is told to enact a truth. Were these
2:8 actions physically performed? Or are they written dramatic

parables? In the case immediately before us, it is quite clear that the action was symbolic. No physical mastication took place. In some of the other cases, it is by no means so clear.

Ezekiel lived in a community where, like any man, he was influenced by the thoughts and acts of his neighbors. The voice

2:9 warns him not to share in the rebellious attitudes that surround him. Instead, he must eat what God gives him. A "hand" extends to him a written scroll. (In Jeremiah 1:9, with which comparison is inevitable, the hand of the Lord touches the prophet's lips.)

A scroll was made of animal skins in Palestine and Babylon, of papyrus in Egypt. A full scroll consisted of many sheets sewn

2:10 together, to a length of twenty or thirty feet. Usually the scroll had writing upon only one side, the "front" as it appeared to the person unrolling it. Sometimes economy would require the writer to use both sides. A person who received a scroll with writing "on the front and on the back" would obviously not be able to add his own words to it. Medieval theologians found a quite different significance in the expression, i.e., that the Scripture has both an outward meaning and an inward, mystical meaning. A scroll would bear a title, summing up its content. The title Ezekiel saw told of "lamentation and mourning and woe." This summary aptly describes the prophet's dreary labors during the next seven years, as he tries to warn his people that folly can but lead to destruction.

Even though the message comes from God, Ezekiel must make it his own by devouring it. The food God gives to us becomes

3:3 bone and muscle in our bodies only if we eat it; similarly the Son of Man must assimilate the message contained in the scroll and then relate it to the people. When he took into himself the message, Ezekiel discovered that it was "sweet as honey" (Psalm 119:103). Readers of Ezekiel's prophecy have come independently to the same conclusion. One first encounters only darkness and destruction. There are many grim passages in the Bible, but none more grim than Ezekiel's writing. Yet the reader discovers, in time, that Ezekiel (like God) delights not in the death of a sinner. Ezekiel (like God) warns the sinner so that he will repent and live. The prophecy Ezekiel wrote is one of the most hopeful books ever composed, but its beauty and joy do not become evident until you have made it your own.

This passage throws some light upon the nature of prophetic inspiration. On the one hand, a prophet does not discover the truth by any reasoning of his own, it is revealed to him by a Power external to himself; on the other hand, it is revealed only to one who has been specially called to receive a word from God. Again, a prophet's inspiration, so far from overwhelming his natural faculties, quickens and uplifts them; not only the language which he speaks, but the particular truth which he has to proclaim, is colored and to some extent determined by his own individuality. He responds with something of his own to the divine approach; so that the truth which emerges is due neither to God's action alone, nor to man's effort alone; it is due to both.

—G. H. Cooke

3. Third Commission, 3:4-11.

The third commission intensifies the warning message of the first. The Son of Man is directed anew not "to a people of foreign speech and a hard language, but to the house of Israel." The colorful expression is "deep of lip and heavy of tongue." Babylon was filled with people from many lands, with whom the Hebrews conversed in many tongues; for communication is necessary to survival. Aramaic was the *lingua franca* of the time. It had been in use for diplomatic purposes for many years (II Kings 18:26f). So quite probably most of the exiles, who were from the ruling classes, were familiar with the Aramaic before they left Jerusalem. But still it was to them a foreign language, spoken and understood with difficulty. At the outset of his prophetic ministry, Ezekiel learns that he might find a readier hearing among the foreigners than among his own people. A similar thought is found frequently through the Bible. Reread the Book of Jonah. Remember our Lord's sad words recorded in Matthew 11:20-24. Yet Jesus told His disciples to begin their prophetic ministry in Jerusalem, where the work would be the hardest (Luke 24:47). To a person experienced in church work today, it is not necessary to point out modern parallels.

Rejection of Ezekiel is relatively unimportant. But the voice says that those who reject him are actually rejecting God. One greater than Ezekiel likewise encountered spiritual deafness (John 12:44-49). In a vivid picturesque phrase the voice describes the people of Israel as "hard of forehead." This alludes to a pushing ox or ram, employed to move carts along rutty roads or across rough fields, while his more tractable companion was pulling in harness.

Evil can be stubborn. Goodness has a stubborn quality too. If you have watched two rams fighting, you can appreciate the **3:9** ironic promise, "Like adamant harder than flint have I made your forehead. Fear them not." Outnumbered and outshouted he would be, but not overcome. Ezekiel receives no promise of physical safety. All that he receives is a duty to perform and strength to perform it. In the early Middle Ages, Agobard of Lyons commented on this passage:

> Not to fear the persecutors of the body is a great gift of God, as the Lord demonstrates when . . . he says to Ezekiel . . . "Fear them not, nor be dismayed at their looks." To fear an enemy who can inflict only bodily injury is a grave defect.
> —*On the Truth of the Faith,* xxi

With the warning of immediate failure, Ezekiel is told to go to the exiles, "to your people" (literally, "the children of your **3:11** people"). There is a bitterness here that is impossible to translate. The term "people" is used for God's chosen nation, Ezekiel's brothers in blood and faith, who are busy rejecting God and will reject Ezekiel. Even so, it is his duty to go to them with the message from the Lord, "whether they hear or refuse to hear." The preacher's task is to proclaim the message faithfully, with all the skill at his command. Neither success nor failure can alter his responsibility.

4. Time for Meditation, 3:12-15.

Jesus, after His baptism, went into the desert to pray. Paul, after his conversion, went to Arabia to meditate. Ezekiel, after **3:12** seeing the vision, went back to Tel-abib to ponder the mystery he had beheld. Still in the state of exaltation, he felt that he was lifted up and carried to the settlement where, we believe, he lived. While he turned from the place where he had seen the vision, he heard behind him the sound as of a great earthquake. The mighty wings raised the chariot-throne, and their throbbing pulsations seemed to chant, "Blessed be the glory of the Lord from his place" (AV). (I cannot accept the conjecture in RSV, which is based upon the supposition that a copyist mistook a C for an M. In the Hebrew alphabet the two letters are somewhat similar in shape, and confusion is quite frequent. But in this case MT agrees substantially with LXX. And in the following pages, the "place" of the "glory of the Lord" is a critical issue. Is it just in Jerusalem? Ezekiel is seeing, as an-

other prophet saw, that "the whole earth is full of his glory"
[Isaiah 6:3b.])

Exalted as he was, Ezekiel returned to Tel-abib in "bitterness." His eyes had seen the appearance of the likeness of the
3:14   glory of the Lord, but he had received a duty to perform that
must necessarily separate him from his friends and fellow exiles.
Yet the "Spirit" lifted him up, and the "Hand of the Lord" was
strong upon him, impelling him to the place he did not wish to
go, to perform the duty that he did not wish to perform.
"Spirit" and "Hand" are different metaphors for the same
reality, acting upon Ezekiel's "spirit," leading him to his post
of duty among the exiles. Not only does the Spirit manifest
Himself to men in periods of ecstasy or superhuman strength.
More significantly, He is with us at all times of bitterness, still
caring, still guiding.

Tel-abib was a Jewish settlement on the banks of the Chebar.
In all probability it was Ezekiel's home (3:24). In the Babylo-
3:15   nian tongue the name is *til abubi*, "the mound of the deluge."
The Hebrew exiles, like any homesick people, took the sound
of the words and adapted it to their own language. The Hebrew
means "hill of corn ears." Archaeologists have discovered evidence of extensive Jewish settlement near Babylon. It has as yet
been impossible to identify any specific location as Tel-abib.

Ezekiel's ministry began in silence. He returned to Tel-abib,
presumably to his own house, and sat in silence for seven days.
He was "overwhelmed" (RSV), "astonished" (AV), "appalled"
(JPS). What word could express the man's feelings? He had
been stunned by his vision of the truth. He had been stunned
by the burden of duty God laid upon him. He needed time to
think before he began to act.

5. Fourth Commission—the Watchman, 3:16-21.

The fourth commission has a burning relevance for the minister today. Here Ezekiel picks up and develops the thought of
individual responsibility that was suggested in 2:7. The same
thought is examined in greater depth in Chapters 14, 18, and
33. Many consider Ezekiel's emphasis upon individual responsibility his chief contribution to our faith. God is beside the
river Chebar, or whatever corresponds to the Chebar in your
life. Because God is there, or here, you are directly responsible
to Him. The fourth commission emphasizes the prophet's re-

sponsibility to speak to the point of moral decision, whether his
hearers listen or no.

In ancient times a watchman stood on a high point overlooking the entire city. He had two duties—to watch and to warn.
3:17   He would watch for invasion from without, and for fire, crime,
or insurrection within the city. The watchman did not want
these tragedies, but if one were to develop, he would sound the
alarm so that responsible citizens could take the necessary meas-
ures to keep the danger from becoming a catastrophe. "Watchman" was thus a natural symbol for a prophet. It is surprising
how seldom the prophets applied it to themselves. Habakkuk
2:1 is the best known example, though it occurs rarely in Isaiah,
Jeremiah, and Hosea.

There is both a similarity and a difference between the duty
of a watchman and that which God entrusted to Ezekiel. The
3:18   watchman speaks to the city. Ezekiel has been ordered to speak
to the whole House of Israel, but more than this, he is responsible to address the individual. Notice the change in focus. "You
shall give *them* warning." "If . . . you give *him* no warning . . .
his blood I will require at your hand." The other prophets had
spoken, each in his way, to the community of faith. Ezekiel did
this, but likewise carried the burden usually borne by the
priests or elders, that of ministering to the individual.

Ezekiel says that the wicked "shall die in his iniquity," if he
does not turn from his wickedness. Christian readers should be
careful not to read NT concepts into the OT. When Ezekiel
speaks of "death" he means, usually, the end of physical life,
sometimes the end of spiritual life. He is not speaking of hell
as understood by Christians. The OT has little to say about the
life beyond, but a great deal to say about the importance of
turning to God while there is time.

Four hypothetical cases are cited, showing the watchman's
responsibility and the hearer's. In the first, the watchman fails
3:19   to warn the individual, who dies in his sin, hence the watchman is guilty of murder. The second shows the watchman faithful, but the hearer persistent in his wickedness. Since the
watchman has done his duty, he is guiltless. (Notice how "life,"
3:20   in this sentence, can mean only "spiritual life.") The third
shows a "righteous" man who turns from his righteousness despite the watchman's warning. This verse has given unspeakable
difficulty to readers in every generation; for it shows God putting

a stumbling-block before a righteous person. The Rabbis (Babylonian Talmud *Yoma* 86b) interpreted the "righteous" man in this verse as one who outwardly obeyed the Law, but denied it in his heart. This person would be "righteous" from the viewpoint of his neighbors. (Has Christian practice really progressed much beyond this concept of righteousness?) God might well place a stumbling-block before such a person. He does not lead an innocent mind to sin, but He uses sin already existing, and punishes it usually with worse sin. Since the watchman has failed to warn this outwardly righteous man, the watchman is

3:21 guilty of his death. We would expect the fourth case to show a sinner who repents at the watchman's urging. But Ezekiel, as we have discovered, is not one to do what we expect. Instead he shows the righteous man (as far as the world can judge) who heeds the watchman's warning and does not sin. Thus his righteousness is both inward and outward. He lives, and the prophet who has done his duty likewise lives.

The focus of attention in the fourth commission is upon the watchman and his responsibility. In later developments of the thought, particularly in Chapter 18, the focus is upon the hearer rather than the one who gives the warning.

6. Fifth Commission—the Blight of Dumbness, 3:22-27.

The fifth commission offers difficulties that have called forth heroic conclusions, of which the chief is that the editor has misplaced what belongs several years later in the prophet's life, and should have been placed in Chapter 24. The difficulties are not imagined; for this commission seems directly to contradict the preceding. In the commission Ezekiel is carried out to the plain, and then ordered to return to his house, a round trip that has given raucous mirth to some commentators. Ezekiel is bound with "cords," though the next pages show him moving about freely. Here Ezekiel is struck "dumb," yet later chapters show him speaking. The difficulties are genuine enough. But our task is not to rewrite the book of Ezekiel, or even to re-edit it; rather we seek in Ezekiel spiritual help for today. I could name at least one clergyman, prone to discouragement, who has found help in studying this passage.

In the first place, Ezekiel says "the hand of the Lord was there upon me." Thus we are dealing with the account of an inward,
3:22 spiritual experience. The trip to the plain did not involve any physical motion. The "cords" were not visible. Others could

hear Ezekiel speak though he was "dumb." Christians sometimes display a curious inconsistency when they act as if the
spiritual is less "real" than the material. The "cords" were
"real" enough, but Ezekiel could not have tied up a package
with them.

3:23

3:24

3:25

3:26

3:27

In the vision the Lord commanded Ezekiel to go forth into
the "plain." There is a clear distinction between visions in the
"plain" (Chapters 3; 8:4, 37), and those by the Chebar (Chapters
1, 10). The term originally meant "valley," but it came to be applied to a vast area, as in our phrase, "the Mississippi valley."
It would be pointless to locate upon a map the "plain" to which
Ezekiel went in his vision. Once more the "glory of the Lord"
was evident. Once more the Son of Man fell upon his face.
Once more the Spirit lifted him up and sent him from the place
of exaltation to the place of duty. We suppose that Ezekiel's
house was in Tel-abib. Quite possibly he had not left it since
returning from the initial vision. Thus interpreted, the passage
means that Ezekiel longed for the rapture of faith, but God
called him to the drudgery. If this interpretation be correct,
then the "cords" with which Ezekiel was "bound" have already
been mentioned, in a quite different figure of speech, as briars,
thorns, and scorpions—impediments that will keep the prophet
from achieving what he longs to accomplish.

What is dumbness? We usually say that it is inability to make
a vocal sound. More often, dumbness is inability to make a
sound that others can interpret as a word. It is inability to make
one's self understood. To take the "dumbness" of Ezekiel as a
physical affliction raises innumerable problems, chief among
them that Ezekiel continues speaking in a natural voice. But
the symbolic meaning of dumbness has already been expressed.
Ezekiel is addressing a rebellious people who will refuse to
hear; "for they are not willing to listen" (3:7). Ezekiel is responsible to declare the message God gives him, whether or
not it falls upon deaf ears.

In less picturesque language, the fifth commission means that
Ezekiel is to carry on his unpopular ministry, speaking to the
few who will listen, until finally the whole House of Israel
turns to seek God's counsel from him. It is a renewed warning
that he will be rejected by those he wants to help, a renewed call
to be faithful despite every discouragement, a renewed promise
that finally God will be heard, speaking through Ezekiel. Thus

interpreted, no re-editing of the prophecy is called for, no delv-
ings into speech pathology are required, and no contradiction
is found with what precedes or what follows. The power of
Ezekiel is his use of symbolism. In the fifth commission he has
used it—powerfully.

II. THE FIRST CYCLE OF WARNINGS, 4:1—7:27.

A. Dramatic Parables, 4:1—5:17.

Here begins a long, drawn out, terrifyingy cry that ruin is to
fall upon Jerusalem. It sounds, at first, like a pitiless cry. A
more careful examination shows that the prophet's own heart
is breaking with pity as he warns of the doom that must fall if
his people continue the course they are following. In later chapters Ezekiel spells out the sins of his people. Here, he foretells
the inevitable result.

The first warnings that we encounter are in the form of dramatic parables. Reading through these parables, one must inevitably ask: were they actually performed, or does Ezekiel use
a literary device to convey an unwelcome truth? First, of course,
we must remember the long history of symbolic action by the
prophets (e.g. I Samuel 15:27). We remind ourselves that superstitious, primitive people believe a symbolic act will help bring
on the thing symbolized, hence an acted parable would be more
meaningful to people in ancient time than to us. But the exiles
were not superstitious primitives, they were the cream of Hebrew
society. A written message could be passed from hand to hand
in the market place, pondered in the council of the elders, and
finally smuggled back to Jerusalem, while an action would be
seen by a few, and then distorted in the telling. We know that
the parables were written out, sooner or later. We know that
the written form of these parables is far more impressive, to us,
than would be the sight of a grown man on the floor playing
war-games. We cannot picture how it would be physically possible for Ezekiel to lie bound upon the floor 430 days, while
performing all sorts of other symbolic actions. In 12:18 Ezekiel
is commanded to eat and drink in fear and trembling. While
the written account conveys actual terror, it is hard to see how
the action would convey anything to the beholder. Any dogmatic statement, either that Ezekiel did or did not act out his

parables, is unjustified. But the evidence supports A. B. Davidson's conclusion that "probably none of them were actually performed."

The message came through, despite the "dumbness" and the "bonds." When Jerusalem actually fell, seven years later, a nucleus of the faithful in Babylon was prepared to accept the judgment of God. They held fast the faith when every earthly reason for faithfulness was destroyed. Ezekiel with his "parables" had enabled them to be strong. ´

Despite the forbidding aspect, the Prophecy of Ezekiel is among the most hopeful books ever written. The reader's first impression is definitely not that of hope. The reader finds so much "lamentation and mourning and woe" (2:10) that he may well miss entirely that the prophet is saying, "Only if you look steadfastly into the storm cloud can you see that the eternal light shines there." With more detail than we enjoy, Ezekiel invites us to examine the storm cloud. As we learn to keep our eyes open against the gritty wind, we see fitful sparks and then dim flickers of light. The prophecy continues, the intermittent shinings of light become more and more frequent, more and more sustained, until the concluding section of the book is one dazzling expanse of glory. The first few expressions of hope are so faint that the reader may not recognize them as hope. Yet even in the fourth chapter, where we are torn between anguish and disgust, we can discern the element of hope that is to become the predominating theme of the book.

1. The Siege of Jerusalem, 4:1-3.

The first parable shows the Son of Man taking a brick upon which he portrays the city of Jerusalem. The Babylonians used
4:2 clay tiles for written purposes. The Hebrews in Palestine did not, but Ezekiel was in Babylon, predicting a Babylonian victory against his home city. Archaeologists have discovered clay tiles with building plans incised upon them. So it would be natural, under the circumstances, for a Hebrew exile to use the Babylonian writing material. The parable shows Ezekiel taking a tile upon which he draws a rough map of Jerusalem. On other tiles he represents the armament of the besieging troops. Tersely he describes the basic elements of a military siege in his day. The "siege-wall" was a wheeled tower from which archers could shoot into the city. The "mound" was a bank of earth raised to the level of the city wall, both for observation and for attack.

The battering "ram" was a Roman invention. (They actually placed a metal ram's head at the end of a heavy beam.) But the Babylonians used the same principle, an iron-shod beam transported by a wheeled tower. Sculptured representations of these lethal tools are frequent among the ruins of Babylon. Sennacherib (704-681 B.C.), in his annals, tells how he used these implements, together with sapping and mining the walls, to subdue the Hebrew cities.

The symbol of the iron plate is not so readily apparent. The plate itself was a griddle used for baking. Many believe that it **4:3** symbolizes only the "iron" severity of the siege. But the verse seems rather to show Ezekiel commanded to enact the part of God, to set his face toward the city, and to press the siege against it. The thought is a bitter distillate of tragedy. The iron plate symbolizes the barrier that the people of Jerusalem have erected between themselves and their Lord. Hence God Himself will destroy the city by means of the Babylonian army. If this interpretation is correct, then in the first words of warning we find the first sign of hope; for the impending tragedy is to come not through the malice of man but through the judgment of God. And the exiles knew—intellectually at least—that God's wrath is governed finally by His love.

2. The Length of the Exile, 4:4-8.

The second parable produces another insoluble puzzle. Ezekiel turns from enacting the part of God to enacting that of **4:4** the Hebrew people. A person standing in Jerusalem, with his face to the rising sun, would have the northern Kingdom of Israel to his left. Hence the left side represents the northern kingdom, demolished in 722 B.C. Israel was already "bound" **4:5** and helpless. Ezekiel, lying on his left side, signifies the punishment of his people. The three hundred ninety days, representing a like number of years, produce the question without any definitive answer. The rabbis long ago determined that probably the days of bondage suggest the period from Rehoboam's splitting the kingdom asunder (c. 932 B.C.) until the fall of Jerusalem in 586 B.C. Thus the period symbolizes Israel's sin rather than the punishment, while Ezekiel speaks of the punishment rather than the sin. For these reasons many students today think it more realistic to accept the reading in LXX, "one hundred ninety." The fall of Samaria in 722 B.C. was almost exactly one hundred fifty years before Ezekiel's vision. Dating from this beginning of Hebrew exile, and adding the forty years symbolized in 4:6, one would thus reach the total of one hundred ninety. Neither of the proposed explanations is wholly satisfactory. Would that this posed the most serious insoluble problem in Ezekiel.

For all the confusion about chronology, our fathers rightly discerned the meaning of the verse. A passage in the Dead Sea Scrolls reads:

> In the Era of Anger, that era of the three hundred and ninety years, when He delivered them into the hand of Nebuchadnezzar, king of Babylon, He took care of them and brought to blossom alike out of the priesthood and out of the laity that root which had been planted of old, allowing it once more to possess the land and to grow fat in the richness of its soil. Then they realized their iniquity and knew that they had been at fault.
>
> —Theodore H. Gaster, *The Dead Sea Scriptures,* pp. 61-62

Though the botanical imagery is poor, Ezekiel's message is well understood. In times that are to us dark and terrifying, God still is working out His purpose. Man has failed. God has not.

4:6   The symbolized forty years representing the punishment of the House of Judah raise almost as many chronological difficulties as the three hundred ninety representing Israel. The period from the deportation of Jehoiachin (597 B.C.) to the return of the Hebrews (538 B.C.) is fifty-nine years. Measuring from the fall of Jerusalem (586) gives forty-eight years. Jeremiah had predicted an exile of seventy years' duration (Jeremiah 29:10). All attempts to read exact chronology into this part of the vision or to reconcile it with Jeremiah have proved futile. Perhaps we can best say that forty years is frequently used in the Bible to express one generation. With our penchant for mathematical accuracy, we wonder why the prophets of old could not be more precise. Ezekiel is proclaiming hope, not statistics. To the exiles, the end of Jerusalem meant the end of everything. Perhaps their individual lives might continue for a few years after the disaster, but faith would be destroyed. Yet even as he warns of the impending tragedy, Ezekiel says that beyond the destruction is the rebuilding of Jerusalem, and that within one generation.

The period of affliction would have an end, but still it would be a period of affliction. In this vision we have two different

4:7   threats—siege and exile. With bewildering rapidity the prophet
changes his role. First he represents exiled Israel, then exiled
4:8   Judah, then the Babylonians besieging the city, and then the
city itself, helpless during the siege. Critics have claimed that
some of these verses are misplaced. In their present order, they
create a vivid picture with the shifting horror of a nightmare.
Nightmares, by and large, are not logically arranged. Phantoms
coalesce into one another. As this parable stands, it shows confusion, but growing out of the confusion is hope.

    3. The Unclean Food, 4:9-17.

    Any lingering doubt that we are dealing with a vision rather
than a physical enactment must be dispelled by the third sym-
4:9   bol; for here Ezekiel is commanded to take grain and make
bread while lying bound upon his side. In a vision such things
are possible. Not only are Ezekiel's actions puzzling, but the
thing being symbolized is likewise puzzling. Again, it seems to
be both the siege and the exile. The odd mixture of grains indicates scarcity rather than ceremonial impurity. (Deuteronomy
22:9 and Leviticus 19:19 do not forbid the mixing of grain in
flour.) Thus the basic symbol represents the siege, but it is
coupled with the mysterious three hundred ninety days (LXX
one hundred ninety) representing exile. From what we know
of the exile, the Hebrews did not suffer rigorous persecution.
In the years following Ezekiel's vision, some of them became
quite wealthy. Their chief sorrow was that they could not fully
practice the dietary and other requirements of their Law.

    The food was crude and unpalatable, and the quantity was
limited. The daily bread ration would be a little more than
4:11 nine ounces, and the sixth part of a hin would be about a
4:12 quart of water. The meager supply of food, cooked in the most
revolting possible way, would be eaten with all the relish that
one would customarily give to barley cakes.

    The passage about the food is disgusting. (So was the siege
of Jerusalem.) Yet this passage makes one of the most important
4:13 points in the prophecy, that faith will be possible when Jerusalem is destroyed. Human dung as fuel is not only revolting,
it is ceremonially impure (Deuteronomy 23:13). To eat food
cooked in such a manner would be a denial of faith. But in the
last days of a siege, when men are reduced to eating rats—or
each other—ceremonial exactness is difficult to observe. Likewise

it was extremely difficult for the exiles to maintain their rigid
dietary code; for they did not control the markets.

The positive message in this horrible parable is so indirectly
stated that many commentators have missed it altogether. The
4:14   exile protests that he has practiced his faith. He has scrupu-
lously tried to observe the dietary code. Whatever the difficulties
of eating Kosher food in a foreign land, Ezekiel had followed
4:15   the Law. God hears and answers the prayer by conceding the
use of animal dung as fuel instead of human dung. Palestinian
farmers today use dried cow dung or camel dung for cooking.
The American west was settled by pioneers who cooked with
buffalo chips that made a clean, odorless fire. In every material
sense this fuel is preferable to the other. However the concession
is made not to Ezekiel's squeamishness, but to his faith. The
former fuel is not only physically disgusting, it is religiously impure to a Hebrew. The latter will bring neither physical nor
spiritual contamination. Ezekiel's point, thus obliquely expressed to the exiles, is that God cares when His people are in
the valley of the shadow. If they strive there to be faithful to
Him, He will make their faith possible.

The parable concludes with an interpretation. In this place
Ezekiel does not show why the harsh judgment of God is neces-
4:16   sary. That explanation will follow in time. Here he announces
the fact of impending doom. "Staff of bread" is a biblical idiom
suggesting man's reliance upon his staple food (e.g., Psalm
105:16). In Jerusalem the staff must be broken. Under King
Hezekiah a tunnel was dug, bringing water from the spring
Gihon into the city (II Kings 20:20). Yet even with this engi-
4:17   neering marvel, the wretched dwellers in the evil city must
drink water "by measure and in dismay . . . and waste away
under their punishment."

4. The Doom of Jerusalem, 5:1-4.

In the fourth brief parable we are dealing once more with
physical actions that would be impossible to one lying bound
5:1   upon the floor. It is questionable, from the grammarian's viewpoint, whether Ezekiel is to take a sword or a razor-sharp knife
symbolizing a sword. In either case the meaning is inescapable.
The invader will scrape the land bare (Isaiah 7:20). Perhaps
there is another allusion. Among the bearded Hebrews shaving
was sometimes thought a disgrace (II Samuel 10:4), and some-

times a sign of mourning (Isaiah 15:2). Balances today signify justice. Probably that is their significance in the parable.

Writing several years before Zedekiah's fanatical revolt, Ezekiel warns that rebellion must end in destruction for the rebels.

5:2 The hairs of his head, each representing a resident in Jerusalem, are divided into three equal piles. Each pile is destroyed, one by fire, one by sword, and one by dispersion to the winds, where the avenging sword still destroys. In this catalogue of

5:4 horror there is a tiny fragment of hope. From the scattered remnant Ezekiel is to gather together what he can and bind the tangled hairs in the skirt of his robe, from which he takes some and casts them upon the fire—not the same fire that had already destroyed the symbolic city of Jerusalem.

Where is the hope? Some will be cast upon the fire, not all. Thus negatively Ezekiel introduces the idea of the remnant. He foresees with devastating accuracy the destruction of all the religious and political institutions that have supported the faith. But the faith itself will live in the lives of the remnant who will remain loyal to God. The faithful will be surrounded by a thousand perils. From the sputtering flame the blaze will spread to the whole of Israel. More prosaically, as a natural result of the rebellion in Jerusalem, new hardships will fall upon the exiles already in Babylon.

5. Explanation of the Parables, 5:5-17.

Following the four parables of horror, Ezekiel adds an interpretation "This is Jerusalem." It is hard for us to appreciate

5:5 what Jerusalem meant to our fathers in faith. We take it for granted that people always have known, "the hour is coming when neither on this mountain nor in Jerusalem will you worship the Father" (John 4:21). To our forebears Jerusalem was the focal point of spiritual life, set "in the center of the nations." The rabbis of old thought that Jerusalem was the center of the earth. This idea persisted at least until the time of Dante (*Inferno*, 34). With our present geographical concepts we believe that the center of the earth is four thousand miles below Jerusalem, or any other city. Politically, Jerusalem never remotely approached being the center of the nations in the sense that Babylon, Egypt, Macedonia, and Rome were power-centers. Yet in a spiritual sense Jerusalem has been, and will be, the moral center of mankind. From this rather insignificant city, the capital of a tiny nation, the knowledge of God has radiated into the whole world. We take for granted what Ezekiel was attempting to tell his contemporaries, that the knowledge of God is what matters, not the physical existence of the stones and mortar men called Jerusalem. To our fathers this was a revolutionary idea.

Jerusalem has received special blessing from God, yet she has sinned "more than the nations." Egyptian and Babylonian legal
5:6 and moral codes show highly developed concepts of right and wrong that in many respects approach the Hebrew Law. Ezekiel claims in effect that for a Hebrew to violate a divine ordinance is more grievous than for a Babylonian to commit the same act. Why? The Hebrews had the divine "statutes" as well as the "ordinances." "Statutes" concern the relationship between man and God, while "ordinances" deal with the relationship between man and man. Jerusalem was a city blessed with the knowledge of God. Because of this knowledge her sin was more culpable than the sins of the surrounding nations (Amos 3:2).

The verse under consideration is filled with difficulties. The verb translated "are turbulent" is of uncertain meaning. Later
5:7 the Hebrew reads "you have acted" while LXX reads, "you have not acted" (cf. 11:12). The Talmud interprets, "In your conduct you have not followed the examples of the righteous Gentiles, but you have copied the evils of the corrupt peoples" (*Sanhedrin* 39b). Probably this obscure verse means that the heathen are living up to their knowledge of right, while Jerusalem is living far below her knowledge. More and more this theme will dominate the first half of the prophecy. Jerusalem
5:8 has sinned. Jerusalem must die. God will execute her "in the
5:10 sight of the nations." Her death will be a hideous example. During the last days of the siege the gaunt defenders will be reduced to cannibalism.

Now, at last, Ezekiel expresses the particular sin that must bring on the judgment. It is idolatry, the worship of things that
5:11 are less than God. As far as crime is concerned, there is no evidence that the Hebrews were markedly more wicked than their neighbors, and considerable evidence that they were less wicked. But they had violated the first of all the commandments. They had placed other beings before God. OT history, from the time of the golden calf to that of the exile, shows an almost unending accomodation to the various nature-religions

of the surrounding people. The prophets called this Baal worship. The nature-gods represented various divinely created powers, chief among them fertility. Strong leaders like Samuel, David, Asa, Hezekiah and Josiah reduced the extent of nature worship. Under weak leaders like Ahab alien practices flourished. During the early years of Manasseh's fifty-five year reign, the king himself built altars for worshiping the host of heaven inside the very courts of the Temple (II Kings 21:5). As Ezekiel will show in later chapters, contaminated faith still flourished in Jerusalem. This is the sin that calls forth the harsh judgment.

5:13   In the early chapters of Ezekiel the signs of hope are few and hard to recognize. Here all the hope that Ezekiel extends is the promise that finally God's righteous anger will be satisfied. As W. F. Lofthouse dryly remarks, "This is the side of Ezekiel's theology which is least evangelical." But the fact remains, however distasteful it may be to contemplate, that evil actions have tragic results. In this case, a false approach to God makes of Jerusalem a talisman, a good luck piece. This false religious belief brings on political folly, rebellion. The rebellion brings

5:14   on harsh retribution from Babylon. Ezekiel sketches the horror of desolation that must ensue. In 36:34ff. he alludes to this passage, using much the same words to express confidence that God will rebuild what the folly of man has destroyed. Here he concentrates upon the immediate, short-term result of sin in human life. Ezekiel will say later that God has no delight in the death of a sinner. He permits suffering and sorrow only that good may result. The specific good mentioned here is that

5:15   the nations will be warned, through the tragedy of Israel, that God is in command of history and that God is righteous.

B.   Oracles against the Land and the People, 6:1-14.

Palestine is a rugged land. An exile in the flat monotonous plain beside the Chebar would long for his native mountains. But in this chapter Ezekiel prophesies against these mountains; for on the hills Jewish people engaged in the idolatrous rites of the nature-cults. The preceding chapters dealt with the sins of Jerusalem, the capital city, while this shows the contamination widespread through the country. In a chapter that is filled with doom, Ezekiel begins to develop the thought of the remnant who will be saved (5:4).

1. Oracle against the Mountains, 6:1-7.

The Lord, speaking through Ezekiel, foretells destruction to the "high places," where the rites of nature worship were con-
6:3 ducted. These were usually hilltops (e.g. I Kings 18:20), but this passage and Jeremiah 7:31 make it appear probable that the term is used for any idolatrous shrine, even when it was located in a ravine or a valley. The "high places" had been religious sites for many centuries when Israel entered the Promised Land. During the early years of occupation the Israelites took these over and used them. Before the Temple was built there were many attempts to centralize the worship of the Lord, and to do away with the ancient shrines. Yet as late as the time of Samuel it was thought proper to worship God upon a high place (I Samuel 9:12). When Solomon's Temple was built, the high places were forbidden to the faithful (Mishnah *Zebahim* 14, 8). The prohibition was not effective.

The objection was not to prayer in this or that place, certainly not to the shade of a tree or the summit of a hill. The objection to worship at the high places was the carry-over of pagan belief and practice into the worship of the Lord. Another prophet excoriated rampant paganism:

> You who burn with lust among the oaks, under every green tree; who slay your children in the valleys, under the clefts of the rocks.   —Isaiah 57:5

The prophetic hatred for pagan religion was not mere provincialism. As Isaiah states, the Canaanitish nature cults practiced sexual license and child sacrifice, and called it religion.

The Lord threatens destruction to the "incense altars," common objects at the Canaanite sanctuaries. They were small lime-
6:4 stone altars with "horns," too small for the offering of any sacrifice other than incense. These, the altars, and the worshipers will be destroyed before the idols. The word used for "idol" is rarely found, in this sense, outside of Ezekiel. It comes from a root meaning "to roll." The word usually refers to a log of wood, which must be rolled rather than carried. A close derivative means "dung." Ezekiel contemptuously uses this term thirty-nine times in reference to idols. Where once lay the
6:5 remnants of animals sacrificed to the "block-gods," the bones of men will lie.

With no sign of a change, Ezekiel turns from addressing the
mountains to the people who inhabit the land, threatening
6:7   total destruction. The threat ends with a solemn cry, "And you
shall know that I am the Lord." This sentence might be called
the theme of the entire prophecy. It occurs fifty-four times in
this simple form and in an expanded form eighteen times more.
Here it is a toll of doom. The next time it occurs it tells of
doom slightly tinged with hope. By the end of the prophecy it
will be a cry of glory and triumph.

  2. The Promise of a Remnant, 6:8-10.

In 586 B.C. Jerusalem fell before the Chaldean army. Nebuchadnezzar dragged some of the Hebrews back to Babylon.
6:8   Some escaped to other lands (Jeremiah 43:7), leaving behind
the lone desolation that had been Jerusalem. Ezekiel's dire
prophecy was carried out to the last grisly detail. Unquestionably the revolt in Jerusalem brought additional rigors to the
Hebrews already in exile, even before they were joined by the
haggard survivors of hunger, fire, sickness, and sword. Yet, as
Ezekiel foresaw, a remnant survived. Jerusalem died, faith lived.
In the fire of exile the dross and impurity were burned from
Hebrew life. The wanton hearts that had departed from God
6:9   were changed. The eyes that had gone leering after false gods
learned to seek the Holy of Hosts. The exile was, in every
sense, a hideous and horrible experience for the Hebrew people.
Yet it was here that the faith was purified, strengthened and
6:10 exalted. Ezekiel   promises, "they shall know that I am the
Lord." His words are not so ominous now.

  3. Renewed Warning to the People and the Mountains,
     6:11-14.

Characteristically, Ezekiel restates what he has already capably expressed. Unfortunately, a difference in customs has led
6:11 to a misunderstanding of his thought here. With us clapping
the hands is usually a sign of joy. Some have actually claimed
that Ezekiel shows malicious glee over the fate of the wicked in
his home city. They cite 25:6, where clapping the hands and
stamping the feet indicate rejoicing. The fact is, these gestures
indicate intense emotion, whether of joy or of sorrow. As Ezekiel
6:12 shows explicitly in 11:13, his prophecy is the cry of an aching,
broken heart, He speaks of divine "fury." He shows the divine
6:14 hand stretching forth to make the land desolate "from the

wilderness to Riblah" (i.e., from the farthest south to the farthest north). And he says once more, "Then they will know that I am the Lord."

Ezekiel's prophecy is not an introduction to sacred studies. The only people among the exiles who gave serious heed to his teaching and writing already knew the biblical teaching about the nature of God. They knew that God can best be described in terms of love. When tragedy and ruin strike love is present. God's essential nature does not change. He still cares. He cares so deeply that He must act to destroy moral evil. But it is a cruel misreading of the prophecy to suggest that Ezekiel—or God—rejoices in the destruction.

C. End of the First Cycle of Warnings, 7:1-27.

The seventh chapter begins with a series of four brief, painfully intelligible oracles that reiterate essentially the same message: *the end has come, disaster after disaster, behold the day, the time has come.* The key words from each oracle are woven into the others. The remainder of the chapter gives a sharp, terrifying picture of the catastrophe, and shows how the invading Chaldeans will occupy the houses in which the Hebrews have dwelt.

The immediate, practical value of this warning ceased as soon as the threat was fulfilled. Yet the threat remains as part of the holy Word of God. Is it there purely because of its antiquarian interest? Or does the basic principle underlying the threat still hold? Ezekiel is profoundly convinced that God, who is present by the river Chebar, is in charge of the entire historical process. In this particular section he is telling us—with all the tact and charm of a pile driver—that God takes moral evil seriously. The message of hope will follow, after the events of history have proved that Ezekiel was right.

1. The End Has Come, 7:1-4.

In words reminiscent of Amos 8:2, Ezekiel foresees an end to "the land of Israel." Although the Kingdom of Israel as a

7:2 political entity had ceased to be in 722 B.C., Ezekiel, a Levite, found it natural to refer to the entire Hebrew community by this term. He warns that destruction will come upon the four

7:3 corners of the land, no city or village will escape. The day of retribution is close at hand, "Now the end is upon you." Hence

we infer a considerable time lapse since the initial vision in
593 B.C. Ezekiel foresees catastrophe, but it is not blind destruction that lies ahead, rather it is the judgment of God, "I
7:4 will punish you for your ways, while your abominations are
in your midst." God's punishment is merciful. His intent is
not vindictive nor destructive, but rather that the sinner may
turn to God and live. In due course Ezekiel will develop this
idea. Here he is emphasizing that, because this is God's world,
evil deeds have evil results.

2. Disaster after Disaster, 7:5-9.

The second oracle offers translating and textual difficulties
that are unusual, even for Ezekiel. At least 30 manuscripts and
7:5 the Targum give the first few words as translated in RSV, but
MT reads, "An evil, one evil. Lo it comes." "One" may be used
in the sense of "singular" or "outstanding." The "one" catastrophe that overshadowed all the rest was the destruction of
the Temple. "The end . . . has awakened" is a play on words
that cannot be translated. Roughly transliterated, the Hebrew
is *hakets hekits*. The predicted "end" will waken from its long
sleep.

Verse 7 contains a word with no known meaning, for which
RSV gives "doom." There is a brief coupling of the cause with
7:7 the inevitable disastrous effect, "the day is near, a day of
tumult, and not of joyful shouting upon the mountains." The
idea of "the day" had a popular meaning among the Hebrews,
and a very different meaning among the prophets. Popularly,
"the day" represented almost any national triumph, as in "the
day of Midian" (Isaiah 9:4). The prophets, from the time of
Amos on, had warned that "the day" represents God's triumph
over the unrighteousness of Israel, as well as His victory over
7:8 the enemy. The popular mind seized upon the privileges of
faith, the prophetic mind upon the responsibilities.

3. Behold the Day, 7:10-11.

The third short oracle gives a brief poetic summary of the
entire chapter. According to MT there are five lines with two
7:10 major beats in each:

> Behold the day.
> Behold it comes.
> Gone forth the doom.
> Blossomed the rod.
> Sprouted the pride.

A verse containing five lines is most unusual in Hebrew poetry. However, one of the best manuscripts of LXX omits the third line, which contains the word of uncertain meaning from 7:7, here translated "doom." If this line be omitted, we have a verse with perfect parallelism, typical of Ezekiel's best terse, allusive poetic style. Whether the line be retained or omitted, the entire verse is an enigmatic expression that the seed of evil has grown into a flourishing tree. "Rod" may symbolize the royal power of Judah (Psalm 110:2), but the Rabbis of old taught that the "rod" represents King Nebuchadnezzar, the agent of God's judgment (cf. Isaiah 10:5). Ezekiel seldom castigates Babylonian sins, but rather speaks to the spiritual need of his hearers, the whole House of Israel.

4. The Time Has Come, 7:12-13.

In a culture that lays heavy stress upon inheritance, selling a piece of inherited property is occasion for deep grief. The

7:12 fourth oracle warns the seller not to grieve nor the buyer to rejoice; for both will be overcome in the approaching invasion. "The day" will end the social conditions that the Hebrew people have known and loved. Possibly Ezekiel alludes to the

7:13 Year of Jubilee (Leviticus 25) when property reverted to its owner by inheritance, saying, "the seller shall not return to what he has sold." The Hebrew is uncertain, a confident translation impossible. But in general the verse means that those driven from the land will not be able to return, and the few who remain will find that the precious laws of inheritance, along with all other social institutions, have perished in the ruin.

5. Summary: Physical and Spiritual Collapse, 7:14-27.

The summary, several years before the fall of Jerusalem in 586 B.C., is in the present tense for vivid dramatic effect.

7:14 Evidently the effect was not quite vivid enough to forestall the insane rebellion that brought on the predicted ruin. Organized

7:15 resistance fails. Beyond the city walls, the sword. Within the walls, famine and disease. The few refugees go to the wildest,

7:16 most inaccessible places and mourn as they realize that the disaster is the result of their sins.

Our English translation shows a vivid metaphor for cowardice, "all knees weak as water." But the Greek makes an even

7:17   more vivid picture by treating the phrase literally, "all thighs
        shall be defiled with moisture." Those who have been so brash
        in bringing on their own ruin will be unable to contain them-
7:18   selves, through sheer terror, when actual ruin comes. In shame
7:19   and humiliation men shave or pluck the forepart of their
        heads (Deuteronomy 14:1; Jeremiah 48:37). Silver and gold are
        rubbish; for they can purchase neither deliverance nor food.
        The word translated "unclean" denotes menstrual impurity.
7:20   Silver and gold have proved a "stumbling block" to those who
        have used these metals, and other things of beauty made by
7:21   God, to make graven images that lure men from God. Because
        the Hebrews have abused God's gifts, God will give their wealth
        to the invaders. This is the bitter message Ezekiel proclaims. Not
        that the wealth will be lost. Not that invaders will seize it. But
        God will take it from those who have misused it and will give
        it to "the wicked of the earth," whose touch will profane it.
        Small wonder that Ezekiel was, and is, an unpopular prophet.
        When the Hebrew people had been despoiled of all their
        material possessions they were forced to put their entire trust
        in God. They had no things left in which they could trust. The
        death of material security turned out to be the resurrection of
        faith. Perhaps Ezekiel foresaw this; certainly God did.
            Even the Temple will prove no sure protection; for God will
        turn His face away from Israel, and robbers will defile the holy
7:22   place. The verse ends (or the next begins) with a bold conjec-
        ture on the part of the translators that illustrates the many
7:23   difficulties offered to the student of Ezekiel. MT may be trans-
        lated "make the chain" on the basis of a rough similarity be-
        tween an otherwise unknown word, a rare verb, and the Arabic.
        If "chain" be the correct translation, then this is another dra-
        matic parable symbolic of exile. But the following passage con-
        cerns the siege, not the exile. And the other dramatic parables
        are introduced by some such phrase as "The word of the Lord
        came to me, saying . . ." LXX gives the phrase "they shall make
        confusion," and the Syriac, "they shall pass through bricks."
        Conjecture is always risky, but this one involves less risk than
        accepting a traditional but indefensible reading.
            Ezekiel seldom mentions the moral quality of the Babylo-
        nians. He was not blind to alien faults, but he was speaking to
7:24   the House of Israel, not to Babylon, and he kept to his subject.
        It is always easy and popular to condemn the sins of the enemy.

It is difficult and unpopular to examine sins closer to home, but this examination was the task of the prophets. In a rare outburst of feeling Ezekiel describes the Babylonians as "the worst of the nations." He does not dwell on the sins of Babylon. He scarcely raises—let alone examines—the question that the instruments of divine judgment are morally inferior to those who are judged. But he shouts aloud the message, confirmed repeatedly by history, that those who abuse their wealth, or privilege, or faith, will lose it.

Ezekiel never directly mentions his elder contemporary Jeremiah, yet his prophecy shows throughout the profound influence of Jeremiah's thoughts, and sometimes it echoes his words. 7:25 reflects Jeremiah 6:14, and 8:11, though at a later stage of historic development. The following verse begins in the general form of Jeremiah 4:20, with allusions to 10:22 and 51:46, and it concludes with a restatement of 18:18, where those who so long have derided God will turn at last to their spiritual leaders for guidance, but will find none.

Zedekiah was on the throne in Jerusalem, but Ezekiel never names him as "king." Throughout the prophecy he exalts God as "King" and calls the earthly ruler "prince," even when describing the ideal community in the future. (The translators of LXX carried this theocratic principle even further. Here they omit the word "king" altogether. They retain it only once, in 17:12. In other places they omit or substitute "ruler" or "leader." So we have reason to believe that the Greek translators sometimes altered the text of Ezekiel for doctrinal reasons, or that they followed a Hebrew text differing from ours. We must frequently use their aid in seeking Ezekiel's meaning, but we must use it always with caution.) The "prince," clothed with terror, was a member of the ruling class, not necessarily of the royal family.

"The people of the land" is a phrase with many meanings. Originally the phrase meant the general mass of people. In pre-exilic time it marked the distinction between the ruling class and the ruled. It came to mean those people who did not know, or did not keep, the Law. But probably in this passage it means "members of the national council," thus providing a perfect parallelism with 7:26—prophet, priest, elders; king, prince, people of the land. Whichever of the meanings is uppermost in

72   *Ezekiel, Prophecy of Hope*

Ezekiel's mind, his conclusion is unmistakable. All will be judged. All will be found guilty. And—finally the thin sliver of hope—all will learn that "I am the Lord."

III. VISIONS OF JERUSALEM'S GUILT AND PUNISHMENT, 8:1—11:25.

A. Jerusalem's Guilt, 8:1-18.

1. The New Image of Jealousy, 8:1-6.

8:1 A new section of the prophecy begins one year and two months after the vision recorded in 1:1-28, in the month Elul (August-September), 592 B.C. The many attempts to reconcile the two dates with the 430 days "immobility" in 4:5f. range from futile to ludicrous. However one may understand the parables and oracles of the preceding year, their effect, though repelling, must also have been fascinating. The elders of Judah, the leaders in exile, were drawn as by a magnet to Ezekiel's house. Perhaps they had been coming to receive his oracles for months. He was obscure and antagonizing, but hear him they must.

8:2 Once more the "Hand of the Lord" was upon Ezekiel. Once
8:3 more he saw a vision of the divine glory. Once more he was transported in spirit. "The form of the hand" from the blazing glory seized the prophet by a lock of hair and dragged him, as an angry master would drag a rebellious servant. Many have attempted to find a distinction between the "Hand" that grasped and the "Spirit" that lifted Ezekiel. There is no difference. Both are metaphors for Him who can neither be imagined nor described. But Jerusalem can be imagined and described. To Ezekiel, as to the other exiles, a few details would bring to mind a precise location within the Temple where once had stood "the image of jealousy."

Solomon's Temple, which Ezekiel in vision was revisiting, stood on the Temple mountain, with the royal palace and the House of the Forest of Lebanon. The Temple and the palace each had a courtyard, and the three were contained in a "great court." Thus the Temple, unlike Ezekiel's or Herod's, had one court of its own, and was surrounded by another which it shared with other buildings. In his vision, Ezekiel went to the well-known place of infamy where, probably, Manasseh had erected an Asherah (II Kings 21:7), an image symbolizing the Syrian mother-goddess. This image had stood within the Temple area where, doubtless, it was worshiped as the "wife" of the Lord. Josiah destroyed the Asherah (II Kings 23:14), but its location was still known as "the seat of the image of jealousy."

The Asherah symbolized fertility in all its beautiful and hideous aspects. The image had commanded the attention of all who entered the Temple. The idol was a "rival" to the Lord. Should the prophet then call Him "jealous?" Jealousy is among the least god-like of human emotions. When we find the term in the Bible, it does not refer to the green-eyed monster, but to something only distantly related. The noun *kin'ah* comes from a verb meaning "to acquire as one's own property." So in human terms the noun means defending one's rights. When the Bible speaks of God as "jealous" it is always in response to the sins of idolatry or licentiousness. These sins—unless repented for—will bring an inevitable disastrous result. Since we must use anthropomorphic language to speak of God, perhaps "jealousy" is the best possible translation for *kin'ah*. But the reader is permitted to use his adult intelligence when he encounters such a term, and to lift the word up to God rather than dragging God down to the word.

There on the spot where "the image of jealousy" had stood, Ezekiel, in his vision, saw the glory of the Lord. The fathers **8:4** had repented of their sin. The glory had not yet departed from the Temple.

The Lord commanded Ezekiel to look to a place outside the Temple courtyard, but within the great court, and there in his **8:5** vision he saw another "image of jealousy." Probably this does not mean that a new Asherah had been physically erected in the great court. Such an act would scarcely have passed unmentioned in II Kings. Rather this is a symbolic statement that the old Syrian paganism was flourishing in Jerusalem, perhaps without official support, but still flourishing at the very gateway **8:6** to the altar. The Lord says, through Ezekiel, that this abandonment of God will cause Him to abandon the Sanctuary.

2. The Hidden Idolatry of the Elders, 8:7-13.

Some argue that Ezekiel was physically in Jerusalem as he witnessed the putrefaction of faith, but his remarkable means **8:8** of ingress to the hidden chamber of idolatry makes it impos-

sible to take this passage literally. In symbol digging still means
making a careful search for truth. God commands Ezekiel to
investigate the thoughts of many leaders in Hebrew society. The
hole in the wall suggests the secrecy with which the elders sought
to disguise their apostasy from the living God.

8:10   In one of the many chambers within the Temple, Ezekiel
finds the walls covered with pictures of bestial and reptilian
"deities" and—savage irony—"all the idols of the House of
Israel." What Ezekiel saw, literally translated, is "every likeness
of creeping things and beasts, abomination and all." "Abomination" thus refers both to the creeping things and the beasts. The
word for beasts usually connotes the larger domestic animals,
but sometimes wild animals. The creeping things are the small
vermin which, understandably, are called "abomination." The
Egyptian cults made idols of the cat, the crocodile, the hawk,
the scarab beetle, and other animals. In view of the threatened
rebellion against Babylon, the passage probably means that the
Hebrew leaders were looking toward Egypt for spiritual and
political support. However, many nations worshiped animal-
gods. Ezekiel makes no reference to exclusively Egyptian religious practices. Possibly the vision has other significance that
must remain unknown to us.

The hole in the wall and the darkness symbolize the secrecy
of the elders' idol worship. It is hard to imagine how a room
8:11   large enough to hold seventy elders could contain any secrets,
while the following verse, if taken literally, means that each of
the seventy had idolatrous imagery in his own cubicle, under
which conditions secrecy would be impossible. But the fact of
idol-worship is in human hearts, not upon walls. Religious
images are but outward symbols of inward corruption. Probably
the paintings were not visible to the eye of flesh. They are
written symbols for spiritual rottenness.

From early times the Hebrews had been guided by a council
of seventy elders (Exodus 24:1). In this case, however, Ezekiel
probably means a round number of prominent citizens, rather
than an official governing body.

The leader in debased worship was Jaazaniah (the Lord
hears) the son of Shaphan (rock-badger). The identity is uncertain. Shaphan was a godly chancellor of Josiah, whose three
sons are mentioned with honor in Jeremiah 26:24; 29:3; 36:11.
If Jaazaniah be another son of this Shaphan, he parted far from

the family tradition, and his example illustrates hideously the truth expressed in Chapter 18.

The elders attempted to hide their idolatry from the public, working their abominations "in the dark." Obviously they were 8:12 not successful, for Ezekiel, five hundred miles away, knew what they were doing. These elders, whose public conduct was doubtless correct, in their hearts were contemptuous of God. They had not ceased to believe that God exists but, far worse, they had decided that God does not care. The sorrows that befell Israel led them to think that God had forsaken the land, rather than leading them to wonder if they had forsaken God.

3. The Women Wailing for Tammuz, 8:14-15.

In the outer court, close to the Temple gate, Ezekiel saw another evidence of spiritual decay, women weeping for Tam- 8:14 muz. In oriental society women were the eternal conservatives, the last to accept a new falsehood—or truth—the last to abandon an old falsehood—or truth. So when the women wailed for Tammuz the sin of idolatry ran deep in Israel.

Tammuz was the Babylonian deity Duzo, the husband (lover or son) of Ishtar. (In the western world he was known as Adonis.) He was the god of vegetation who controlled the floods of the Tigris-Euphrates valley. Each year, when the rivers ran dry and the fields were parched, the Babylonians believed that he had descended to the Underworld. They commemorated his descent with public weeping, as they hailed his return with great joy. In Babylon the weeping took place in the month of Tammuz (June-July). Ezekiel's vision of Hebrew women weeping in Elul may indicate that the Palestinian rite was held at a different time; but more probably we should recognize that time and space are telescoped together in a vision. Ezekiel is expressing his disgust—and God's—rather than giving a literal description of religious error. The cult of Tammuz persisted in Kurdistan down into the twentieth century.

John Milton describes the scene:

> the love tale
> Infected Zion's daughters with like heat;
> Whose wanton passions in the sacred porch
> Ezekiel saw.

While there was much wanton passion in the religious practices of the sixth century, this is not what Ezekiel is mentioning here.

The women are weeping for a nature-god whose recurring death suggests that all things must decay. In later ages, despair was included among the seven deadly sins.

4. Sun Worship in the Inner Court, 8:16-18.

Each vision of horror has ended with a warning that the prophet will behold yet worse. The previous visions were seen **8:16** at the gates of the Temple, or in the chambers that constituted the Temple walls. But now the prophet is led to the inner court of God's house, where he sees a group of about twenty-five men with their backs toward the Temple. (LXX reads "twenty," the number of the Babylonian sun-god.) We cannot infer from the place where they stood that these men were necessarily priests or Levites, though we gather from 9:6 that they were religious leaders. Priests customarily prayed facing the Temple. The twenty-five were facing the other way to signify that they had renounced the Lord, and were looking to Shamash, the Babylonian sun-god.

In later years as the Hebrews celebrated the Feast of Tabernacles they recalled the sin of their fathers. The Mishnah records:

> When the celebrants reached the gate which leads out to the east, they turned their faces from east to west [thus facing the Temple] and said, "Our fathers who were in this place stood with their back toward the Temple of the Lord and their faces towards the east, and they worshiped the sun towards the east; but as for us, our eyes are turned to the Lord."   *Sukkah*, 5, 4

To us it seems strange that Ezekiel lays such heavy stress upon religious transgression, and comparatively so little upon social **8:17** righteousness. The other prophets amply confirm that religious laxity and social injustice went hand in hand. Here Ezekiel says merely that they "fill the land with violence." If the root of faith is severed, there can be no fruit of righteousness. For Ezekiel it is enough to show that the root has been cut.

The crowning abomination must remain unknown to us. "They put the branch to their nose." This was evidently a supreme insult to the Lord. A Rabbinic tradition calls this phrase an "emendation of the scribes," a change made in the text for reverential reasons. The original reading was, "They put the branch to My nose." Whatever the phrase may have meant, it indicates some obscenity that is just as well buried in the ancient past. LXX reads, "Behold, these are as mockers."

Running through the ominous chapter is a question, often repeated, "Have you seen this, O Son of Man?" The question is 8:18 to rise again, almost at the close of the prophecy (47:6). There the question is, in effect, "Have you seen God's victory?" Here the question is, "Have you seen the actions that call forth God's judgment?" The conclusion of the chapter restates one of Ezekiel's key thoughts: actions have consequences; evil actions have evil consequences. But the prophecy as a whole expresses a far more positive key thought: the God who smites is the God who heals; turn to Him today, and be whole.

B.   The Judgment of Jerusalem, 9:1—11:25.

As the preceding chapter described in vivid symbols the spiritual corruption of Jerusalem, this chapter foresees, symbolically, 9:1 the wages of sin. In 592 B.C. Ezekiel forecasts with terrifying accuracy what actually took place in 586 B.C. The prophet hears a loud voice—not addressed to him—summoning the executioners. Six men answer the summons, coming from the north 9:2 with their weapons in their hands. Although the Rabbis understood the six men to be angels (Babylonian Talmud, *Shabbath* 55a), it is more likely that they represent the generals commanding Nebuchadnezzar's army. Actually this is a distinction with little practical difference. An angel is an agent who consciously carries out the will of God. Ezekiel's prophecy, however one may dislike it, is that God will destroy evil in Jerusalem through the agency of the Babylonians who, naturally, will descend upon the city from the north.

With the six men is another who wields a pen rather than a weapon. The seventh man is clad in linen, the material used for the clothing of priests and others in authority. (In Daniel 10:5f. the "man clothed in linen" is unmistakenly an angel.) Attached to his girdle is a pencase (not "inkhorn"). In Palestine at the time most writing was done with reed pen and ink, usually upon papyrus or parchment. A scribe carried his pens in a writing case which contained a receptacle for mixing ink. The pencases carried by high officials often were made of silver elaborately and beautifully engraved.

The seven agents of God entered the Temple and approached the bronze altar. Lacking a ground-plan of the Temple, we cannot be sure where this altar stood. When King Ahaz built an altar, probably of stone, he moved Solomon's bronze altar (I Kings 8:64) "from the front of the house" to a new location "on the north side of his altar" (II Kings 16:14).

The verse means that destruction will come to Jerusalem *from the altar.* Many reject the idea that God, who is love, has any connection with disaster. But what can they put in its place? They can say that the malice of man, or some demonic power, or the blind, unthinking, uncaring process of nature has brought a particular disaster into a particular life. Tragedies occur, we know. Where do they come from? Ezekiel teaches that God dominates history. He controls the malice of men, the unseen powers of darkness, and the processes of nature. This idea, widely rejected today, is the rational ground for religious hope in times of darkness. It was by teaching this unwelcome idea to those who would hear that Ezekiel was able, under God, to salvage his nation.

Ezekiel's basic subject is the glory of God. A constant danger of theology, in Ezekiel's day as in ours, is choking the glory

9:3 out of faith, reducing it to a neat series of propositions about the nature of God and human duty. In the process of reducing theology to a system, men lose the qualities of amazement and wonder, without which faith becomes a mere branch of religious philosophy, and worship an expression of liturgics. Perhaps the gravest reason why the prophecy of Ezekiel is neglected today is the prophet's inability to make others sense what he sensed of the divine glory. With their terse economy of expression, Isaiah, Jeremiah, the Psalmists, the Joban poet, and others were able to communicate what Ezekiel sensed, and expressed in many words that reach our minds but not our hearts.

In 8:4 we read that the glory of God was "there," without reference to the chariot-throne. Presumably we are to understand the Holy of Holies, where stood the ark with its gigantic cherubim, above which God was believed to be enthroned (Psalm 80:1), the place where a Hebrew would be most conscious of His presence. In a vision the divine glory might be visible and audible, rising from the cherub over which it hovered, coming to the threshold, and crying to the man clothed in linen. It is both difficult and unnecessary to construct a precise itinerary for the divine glory, correlating the few scant details here, in 8:4, and 10:4. Those who attempt such an itin-

erary are but maiming the wonder of the vision, and its clear
message that God is in the midst of disaster. When the way of
faith leads to a cross, is God defeated?

In Jerusalem there were some, perhaps many, who had not
succumbed to the general idolatry, but had grieved for the sin
9:4 of their neighbors. Yet these too must be involved in the impending tragedy. The Lord commands the scribe to go through
the city, seeking out the faithful, and placing upon their fore-
heads a "mark." This mark was a *tau,* the last letter in the
Hebrew alphabet. One rabbi of old taught that God commanded the angel Gabriel to mark the righteous with a *tau* signifying *tichyeh* (you shall live) and the wicked with a bloody *tau*
signifying *tamuth* (you shall die), (Babylonian Talmud, *Shabbath* 55a). But Christian theologians, from the time of Origen,
have found another meaning. The *tau,* in ancient Hebrew
script, was a cross mark. It was used by illiterate persons to sign
documents for exactly the same reasons that such persons use
an X now. The scribe, of course, would use it as the most convenient mark, just as we do today. Is it a mere coincidence that
those who were saved bore the sign of the cross?

The six agents of destruction are sent throughout the city
upon their savage errand, beginning at the sanctuary with the
9:6 elders who have corrupted the holy place. Ezekiel is aghast as
9:7 he envisions corpses rotting in the Temple. He permits us a
rare glimpse of the personal anguish it brought him to convey
his hideous warning, asking if God will "destroy all that remains of Israel." The bulk of Israel had already been destroyed
when Samaria fell in 722 B.C., many Israelites had been deported, and colonists from other regions, with other beliefs, had
moved into the land. Now Ezekiel asks if the remnant of the
remnant must likewise be wiped out.

The Lord's answer is stern and uncompromising as He con-
nects the impending doom with the present shabby faith. He
9:9 reminds the hearer of what must have been a widespread saying (Ezekiel quotes these current proverbs thirteen times), "The
Lord has forsaken the land, and the Lord does not see" (see
8:12). This attitude was based upon a belief, by no means ex-
tinct, that worship and righteousness are the price men pay for
good luck. When calamity strikes, such shallow faith can decide
9:10 only that God is powerless to prevent it, or that God no longer
cares. The prophets were stoned and sawed asunder for pro-

claiming that God cares so deeply that He will destroy moral evil among His people.

The scribe returns to report that he has obeyed the Lord's command. Yet, despite the grim report God answered Ezekiel's prayer of intercession. Jerusalem, the city of stone, and the Temple, the building of stone, were destroyed. But the faithful lived.

9:11

C. The Vision of the Glory of the Lord, 10:1-22.

One would expect Ezekiel to follow Chapter 9 with a lurid description of Jerusalem's destruction. Instead he shows, symbolically, that this destruction is part of God's providence. The renewed vision is, in the main, a repetition of that recorded in Chapter 1. It differs chiefly in increased emphasis upon the glory of the Lord, and decreased emphasis upon the mechanical details of the chariot-throne. Critics have rivaled Ezekiel's vivid imagination in explaining the similarities and the differences between the two visions. Undeniably the chapter contains difficulties that may or may not indicate textual corruption. As it stands, the chapter is a powerful piece of dramatic writing. Power is seldom attained by corruption. A more restrained explanation of the difficulties is possible.

> It ought not to surprise us that the chapter contains frequent breaks of thought, and that in many verses it does not hang well together. What would be otherwise difficult to explain without plentiful recourse to hypothetical—and bungling—scribes and redactors, become natural if we regard Ezekiel as describing the rapid transitions of a trance; rapid as are these transitions, they only answer to the rapidity of thought when freed from communion with its normal environment.   —W. F. Lofthouse

In this chapter the "living creatures" that pilot the chariot-throne are identified with the "cherubim." Since it never occurred to us that they were anything else, we find it strange that Ezekiel lays such emphasis upon the identity. But look at the picture in its setting. Here is an exile who has seen a vision. He has duly reported this vision to his fellow-exiles, and has followed it with grave warnings that Jerusalem must be destroyed. Some listen. Many mock, "Ezekiel, you are mad. Jerusalem is impregnable. That is where God is enthroned between the cherubim. Remember what happened when Sennach-

10:2

erib besieged Jerusalem? Well, if Nebuchadnezzar tries, the same thing will happen to him. We'll believe you saw a vision, if you tell us so, but you didn't see God. He is not here, He is in Jerusalem, enthroned between the cherubim." Until Jerusalem actually fell, Ezekiel was under the blight of "dumbness." Others could not, or would not, hear what he said. This whole chapter is a powerful, yet pathetic, cry of a man to those who will not listen.

The fire beneath the cherubim is both a holocaust that will destroy smug security and a beacon of hope that will prevent total despair. Jerusalem must burn, but its flames will come from God. Six years later, when the physical city Jerusalem was gutted with physical fire, it must have taken a robust faith to recognize this as the fire of God. Thanks chiefly to Ezekiel, some had this robust faith.

In reporting his vision Ezekiel insists, to the point of weariness, that the living creatures he saw in vision by the Chebar were actually cherubim. To us, cherubim are a distraction from God. To our fathers in exile, cherubim were a means of thinking intensely about Him. The idea of winged creatures associated with the deity was widespread through the ancient world. Some such representation was upon the primitive Ark, symbolizing the presence of God (Exodus 37:7-9). Since cherubim had blocked the way for Adam and Eve to re-enter the Garden (Genesis 3:24), they likewise symbolized that man may not approach too close to deity. The Hebrews felt that God's presence was manifest between the cherubim (I Samuel 4:4), thus they symbolized, more than anything else, that He dwelt in the midst of His people.

In Solomon's Temple the cherubim were gigantic statues that towered above the Ark. These statues were carved of olive wood and overlaid with gold. They stood ten cubits (about fifteen feet) high, and their wings were an additional five cubits (I Kings 6:23-28). The Hebrew people believed that God's "throne" was between, or above, the cherubim (Psalm 99:1). Such a belief was subject to crude misrepresentation. It could, and sometimes did, turn into fetishism. Ezekiel has savagely attacked, and will again attack, the idea that God's presence is a good-luck charm. Yet the belief was more refined than its modern critics make it seem. Recall Solomon's prayer, where God "dwells" in heaven, but His "name" is in the earthly

10:3

house (I Kings 8:27-30). In the Targums this belief underwent
further refinement, as the rabbis distinguished the *shekinah*
(tenting place) between the cherubim, from God's *yashbah*
(dwelling place) in heaven. Though it may be difficult for us
to enter sympathetically into the exiles' frame of reference, we
must at least agree that when they thought of the place between
the cherubim, they were more conscious of God's nearness than
at any other time.

The real subject of Chapter 10 is "the glory of the Lord," not
the cherubim. "Glory" is the means by which men apprehend
10:4 God's presence. In their desert wanderings the Israelites were
guided first by the pillar of cloud and of flame (Exodus 13:21ff).
Then the Ark of the Covenant, with its cherubim, became the
visible sign that God is at hand (Exodus 25:10-22). Centuries
later, when the Ark was temporarily lost, the widow of Phineas
named her newborn son *Ichabod,* "the glory has departed"
(I Samuel 4:21).

The Hebrew word for glory is *kabod.* Basically it means
weight, or substance, thence wealth. A wealthy man would show
his position by his appearance and bearing; so these came to be
called *kabod.* Since such a man would receive honor and respect
from others, these too were *kabod.* So the word came in time to
embrace the ideas of honor, dignity, noble bearing and worthi-
ness, as well as indicating mere wealth. Such is the word Ezekiel chose to denote the "glory of the Lord." When he uses the
term he means man's consciousness that God is at hand. In the
NT, the corresponding word has even greater depth of beauty
and meaning.

Ezekiel describes God's glory as ineffable radiance; while
the house from which the glory has departed is filled with darkness like that of a dense cloud. In our literal minded twentieth
century, many seem to believe that the light of God, so often
mentioned in the Bible, must have been measurable with a
photometer. One may believe deeply in the light of God without believing that the optic nerve can perceive it.

Today some find distasteful Ezekiel's picture of a light that
moves about the Temple area, to the thundering pulse of the
10:5 cherubims' wings as they prepare to depart. Yet this quasi-phys-
ical picturing of the divine glory expresses imaginatively what
actually happened. The place where many had known the glory

of the Lord became the haunt of the moles and the bats. As Ezekiel has already told us in Chapter 1, the glory of the Lord is
found where faith in Him exists, be it even by the river Chebar.
No spot on earth is hallowed for its own sake. God's relation
with man is spiritual, not geographical. We do not need to be
convinced of this. The exiles did. To us it seems perfectly
obvious. It is obvious because Ezekiel and men like him have
made it so.

In a slightly expanded repetition of 10:2, Ezekiel presses home
the point that the destroying fire comes from God. He has never
10:6   identified the man in linen. Later generations were to announce
10:7   confidently that he was the Angel Gabriel. But the hand that
conveys the destructive fire is that of a cherub. There can be no
mistaking the prophet's meaning.

One expects a lurid description of the burning city, but it
does not follow. Instead the prophet describes again the chariot-
10:14   throne, with several minor variations upon his description in
1:4-28. Chief among these variations is "the face of the cherub"
instead of "the face of an ox" in the earlier description. Long
ago a rabbi gave a charming interpretation, saying that Ezekiel
asked God to remove the face of the ox because it was reminiscent of the golden calf, and "an accuser cannot be an advocate"
(Babylonian Talmud, *Hagiga* 13b). It is less charming but perhaps more accurate to say that this is another way of sealing
the identity of the living creatures and the cherubim. The chariot is south of Ezekiel, moving toward the east. Hence Ezekiel
sees the ox-face on the left side of the leading cherub, and he
uses the general term "cherub" to include the particular aspect
"ox." Apparently the Hebrews in ancient times were content
to treat symbolism as symbolism, and not as case studies in angelic morphology. (See e.g., Psalm 18:10 where glorious spiritual
concepts are expressed in physical imagery including "he rode
on a cherub and flew.") The meaning of the vision is what matters, not the anatomy of the charioteer.

Tersely, Ezekiel sums up the significance of the chapter. The
cherubim were the living creatures that he saw in vision by the
10:20   river Chebar. To the minority of exiles who gave serious heed,
these words were a flame of hope. Ezekiel had spent years telling them about the plot to rebel against Nebuchadnezzar, and
that this plot must end in disaster. Now he tells them that, al-

though Jerusalem will be destroyed (and the gold-plated statues
10:22 with it), their historic faith will go on. God will be with His
people in exile, still moving "straight forward."

D. God's Judgment on the Leaders, 11:1-13.

The section about God's judgment upon the leaders of the
people offers several difficulties that have led some to think that
this section originally followed Chapter 8, and others to think
that it was originally an isolated prophecy that the editor attached, somewhat clumsily, to the general section dealing with
the judgment of Jerusalem. The number twenty-five and the
name Jaazaniah tie it in with the former. The fact that Jerusalem has already been destroyed, in symbol, isolates it. In the
prophecy of Ezekiel as it stands today—not the first edition—
Chapters 8-11 are the report of a vision, where both distance
and time are suspended. The total impact of the vision, as reported to the exiled elders, is unmistakable and powerful: Jerusalem will die, but the faith will live. Did the need for this
message cease in 586 B.C.? Were there no further perils to the
faith in the years and centuries that followed Ezekiel? Whenever
the prophecy may have assumed its present form, this section
makes its own unique contribution to the total impact.

The Spirit lifts Ezekiel and carries him to the east gate. Evidently this implies a new element in the vision, and not a sequel
11:1 to Chapter 8; so the twenty-five men probably should not be
identified with those mentioned in 8:16. Among them were two
"princes of the people." One prince bears the name Jaazaniah
(the Lord hears), like the idolator in 8:11. Since the two men
have different fathers, this must be a coincidence of names.
Jeremiah's bitter opponent Hananiah was likewise a son of
Azzur (Jeremiah 28:1). Possibly Hananiah and Jaazaniah were
brothers. The other prince was Pelatiah (the Lord has deliv-
11:2 ered). The meanings of the names do not fit into any symbolic
pattern. Probably we are dealing with historic persons who were
confidently giving wrong advice to the city.

The nature of the advice about house-building is not clear.
The Hebrew reads, "not in the near [future] the building of
11:3 houses." This can mean that the immediate task is to make
preparations for war against Babylon. But the phrase can also
be translated, "It [destruction] is not near, let us build houses."
To complicate matters, LXX reads, "Have not the houses lately

been rebuilt?" The word "house" may refer to the royal dynasty rather than to a residence. With this wealth of possible interpretations before us, we are justified in understanding no more than that the twenty-five were engaged in some sort of conspiracy, behind a smokescreen of rhetoric. The expression about the flesh and the cauldron was probably a current proverb, suggesting "As the flesh is for the pot (or the hand for the glove) so the city is for us." This cryptic expression may also mean that the leaders left in Jerusalem considered themselves the "flesh" (we would say "cream") of society, while the bones and offal had already been exiled. (See Jeremiah 24.) Much as the cauldron protects the meat from the fire; so the walls of Jerusalem would protect the villainous leaders.

The prophecy as it stands today shows Ezekiel in Babylon. In vision he is transported to Jerusalem, where he has seen various disheartening sights. Now he confronts some flesh and blood men and speaks to them with devastating result. Some have sought a way from the difficulty by saying that Ezekiel was physically in Jerusalem at the time. This assumption raises at least as many questions as it settles. Yet there is no way out of the difficulty without making some assumptions. Should one assume that the prophesying to the twenty-five is symbolic, the procedure seems rather pointless. Should one take seriously that Ezekiel was in Babylon, it is hard to understand how the leaders in Jerusalem could be affected by what he said. Should one assume that Ezekiel was in Jerusalem, it is hard to see why the elaborate camouflage of the ten preceding chapters to cover a fact with no negative bearing upon the total prophecy.

While still in the visionary state, Ezekiel was compelled to prophesy on behalf of the Lord. The content of his prophecy is far more understandable than were the cryptic remarks of the leaders. Their words were designed to conceal the true meaning; his are designed to expose it. The Lord accuses the leaders of having multiplied their "slain" in the streets. Possibly this means that there had been some judicial murders of political opponents, but the Hebrew usage also connotes the "oppressed." (See 7:23; 22:25.) The proverb in 11:3 receives a savage twist in meaning; the victims are the "flesh," the victimizers will be brought forth from the safety of the "cauldron." (Many Hebrew manuscripts and LXX read "I will bring you forth.") The verse implies some sort of judgment after earthly death and

11:4

11:5

11:6

11:7

God's final vindication of the righteous, though the idea is not
developed here or elsewhere in the OT. Those who show such
11:8   verbal bravery acted the coward's part in 597 B.C. when Jerusalem was invaded and Jehoiachin deported. Now in their turn
11:9   they will face the sword and the terrors of exile. God will judge
them at the border. Nebuchadnezzar actually meted out his
cruel punishment upon the rulers of Israel at the border city of
Riblah (II Kings 25:6-7). Some argue that the reference to the
border demonstrates that this section was written after the
event. Possibly so, but any reasonably competent writer today
could describe with devastating accuracy the destruction of a
modern city, just from his general knowledge of military facts,
and Ezekiel was a competent, well-informed writer. Those who
have fled from the righteousness of God will learn, finally, "I
11:12 am the Lord." Are these words of hope or despair? That depends entirely upon the life one brings to the hearing of them.
    While Ezekiel was prophesying Pelatiah died. Critics who
approach Ezekiel without reverence find this passage quite
11:13 amusing. Ezekiel in Babylon envisions Pelatiah in Jerusalem.
Ezekiel speaks words of judgment, and Pelatiah, five hundred
miles away, falls dead. Certainly this is no place for dogmatism,
but neither is it the place for mirth. Some think to demonstrate
their reverence by assuming that Ezekiel had the gift of clair-
voyance. Ezekiel was a "clear seer," but he was not a "clairvoyant." What then?
    It is probable that Ezekiel kept well informed about events
in Jerusalem. Information traveled slowly, but it traveled. (Jeremiah 29 shows that, at the other end of the long road, Ezekiel's
brother-prophet had detailed information about life among the
exiles.) A keen student of politics in Jerusalem would know of
the conspiracy against Babylon, of Pelatiah's part in it, and of
Pelatiah's death.
    In the vision as it is reported to us time sequence is supended.
The symbolic fire of God had already been cast upon the city
(10:2) as the physical fire of Nebuzaradan was, in due course,
to blaze (II Kings 25:9). So there is no *a priori* reason why time
sequence should suddenly become important. Pelatiah was dead.
Ezekiel knew it. The exiled elders knew it. Now in his vision
Ezekiel weaves the historical element into a symbolic pattern,
where particulars represent universal truths. The death of Pela-

tiah signifies the destruction of all shabby compromise and greedy political leadership.

Dr. Howie suggests a somewhat similar interpretation of the passage. From his general knowledge of conditions in Jerusalem Ezekiel delivered his stunning prophecy to the exiles in Babylon. At about the same time Pelatiah died in Jerusalem. Years later when he wrote his prophecy Ezekiel commented upon the coincidence of dates. He does not claim that Pelatiah's death is an effect of Ezekiel's words. His claim is much deeper and more significant, that both the prophecy and Pelatiah's death were direct acts of God working in history.

Again Ezekiel's own feelings break through his iron self-control. He fears that the death of Pelatiah signifies more than the end of evil in Jerusalem, that it forecasts the end of faith and righteousness as well. He falls to his face and repeats the cry of 9:8. This time there is an answer, the strongest ray of hope that has yet lightened the gloomy pages of the prophecy.

E. The Promise of the Return, 11:14-21.

Ezekiel has infrequently alluded to one of his heaviest burdens in exile. It was the attitude of the Hebrews remaining in

11:15 Jerusalem toward their brothers by the Chebar. In 597 B.C. Nebuchadnezzar had conquered Jerusalem and had deported some of the finest citizens, including Ezekiel. He left behind "the poorest people of the land" (II Kings 24:14). One would think that the ties of faith and common decency would have bound those in Jerusalem close to their exiled brothers. But some who remained began to pride themselves that their superiority had saved them, that God had given them the land for a possession by choosing the exiles for special punishment because of their sins. It is hard enough to bear the reproaches of an enemy, but the lonely exiles must likewise bear the contempt of their own brothers. The Lord, speaking through Ezekiel, rebukes this haughty attitude. With a fullness of expression unusual even in Ezekiel, He says, "your brethren, even your brethren, your fellow exiles, the whole house of Israel, all of them" have smarted under the reproach. This fullness is not mere redundancy. The Lord is gathering together and calling His own all who were exiled, from the fall of Samaria in 722 B.C. down to the time of the vision.

The scattered exiles, rather than those who remained in Jeru-

salem, will become the saved, and saving, remnant. The AV
11:16 reads, I will "be to them as a little sanctuary." This translation,
though charming, is not accurate. It suggests a gracious promise
rather than an already demonstrated fact. Sanctuary has acquired the meaning of "refuge." It is doubtful that Ezekiel had
this in mind. The Jewish people in Jerusalem were physically
close to the "sanctuary," the central Temple area. They thought,
erroneously, that their physical proximity to a place of worship
imparted some spiritual virtue to them. They demonstrated the
inaccuracy of their thought by despising the exiles, who were
physically remote from the sanctuary. The Hebrew reads, "I
have been a sanctuary to them for a while" or "in small measure." According to the rabbis, the phrase means that, although
the exiles were unable to worship in the Temple, they had not
lost the presence of God, the reality that made the Temple holy.
The exiles learned that it was possible in Babylon to have
houses of prayer and learning, in which the Spirit of God was
present (Babylonian Talmud, *Megilla* 29a). Even today Hebrews call their synagogue "a little sanctuary" in allusion to
this verse.

Speaking for the Lord to the exiles, Ezekiel makes the promise that they will return from the nations to which they have
11:17 been scattered, and will possess the land instead of those living
11:18 there at the time of the vision. The returned exiles will purify
11:19 the land of all idolatrous excrescences, and the Lord will give
a spiritual renewal to those who have been through much
turmoil.

The language describing the return and renewal is taken
from Deuteronomy 30:1-6 and Jeremiah 32:36-40, with allusion
to many other passages in these two books. Here at last is a
clear, though muted, song of hope, to be repeated, fortissimo,
in Chapter 36. God will renew His people. In Hebrew, "heart"
refers to mental activities more than to the emotions. "Spirit"
refers frequently to God; when used in reference to man, it
suggests divine activity in human consciousness. So the renewed
heart and spirit, in place of the old heart of stone, means that
men, individual men who comprise the nation, will be infused
with a new divine energy. Ezekiel traces all that is good to God's
activity in human life. He bases the nation's welfare upon individuals who are responsive to God's will. When such people
11:20 occupy the land after the cleansing fires of the exile, then true

worship will be restored and the people will live in covenant with God.

Popular piety assumed with little serious thought that God was bound to His people as with ties of kinship. God gave the prophets the unwelcome task of saying that the ties between God and His people are moral. Jeremiah emphasized heavily the double promise (e.g. Jeremiah 7:23) which here becomes a controlling *leit-motif* in the prophecy of Ezekiel, "They shall be my people and I will be their God."

F. The Glory Forsakes the Temple, 11:22-25.

The glory of the Lord arose from the place that was once hallowed, and went to the mountain which was upon the east side **11:23** of the city. This can mean only the Mount of Olives, a place of glory known to Christians. The rabbis had a tradition that the glory rested upon the Mount of Olives for three and one-half years, hoping in vain that Israel would repent (Midrash *Rabbah to Lamentations,* Proem 25). So the vision came to an **11:24** end, as Ezekiel returned in spirit to the exiles by the Chebar, **11:25** and reported all that he had seen and heard. There was no need to trace further the path of the chariot-throne. Ezekiel had already seen it near Tel-Abib.

IV. THE SECOND CYCLE OF WARNINGS, 12:1–19:14.

The second cycle of warning is not dated. However, it is clearly distinguished from the preceding visions and from the third cycle of warning (Chapters 20-24).

In this cycle Ezekiel reaffirms the judgments, both negative and positive, that he has already given. It seems to us that he has stated his negative case at sufficient length, but we are living after the event that Ezekiel foresaw with such horror. There is much repetition in this section; there is likewise much advance. Thoughts that previously were only suggested are developed here with deep insight.

Ezekiel is attempting to influence events in Jerusalem. For this reason, some have decided that much of his ministry actually took place there, rather than in Babylon. Yet the preceding chapter has indicated that Ezekiel's hope for the future lies not so much with the people in Jerusalem as with those already

in exile, soon to be joined by the ragged, exhausted survivors of
the forthcoming siege. His primary hope is to build up in Babylon a strong, disciplined cadre of the faithful who will receive
the next group of exiles and help them to realize that, if Jerusalem is dead, God still lives. Joined to this primary mission is
a secondary hope that Ezekiel through his writings might be
able to impart some sanity to those in Jerusalem, and to keep
them from making hideous mistakes that must inevitably bring
destruction.

A. Dramatic Parables, 12:1-20.

1. Exile and Flight, 12:1-16.

The ominous threat that was so clear to Ezekiel was invisible
to many of his companions in exile. They had been through
12:2   the same harrowing experiences he had endured, but still many
shared the general superstition that Jerusalem was a charmed
city to which they would speedily return. Perhaps the elders
had begun to harken to the lonely prophet, but many among
the exiles were as yet rebellious. They would not acknowledge
the facts spread before them.

At God's commandment, Ezekiel presents yet another dramatic parable. This one imposes no physical impossibilities. It
12:3   is clearly defined, painfully understandable. The exiles could
all remember how they had gathered together the pathetic few
belongings a person could carry, and how they had trudged mile
after dusty mile on the hopeless road to Babylon. The parable
must have been vivid to those who had known the ache of exile
in their bones and muscles.

In the last desperate days of a siege those in the city would
attempt to escape through breaches in city walls and then
12:5   through the surrounding enemy. As a sign of ruined homes and
12:6   despairing efforts to escape, the parable shows Ezekiel tunneling
through the adobe wall of his house, hoisting his baggage to
the shoulder, setting off into the darkness, and covering his face
so that he cannot see the land. A few years later King Zedekiah
and the remnants of his army attempted an escape "by night by
way of the gate between the two walls." The Babylonian troops
overtook the fugitives on the Plains of Jericho. They carried
Zedekiah to Riblah, and there they blinded him, after first killing his sons "before his eyes" (II Kings 25:4-7). How many oth-

ers were blinded we do not know. The Babylonian troops on a punitive expedition were not inclined to be gentle.

It must have been an obtuse exile indeed who failed to perceive Ezekiel's meaning. But many did not see because they 12:9 would not, they did not hear because they would not. When they asked innocently, "What are you doing?" Ezekiel answered, 12:10 The "oracle concerns the prince in Jerusalem." Literally he says, "the prince this burden," *hanasi hamasa*. This is even more cryptic than usual in the prophecy. There are several possible understandings of the "burden" that Ezekiel has borne in his parable. First, it is not a flattering description of the prince. Second, there follows a weary picture of the prince shouldering his baggage and trudging off into exile with the others. But the word "burden" likewise denotes a prophetic message. This sense is uppermost, and is correctly translated in RSV as "oracle." The English gives the major meaning without the undertones. There follows another subtlety, "all the house of Israel who are in it [Jerusalem]." Ezekiel was given a message to "the house of Israel" (3:1). He has proclaimed this message to the exiles already in Babylon, while some in Jerusalem were arrogantly proclaiming that they were the true Israel. Here Ezekiel states, quietly, that Israel is already scattered abroad, though some who belong to the spiritual community still live in Jerusalem.

In blunt words that no one could possibly misunderstand, Ezekiel spells out his message. Exile, captivity, the long, long 12:11 road to Babylon, blindness. But this is not the heart of the 12:12 message. Any skilled political analyst could have foreseen as much. Ezekiel was both a skilled political analyst and a prophet. 12:14 His message is, "I [God] will scatter toward every wind" those 12:15 who have trifled with My holiness, and "they shall know that I am the Lord." Ezekiel has said this many times before to deaf ears. Are our sophisticated twentieth century ears still deaf to the message? Is a burning desire to know and to do the will of God the guiding and controlling force in modern politics? Do people in high places ever trifle with the righteousness God demands of all in authority? As always, part of the judgment is 12:16 the hope. God will save a remnant. When His ways are most contrary to our human longings, still His purpose is to redeem.

2. The Siege, 12:17-20.

Ezekiel has already symbolized vividly the starvation diet in

a besieged city (4:9-17). Again he signifies much the same thing,
12:18 with much the same symbolism. But this is not a mere repetition. Formerly he foreshadowed the scarcity of food during a siege. This time he depicts the acute terror that shakes the people when an enemy surrounds the city. His word, translated "quaking," is frequently used to describe an earthquake. It is difficult to see how the acted symbol, as described, would convey anything to anybody without the written commentary showing that this parable concerns the "people of the land."
12:19 Most of Ezekiel's barbs have been directed toward the leaders who were skillfully steering the nation into disaster. But the working people in the villages and farms will share in the tragedy when it comes. All of Zedekiah's kingdom must be laid waste before the people can "know that I am the Lord."

B. Prophets and Prophecy, 12:21—14:11.

The section under discussion deals with prophets and prophecy. Today many believe that prediction is the important element in prophecy. For those who hold this belief Ezekiel is a happy hunting ground. The book is filled with allusions and symbols that can easily be applied to Russia, China, Brazil, or any other nation in modern times.

Ezekiel predicts. For eleven chapters we have been reading his prediction that Jerusalem will fall, and in later chapters we shall examine his prediction that Jerusalem will rise. These predictions are based upon facts as interpreted by the light of faith. Negatively, since God is God, evil actions will have evil results. Positively, since God is God, He will be faithful to His covenant. Other prophets, more than Ezekiel, carried this latter prediction another step forward. Since God is God, He will send His anointed One into the world to save the faithful. This is prediction, but it is not a timetable of forthcoming catastrophes and triumphs.

A friend of mine holds vehemently to the predictive importance of prophecy. With Ezekiel in hand, he forecasts the rise and fall of empires with awe-inspiring assurance. I have made him a standing offer. If he can predict exactly what will be the price of butter on September 1, then he and I together can make a few million dollars in the butter market, and donate it all to charity, and I will rethink my attitude toward prophecy and prediction. He tells me that I am being frivolous about

sacred things. I was never more serious in my life. I believe
that empires stumble and fall over commodity prices and a
myriad other factors. If one cannot predict what is little, how
can he predict what is great? In this tangled, confusing world,
I need the faith that Ezekiel had, faith in God who will not let
me trifle with His holiness, yet who is with me always, even unto
the end of the world. If Ezekiel's flaming visions and searing
judgments help me to share this faith, it is enough. I do not ask
to see the distant scene. Prediction is an important, but minor,
part of prophecy. Ezekiel predicts. So did the false prophets. Of
course they were sometimes right. But their occasional right-
ness did not make them spokesmen for God.

The English word "prophet" comes from the Greek *pro-
phetes*. *Phetes* means "teller." *Pro,* in Greek as in English, has
a double meaning, "forth" and "fore." The word *pro-phetes*
means primarily a "forth-teller," only secondarily a "fore-teller."
In classical Greek, the one who had ecstatic visions was called a
mantis. He who "told-forth" the vision in rational terms was the
pro-phetes. The primary duty of a biblical prophet was to "tell
forth" the basic character of God, and the righteousness that
God exacts of man.

The Hebrew term for "prophet" is *nabi,* "one who announces." The OT applies this term to some exalted persons,
like Abraham (Genesis 20:7), and to some who were less exalted
(I Kings 18:19). The *nabi* was one who spoke, or claimed to
speak, for God. When we think of "prophets" we think of giants
like Ezekiel, Jeremiah, Hosea, and Amos. The following chapters show that many pygmies likewise bore the title. The lowest
kind of "prophecy" might better be called "sorcery." Among
the exiles were "prophets" who used amulets, incantations, talis-
mans, and the other sorry apparatus of man's long attempt to
control the Almighty.

Many others besides Ezekiel dreamed dreams and saw visions
and called it "prophecy." Dreams and visions often are accompanied by outward physical manifestations. In ancient times
these were sometimes considered essential. The Egyptian hiero-
glyphic sign for prophetic possession shows a human figure in
an epileptoid convulsion. In the earlier days of Hebrew prophecy, physical manifestations were frequent. When Amos avowed,
"I am no prophet *(nabi)* nor a prophet's son" (Amos 7:14) he

probably intended to distinguish himself from professional ec-
statics.

If prediction and mystical ecstasy are not the distinguishing
marks of a prophet, what are? The question is easier to ask than
to answer. Perhaps we can best examine this by contrasting the
true and the false prophets.

With the wisdom of twenty-five centuries to guide us, we find
it easy to distinguish between the "prophets" and the "false
prophets." We say glibly and correctly that the prophets rightly
represented God, while the false prophets misrepresented Him.
But how were our fathers to tell? The prophets bore no visible
sign of divine approval. The false prophets did not look or
sound fraudulent. Jeremiah names three exiles with Ezekiel who
forecast an optimistic, attractive future, and sent back cheerful
letters to Jerusalem, possibly while Ezekiel was laying symbolic
siege to the city (Jeremiah 29:20-32). These three and many
others were "false prophets." But how could our fathers know?

The OT does not employ the convenient (NT) term "false
prophets," even when it speaks of those who prophesy falsely.
Among these were doubtless men with wit and charm. It is not
needful to suppose that they were intentionally deceitful. Possibly most of them uttered their soothing platitudes in the
thought that they genuinely were speaking on behalf of God.
The true prophet bore no external credentials to certify his
right to speak. Later generations have united in agreeing that
Ezekiel and Jeremiah were indeed prophets of God, but the
majority in their own time rejected them in favor of a more
immediately gratifying "gospel." Yet both of these true prophets
reached some who dared to apply tests that are still valid for
distinguishing between religious truth and religious poppycock.

Does this message take God's holiness seriously? Is this message God-centered or man-centered? Does the message take sin
and forgiveness seriously? Is the message consistent with the
facts of experience and of faith? Does the message call for self-
examination and repentence, or for easy satisfaction with things
as they are? We can apply a test that the exiles could not. Hold
the alleged truth up against the cross of Christ. Does it make
the cross a mockery? Or does it demonstrate that Christ's suffering and death have meaning, purpose, and victory? Finally, One
greater than Ezekiel gave us the supreme test: "He who does
what is true comes to the light" (John 3:21).

1. The End of Delay, 12:21-28.

Two brief oracles emphasize the same basic point: God will fulfill His word. As Ezekiel has done before, he alludes to a proverb that probably was popular in the homeland long before the exile. In effect the proverb sneers at the prophet because God's warnings are not immediately and smashingly fulfilled.

God keeps His promises. His warnings are conditional. He does not *want* the death of any sinner. He warns the sinner to repent and live. Time passes, and the dire warning is unfulfilled. Why? God's threats are contingent, uttered in love, in order that they may not be carried out. He gives His warnings with a moral purpose, not as mere predictions of the future, but that living men may know the will of God, and change their lives while there is time. (See Jeremiah 18:7-11; II Peter 3:4.)

As he has done before, Ezekiel gives a grim twist to the proverb, changing its meaning completely. He announces the end 2:23 of the flattering divination that has supported the popular, 2:24 easy-going faith. Divination originally meant the use of external devices to interpret the mind of God. The flight of birds, examination of livers, astrology, and a thousand other techniques were employed. It is not known that the false prophets in Ezekiel's time used such devices, but their teachings were just as valuable as if they did.

The second oracle is addressed to those who have grudgingly conceded some measure of truth to Ezekiel's message, and have 2:27 assumed that fulfillment lies in the distant future. To these 2:28 Ezekiel gives the same response, "None of my words will be delayed any longer, but the word which I speak will be performed."

2. The Foolish Prophets, 13:1-16.

For those who are concerned about the way Ezekiel was written, the section about the foolish prophets offers many fascinating problems, chief among them the violent switch back and forth between "you" and "they." For clergymen, at least, who are concerned primarily with the message of Ezekiel, the problem is more personal. We cannot keep from asking, "Lord, is it I?"

The name "prophets of Israel" is a mixture of irony and despair. While Ezekiel was "dumb," the purveyors of flattering

13:2   lies had a large attentive hearing. The first and most scathing denunciation Ezekiel brings against them is that they "prophesy out of their own minds." It is a grave sin for a man to present human ideas under the guise of divine truth.

     Ezekiel calls his adversaries "foolish prophets." There is a gentle play on words here. "Prophet" is *nabi,* and "fool" is

13:3   *nabal.* In contemporary English, a "foolish" person lacks intelligence. In Hebrew *nabal* denotes a person who is blind to spiritual claims, who says in his heart that there is no God

13:4   (Psalm 14:1). Ezekiel likens the foolish prophets to foxes in the ruins. The fox, in popular folklore, is clever but unscrupulous, mischievous, and destructive. "Ruins are congenial to them; a condition of decay is their proper sphere; there they can burrow as their instincts prompt them . . . Their operations only increase the devastation and undermine . . . anything that may yet be standing" (A. B. Davidson).

     Turning now to the prophets, Ezekiel thunders that in the hour of peril they did not man or even help build the defenses.

13:5   As a soldier's duty is to be in the place of danger; so it is the prophet's duty to speak the truth that God gives him. But the foolish prophets neither prepared the people for the crisis nor helped when the crisis came, presumably the crisis in 597 B.C. Instead they projected their own fantasies and desires as the

13:6   will of God, hoping that events would prove them right. They dared to speak for the Lord when the Lord had not spoken, at least not to them.

     Because God is God, He must oppose those who misrepresent Him. His Hand, that has meant such encouragement and

13:9   strength to Ezekiel, will be against those who have courted popular favor rather than divine. Three stages of God's disapproval are mentioned. First, those who have known leadership and influence will be excluded from the council. Second, they will not even be included in the register. (Ezra 2 and Nehemiah 7 give such a register. We would call it a civil document, but in Israel it had spiritual import.) And finally, when the exiles return to their home, the foolish prophets will not return with them.

     It would be distressing to draw modern parallels, pointing to those who cry " 'Peace,' when there is no peace" (See Jeremiah

13:10   6:14; 8:11; Micah 3:5). The Hebrew *shalom* denotes national prosperity and security as well as personal contentment. To ensure the peace in Ezekiel's day, kings built gigantic walls about their cities. So, figuratively, Israel has built a "wall" of political and spiritual defenses. As Ezekiel has already told us at great length, this "wall" was shabbily constructed. Here he uses a rare word that suggests a wall built of stones but chinked together with mud rather than cemented with mortar. Such a wall might look quite impressive, but it could not stand up in a driving storm. While the true prophets were begging their people to build firm walls, the foolish prophets daubed the flimsy walls with whitewash. They failed to show that man's only sure defense is complete acceptance of God's will. They gave a religious sanction to human designs.

Ezekiel has predicted the coming destruction many times. Here he presents it imaginatively as a storm of rain and hail. The whitewash will offer no protection. The mud and chinking will become slippery. The stones will slither apart. The wall will crumble, and the foolish prophets will perish in the ruin. And, "You shall know that I am the Lord." The figure of speech is not quite clear. Ezekiel has been addressing the foolish prophets in Baylon. The crumbling wall surely suggests the destruction of Jerusalem. When Jerusalem fell, the foolish prophets in Babylon did not lose their lives. But they did lose their influence. Probably this is what Ezekiel means to suggest in his vivid picture of the destroying storm.

Many higher critics believe that the section about the foolish prophets reached its present form long after the time of Ezekiel, when the editor took various prophetic oracles and brought them into one, adding a few comments of his own. If this analysis be accepted in its totality, it detracts not one whit from the present-day value of the passage. There is no value today in throwing stones at individuals who died twenty-five centuries ago. Neither was there value in throwing stones at them twenty-four or twenty-three centuries ago. The value in this passage is its continuing up-to-dateness. The false prophet is not an individual always, but a constant temptation in the life of every believer. The finest commentary on this passage is to be found in Matthew 23:27-28, where the title "foolish prophet" has changed, but the reality remains the same.

3. The False Prophetesses, 13:17-23.

The Bible tells of a small but worthy number of women who prophesied: Miriam, Deborah, Huldah, Noadiah. Beyond these

13:17   there may well have been hundreds of others who faithfully
         represented the Lord in their several communities. In addition
         there was a miserable gaggle of crones who practiced what we
         would call "sorcery" though they called it "prophecy." Some of
         them apparently were among the exiles, vending witchcraft in
         the name of the Lord. Since the exiles represented the best of
         the Hebrew population, we must conjecture that sorcery was
         widespread throughout Israel. Ezekiel's most telling condemna-
         tion is that the false representatives of God—like their mascu-
         line counterparts—"prophesy out of their own minds."

              The details of magic-practice are obscure to us; yet today
         people do much the same things with horoscopes, tea leaves,
13:18   playing cards, crystal balls, palm reading and other such trump-
         ery. The "magic bands" were probably amulets, supposed to
         transmit the powers of the sorceress to her customer. Babylonian
         inscriptions tell about tying or sewing knots as a normal part of
         witchcraft. Sixteen small leaden figures were unearthed at an
         excavation near Hebron. Each of these figures has a wire twisted
         about the ankle or wrist. We cannot tell today whether this
         sympathetic magic was intended to work good or harm upon the
         person symbolized. We do not know the function of the veils.
         Yet in a verse that is filled with ancient obscurity, Ezekiel asks
         a question that has a terrifying contemporary ring. "Will you
         hunt down souls belonging to my people, and keep other souls
         alive for your profit?" What is the motive behind religious ac-
         tivity? Those who spend their full time in religious work need
         to eat. So churches receive offerings, and ministers draw salaries.
         Is church work just a job, to be done for the pay check? Or is
         the pay check a necessary means, enabling the church worker
         to do God's work in the community? Ezekiel has suggested an-
         other test of true prophecy. Is the alleged prophet concerned
         with souls for his own sake, or for God's sake?

              Barley and bread are not the wages of a sorceress, but mate-
         rials used in divination. These materials were used in the ritual
13:19   of sacrifice; hence the Lord cries that their use to achieve human
         ambitions is a profanation of His name. Probably putting per-
         sons to death should be understood as a figurative expression
         for discouragement, suggesting what is said literally in 13:22. A
         troubled person would come to the sorceress, inquiring about
         his trouble. She would crumble some bread, scatter some barley
         flour about, look at the mess, and deliver a verdict. A person

who took an unfavorable forecast seriously would be deeply discouraged, perhaps to the point of death. The horror is not that people longed to know the future, but that some would dare to influence the destiny of souls, in the name of God, because of a few crumbs on a plate.

God's attitude toward witchcraft is stern. He promises to tear away the apparatus of mumbo-jumbo and to liberate the people 3:21 whom the magic-mongers have captivated. The women who 3:22 have prophesied falsely have sold good luck, not righteousness. They have discouraged some, and in others they have strengthened a free, easy confidence that has kept their victims from the 3:23 turmoil of repentance, the only way to life. So God will put an end to their delusive visions. He will liberate His people from their clutches. "Then you will know that I am the Lord."

4. False People Who Demand False Prophets, 14:1-11.

Ezekiel is not finished with false prophets. Here he turns his attention to the people who demand, and get, flattery instead 14:1 of truth. Probably the "elders of Israel" are the same as the "elders of Judah" (8:1). Some of them come to Ezekiel. Presumably they ask him a question, which he refuses to answer. The 14:3 Lord, speaking through Ezekiel, thunders that these men have "taken idols into their hearts." In view of the widespread idolatry in Jerusalem, there must have been much contagion among the Hebrews in Babylon. The form of the accusation does not imply that the elders actively engaged in idol worship, but that their minds were influenced by pagan thoughts and practices. The Lord raises a question. When people have made themselves unfit to hear divine truth, is it right for God to hear and answer them? Yes, God will answer the idolator "according to the mul-14:4 titude of his idols" (AV). God will answer in judgment, not through the lips of a true prophet. God's purpose in judgment 14:5 is positive, "that I may lay hold of the hearts of the house of Israel." As long as men welcome iniquity into their lives they cannot hear and respond to God's truth, any more than a filthy cup can hold clean water. But God can—and will—cleanse the cup.

Before the judgment falls, God calls his people to repent. He warns both the house of Israel and "the strangers that sojourn 14:7 in Israel." This expression shows that Ezekiel is concerned for the entire community of faith, not only for his fellow exiles.

While Shemaiah was sending his cheery messages back to Jeru-salem (Jeremiah 29:25), Ezekiel was writing down his gloomy oracles and sending them back too, in the faint hope that some might read and act upon them. (The great Jewish commentator Kimchi said that the "strangers" were Babylonians who had embraced the Hebrew faith.) Whoever the person be, if he takes idols into his heart and then comes to a prophet for divine guidance, God will answer him directly, with judgment.

An idolator comes to a "prophet." He asks guidance from God, without preparing himself to receive guidance. A true prophet, like Ezekiel, gives the fundamental answer, "Repent." The false prophet, like his hearer, has "taken idols into his heart." He speaks. He cannot do otherwise. His reputation depends upon delivering pretty oracles when required. His oracles turn out to be false. The Lord says, "I, the Lord, have deceived that prophet." Here Ezekiel touches upon, but does not examine, the question of divine causality. Taken out of their context, his words make God look morally capricious.

14:9

As a usual thing, Ezekiel looks beyond the secondary causes, by means of which we "explain" events in the world, to the primary Cause of all, and he hears the Lord saying, "I, the Lord, have deceived that prophet." With our view of secondary causes, we would say that the prophet deceived himself. The false prophet has violated God's moral law. He has abused his talents; so the powers that were given to him for good are turned into evil. He speaks falsehood. He uses the vocabulary of faith without the reality. God's "deception" of the false prophet has not infringed upon his free will. The false prophet is in the same position as any other sinner who abuses God's good gifts and finds that they turn sour. The gifts still come from God.

14:10

14:11

Over a long period of time people get about the kind of spiritual leadership they really want. People who are estranged from God demand, and get, false prophets. False prophecy encourages and develops shabby faith. Each helps to create the other. Divine justice will fall with equal weight upon the deceivers and those who have cried to be deceived. But God's purpose in inflicting judgment is redemptive, "That the house of Israel may go no more astray from me, nor defile themselves any more with all their transgressions, but that they may be my people, and I may be their God." In earlier chapters, the signs of hope were almost invisible. Here is hope, clear, visible, radiant. One can scarcely accuse Ezekiel of unthinking optimism. He looks steadfast into the teeth of the storm, and sees through the blackness the eternal light.

C. The Righteous Cannot Save Jerusalem, 14:12-23.

When Sodom was threatened the Lord promised Abraham that He would spare the city if even ten righteous men were to be found in it (Genesis 18:22-32). A similar thought doubtless comforted many while Ezekiel warned that Jerusalem must be destroyed. This section is an answer to those who express such confidence. Everyone must concede widespread idolatry and the moral laxity that was its constant partner. But everyone knew, likewise, that many in Jerusalem were striving to live their faith. It was an understandable hope that God might spare the city for the sake of these righteous persons. Ezekiel must demolish this hope. He has already emphasized the doctrine of individual responsibility, and he will develop this idea more thoroughly in Chapter 18. Here he stresses the doctrine in both its negative and its positive aspects.

The Lord, speaking through Ezekiel, announces a general principle. A nation that defies fundamental righteousness cannot long survive, though the righteous in it will live. Neither Ezekiel nor his hearers could know that this principle was actively at work undermining Nebuchadnezzar's empire. (A good many Christians in the twentieth century seem likewise to have forgotten it.) Ezekiel has mentioned those who bear God's mark who will be saved from destruction. Could not their mantle of safety be cast over those who have cried aloud for destruction?

4:14 God answers sternly that the most righteous cannot deliver others by their righteousness. Jeremiah 15:1 develops much the same thought, showing that even if Moses and Samuel were to pray for Jerusalem, they could not deter God from His judgment (See also Exodus 32-30-33). Jeremiah's choice of heroes is understandable, Ezekiel's less so. Why of all the great men of faith did he select Noah, Daniel, and Job? In the case of Noah and Job we see folk heroes who lived when others died. The name of Daniel here and the name of the prophet are spelled differently. This is one time when we cannot cry textual corruption; for every instinct of a scribe would urge him to amend Ezekiel's spelling to the more familiar form. Beyond this, at the time the prophet Daniel was but a lad. It is scarcely probable that Ezekiel would refer to him in terms applicable to Noah and Job. The Ras Shamra texts, from the fifteenth century B.C., name a heroic Daniel who was "the righteous judge of the cause of widows and orphans." Possibly Ezekiel refers to him. We do not know why Ezekiel selected three particular folk heroes to illustrate the principle of divine justice. It is perhaps more important that we strive to live what we do understand in Ezekiel than that we fret overmuch about insoluble puzzles.

Three times the essential judgment is repeated with the same conclusion. The forms of the catastrophic judgment correspond

14:21   with those in Leviticus 26. In 14:13-20 the fourfold destruction was discussed as a general principle concerning "a land." Now Ezekiel applies it directly, tragically, to Jerusalem. Yet some of

14:22   the wicked will survive, along with those who have borne the mark of God. When these have come to Babylon, and the exiles

14:23   have seen "their ways and their doings" then they will know that God's action was just.

D. The Parable of the Grapevine, 15:1-8.

The brief passage about a worthless grapevine amplifies the concluding thought of the preceding chapter, that God's justice

15:2   requires Him to destroy Jerusalem. Ezekiel takes an old, familiar figure of speech among his people. Genesis 49:22 likens Joseph to a fruitful bough. The same figure is found again and again in the Bible, reaching its culmination in John 15. Other prophets compared Judah to a grapevine, stressing the lack of fruit (Hosea 10:1; Jeremiah 2:21). Ezekiel does not even mention the fruit; there is not enough to mention. He examines the wood of the vine and finds it worthless. His harsh question might better be translated, "How does the wood of the grapevine surpass the wood of any other vine among the trees of the

15.3   forest?" Wood from trees has value, but the wood of vines has none. Men do not choose vine wood even for such a humble

15:4   purpose as making pegs. Contemptuously, they cast it on the fire. Before vine wood is charred, it is worthless. After charring, is it useful for anything?

The application of the parable is sharp and painful. Israel is smaller than other nations, at best a vine among trees. And the

15:6   vine has been fruitless. The people and their leaders have not measured up to God's standard of faith and life. God has al-

ready acted in judgment. He must act again. First the Northern
Kingdom fell in 722 B.C., then Jerusalem itself was invaded
in 597 B.C. and the king sent into exile. What remains is com-
15:8 parable to a piece of charred vine wood fit only to be cast back
upon the fire. At the end the prophet drops the metaphor and
makes a literal prediction that the land will be "desolate." This,
the archaeologists assure us, was literally fulfilled.

E. Historical Allegories, 16:1—17:24.

Here Ezekiel takes up and elaborates the concluding thought
of the preceding chapter. God's judgment, though harsh, is
just. First, the prophet examines the long history of Israel in
terms of an ancient folk tale, which he applies symbolically to
his people from the beginning of their history as a nation. Then
in Chapter 17 he turns from the ancient past to the sins of the
present, again presented in allegorical terms. He concludes that
evil actions have led inexorably to tragic results, that God must
punish sin; but even so, God is faithful to His convenant. Each
chapter begins in despair and ends in hope.

1. Faithless Jerusalem, 16:1-63.

The chapter is divided into four sections, of which the first is
again divided several times. The chapter concerns Jerusalem.
16:2 The word is used here in simple metonymy for the entire Kingdom of Judah. The prophet traces Jerusalem's history first in a
long, ornate allegory of a foundling bride who is faithless. In
verses 44-58 the allegory changes to Jerusalem being the "sister"
of Samaria and Sodom. Chapter 16:59-63 is the promise that
God's ancient covenant will be renewed. These last sections
contain the longest sustained expression of hope in the prophecy to this point.

a. The Royal Harlot, 16:1-43.

Ezekiel took an old, familiar folk tale and used it as the basis
for his most developed allegory, save that of the rebuilt Temple
in Chapters 40-48. Some minor details in the legend do not quite
fit the allegorical application. Wisely, Ezekiel did not crowd the
ultimate possible amount of significance into his parable. We
should respect his aim and try not to squeeze from each detail
a deep meaning that is not there. It is sufficient if we receive
the chief message.

Most twentieth century readers will find details in the al-

legory quite offensive. We have noticed by this time that Ezekiel frequently is blunt. He is dealing with the filthy business
of sin. He does not attempt to hide his thoughts behind a disguise of polite phraseology. The reader should examine this
chapter carefully, however the details revolt him, for here
Ezekiel develops some of his key thoughts.

Other prophets described the relationship between God and
His people in marital terms (e.g. Hosea 1-3; Jeremiah 3; and
Revelation 21:9). Sexual imagery in religious writing and art
is widespread throughout the world. Mystics almost everywhere
have compared mystical union to marital union, the point of
the comparison being bliss. Probably religious eroticism reached
its unsavory peak in the Sakta and Tantric developments in
India, but the cults of the near east followed close after. The
only possible defense of these cults is feeble. The orgy was
justified, not for its own sake, but by the magical powers of
fertility in field, animal and wife that it was supposed to
develop. The end of licentiousness was production. But the
participants were often masters of the everyday skills of licentiousness, not needing to go to the trouble and expense of
"ecclesiastical" sanction when hedonistic values were the only
ones in sight.

The negative side of marital imagery, where infidelity serves
as the outstanding symbol for rebellion against God, is found
only among the Hebrews and the Christians. The idea of the
Chosen People gives the depth and beauty or tragedy to the
biblical usage. Both Israel and the Lord might have covenanted
otherwise; for each had many available choices. But Israel and
the Lord were pledged to each other as by ties of marriage.
Hence infidelity to God is comparable to adultery. Hosea ex-
plores this symbolism in the fullest depth of tragedy. If we can
enter into Ezekiel's framework of thought, looking beyond the
physical symbolism to the thing symbolized, then we can see
that Ezekiel here is developing a central prophetic theme with
a profundity surpassed only by that of Hosea.

This passage is not included among the prophetic readings in
Orthodox Hebrew worship (*Megillah* 4,10) because it so violently denounces the disloyalty of Israel. For quite different
reasons, it is seldom read publicly in the Christian Church.

(1) The Foundling Queen, 16:1-14.

Of all the prophets, Ezekiel is the one who sees Israel's history

in the harshest colors. Most look back to a purer age of faith in
16:3 the past. Ezekiel sees that from the beginning Jerusalem has
been a Canaanitish, hence idolatrous, people. The Hebrews
came from an Aramean background (Deuteronomy 26:5) and
immigrated into the land of Canaan, but they were racially
akin to the Canaanites, who also were called "Amorites" (Westerners). The Amorites once were a powerful nation. In the
third millennium B.C., the Babylonians called Syria and Palestine the "Land of the Amorites." They were still a powerful
tribe at the time of the Hebrew conquest. Ezekiel shows that his
people had considerable intermixture with the Amorites, both
by marriage and by the intrusion of pagan elements into Hebrew faith and practice. "Hittite" should not be confused with
the once great civilization in Asia Minor. Apparently it was a
loose general term for the Subaraeans, a non-Semitic people who
formerly occupied a vast territory north and west of Babylon.
At one time the Subaraean domain extended down as far as
Palestine. The whole land of Canaan is indifferently described
as "the land of the Amorite" (Amos 2:10), or "the land of the
Hittites" (Joshua 1:4). The reader today should hesitate to
criticize ancient usage, remembering that when he speaks of
Aztecs, Ontarios, Caribs, or Navajos, he calls them all "Indians"
though their relationship with India is founded upon a navi-
gator's mistake.

Pagan parents gave birth to a child, and denied her the
minimum essentials for survival. Instead they exposed her to
16:4 die in the open field, a bloody, filthy object of loathing. The
16:5 Hebrews became a people in the land of Egypt. And why were
they in Egypt? Israel was a nomadic shepherd in Canaan. His
son Joseph went to Egypt as a slave because of base treachery
among his brothers. A famine came upon the land. The family
of Israel fled to Egypt, and eventual slavery, to escape starvation. In terms of the allegory, the Prince saw the infant "welter-
16:6 ing" in her "blood." Ancient Hebrew commentators read much
deep significance into the "blood." Probably, for once, we
should take Ezekiel literally here. A newborn child, unwashed,
is far from beautiful.

The Prince commanded the child to "grow up like a plant
of the field." She grew to womanhood, but she was "naked and
16:7 bare," figuratively, "unmarried." The children of Israel became
a people in Egypt, but they were a people in chains, with no

hope for the future. Nothing lay ahead but the living death of slavery and the gradual forgetting that once the Lord had made
16:8   a promise to Abraham. Then God sent Moses. The Prince spread his skirt over the pauper, a symbolic act of betrothal
16:9   (Ruth 3:9). He cleansed her from menstrual blood, purified her for marriage (Ruth 3:3), brought her out from her squalid
16:11   surroundings, lavished priceless adornments upon her, and
16:12   crowned her as his royal bride. The children of Israel were slaves. God, working through Moses, brought them out of the land of Egypt, out of the house of bondage. At Sinai He entered into a solemn covenant with them. (Proverbs 2:17 speaks of marriage as a covenant with God.) Through the harsh desert He led them, at last, into the Promised Land.

The tribes of Israel slowly became a nation. Their leaders mastered the techniques of war, administration, and commerce,
16:14   until finally, under Solomon, the Kingdom attained a considerable size and great fiscal prosperity. In literal fact, her "renown went forth among the nations." God bestowed great blessings upon Israel. This is the undebatable message of the parable. There are almost as many interpretations of detail as there are commentators. But no one can deny Ezekiel's central theme that God bestowed great blessings upon the chosen people, not because of their merit, but because of His love.

(2) The Harlot, 16:15-34.

The Queen trusted in her own beauty. She looked lustfully to other men, taking for granted the wealth and security her
16:15   husband had given her. Less allegorically, Jerusalem turned to idol worship. Here Ezekiel describes idolatrous faith as harlotry. This was a vivid figure of speech developed by Hosea and used subsequently by many prophets. But it is more than a revolting metaphor. Many Canaanitish religious cults practiced temple prostitution, homosexuality, and other aberrations as acts of "worship." Since Israel adopted some of these practices, Ezekiel calls the wanton Queen a harlot.

The bride took the garments her husband had lavished upon her and used them to drape the couches where she welcomed
16:16   her own destruction. (RSV misses the point, translating *bamoth* "high places" as "shrines.") Literally, the Israelites took materials that God had created for better use, and on the "high places" they erected tents, lavishly hung with rugs and draperies,
16:17   for the worship of Asherah (II Kings 23:7). The bride made

"images of men" from the precious metal and jewels her husband had given her. The allusion is not quite clear. There may have been images in human form, but, usually, when idolatrous Israel represented the deity it was in the form of a bull calf, while the most popular Canaanite deities were female. The Hebrew may be translated "male images." Since Jerusalem is a wife unfaithful to her husband, any false god whom she might worship would—for purposes of the allegory—be called a "man." Ezekiel makes no distinction between idols representing pagan deities and those representing the Lord. It was but a short step from the use of religious statuary symbolizing God to the lascivious rites of the pagan neighbors. The grave spiritual danger in the pre-exilic period was not open denial of God, but amalgamation of pagan forms, beliefs, and practices into the pure faith. (See Exodus 32).

The most hideous aspect of idolatry was the descent to human sacrifice. When the Israelites entered the Promised Land, 16:20 the practice was highly developed among the Canaanites. During the period of the Judges it continued among the pagan neighbors, and extended sometimes into the Hebrew community (Judges 11:39). Ahaz "burned his son as an offering, according to the abominable practices of the nations whom the Lord drove out before the people of Israel" (II Kings 16:3). Manasseh likewise sacrificed his son (II Kings 21:6). We gather from Micah 6:7 and many other passages that such grisly sacrifices—sometimes at least—were offered to the Lord. Under the influence of the prophets, politically implemented by Josiah, the horrible practice was ended. But apparently superstitious Israelites considered child sacrifice of great effect when ordinary religious rites had failed (II Kings 3:27). And so, unhappily, the practice revived during the last days of Jerusalem (Jeremiah 7:31; 19:5; 32:35). Ezekiel contends that Jerusalem must be 16:21 destroyed. Think what it means to slaughter a child and burn his body as a sacrifice to God. Then disagree with Ezekiel, if you can.

It is difficult to horrify people in the twentieth century, but the practice of child sacrifice achieves this difficult result. Eze- 16:22 kiel traces this horror, and every other sin, back to the basic sin of pride. Jerusalem had forgotten from whom her blessings —including her children—came.

Ezekiel turns his attention from "religious" sins to "political"

16:23 sins, though he would not acknowledge the distinction. He contends here and always that departure from God leads inevitably to wrong conduct in the home, the Temple, the shop, and the palace. Jerusalem had made foreign alliances of dubious moral worth. These alliances sometimes brought with them foreign idolatries, ideas, and customs. Hence Ezekiel, with other prophets, stigmatizes them as harlotry (Hosea 2:4; Isaiah 57:7ff).

16:24 We do not know how many shrines were erected to foreign deities within the city Jerusalem. (The Greek, Latin, and Syriac versions interpret these "vaulted chambers" as brothels.) But enough were built in conspicuous places at the major intersections that Ezekiel accuses Jerusalem of being a harlot who
16:25 throws herself at every passerby.

16:26 The first alliance with Egypt was Solomon's (I Kings 3:1). We are not aware that the Egyptians exported their religion to any major extent. We find no mention of Egyptian religious influence even in I Kings 11:4-8, and the Egytian idolatry in 8:7-13 is probably symbolic. So the "harlotry" with Egypt should probably be understood as political alliances rather than the adoption of Egyptian religious practices.

16:27 Egyptian alliances were seldom profitable. When Hezekiah appealed to Egypt for help, Sennacherib the Assyrian stormed in and seized several Judean cities and gave them to Philistine kings (II Kings 18:13). Ezekiel says that the Philistines "were ashamed of your lewd behavior." Presumably this irony is part of the allegory. It was difficult to shock the Philistines.

16:28 Insatiable Israel had likewise sought alliances with Assyria. Probably this refers to the pro-Assyrian policies of Ahaz and
16:29 Manasseh (II Kings 16:7ff). Again Jerusalem had trafficked with Chaldea. Indeed she had looked anywhere and everywhere for help, save to Almighty God.

16:31 The allegory rises to new heights of savagery as Ezekiel cries that Jerusalem is even worse than a common harlot who has at
16:32 least the excuse of economic need. Instead the adulterous wife
16:33 has paid men to come to her. Ezekiel's word "gifts" closely
16:34 resembles the Babylonian word for "bridal dowry." Even this the faithless wife has given away in bribes to strangers. The Hebrews had long considered Jerusalem different from other people. Brutally Ezekiel concedes the point. Jerusalem is different. She is worse.

(3) The Harlot's Punishment, 16:35-43.

Ezekiel has unsparingly condemned the sin of Jerusalem. Now with unmatched severity he turns to her punishment, summoning together all his anger and sorrow with the bitter epithet, "O harlot."

16:35

In Israel the punishment of an adulteress was death by stoning (Deuteronomy 22:21). Ezekiel pictures God gathering together Jerusalem's "lovers" and those whom she has hated (presumably the Philistines and Edomites, with whom there had been no alliances). They will strip her bare, exposing her shame. And God, through their agency, will carry out the punishment upon a faithless wife or a child murderer.

16:37
16:38

The figure begins to coalesce with the reality. The attackers stone the harlot and hack her to bits with their swords. According to Rabbi Kimchi, the great medieval commentator, people used to throw stones at an adulteress, stab at her, and burn her house. This resembles what happened to Jerusalem. And so, says the Lord, "I will make you stop playing the harlot." Finally when God's "fury" is satisfied, He will be "calm" (the first word of hope in forty-two long verses).

16:40
16:41

16:42

> Any judgement as to the seeming harshness of this "anthropopathism," whereby Yahweh is represented as "raging himself out," should be modified by recollecting that we are not free of the allegory. —W. F. Lofthouse

b. The Sisters, 16:44-58.

The allegory of the sisters is closely linked to and yet sharply differentiated from the preceding. Both depict Jerusalem as a faithless woman. In the former allegory Jerusalem symbolizes the entire Hebrew community. In this Jerusalem represents the Kingdom of Judah.

16:44

Ezekiel quotes yet another proverb, "Like mother, like daughter," in renewed reference to Jerusalem's "Hittite" ancestry. Never one to court cheap popularity, the seer points out that the Amorite and the Hittite had other children. Jerusalem could not help acknowledging her kinship with Samaria, the capital city, symbolizing the Northern Kingdom of Israel. Until its defeat in 722 B.C., the Northern Kingdom was in every respect larger and stronger than the Southern, hence Ezekiel could, without offense, call Samaria the "elder sister" who lived with her daughters (small cities and villages) to the

16:45

16:46

north of Jerusalem. Samaria was destroyed. Many in Jerusalem, who received the wrong message from the prophet Amos, said complacently that she was destroyed because of her sins.

The younger sister, who with her daughters lived to the south, was Sodom—the outstanding biblical symbol of evil. Sodom was the city of the plain south of the Dead Sea where Lot settled. Despite Abraham's fervent prayer, Sodom was destroyed for its rampant wickedness. The particular sin that is mentioned in the Bible is widespread homosexuality (Genesis 19:4-8).

It was no surprise or offense when Ezekiel related Jerusalem to Samaria, but kinship with Sodom was unheard of and

16:47   thoroughly unwelcome. Sodom remains, even today, as a symbol of all that is vile, horrible, and worthy of destruction. Ezekiel drives the point home with a sledge. Samaria was evil. Sodom

16:48   was more evil. And Jerusalem is worse than either.

The outstanding sin that Ezekiel sees in the hideous past of Sodom is not sensuality or unnatural vice, but pride due to

16:49   material plenty. The smug Sodomites revelled in their own
16:50   prosperity and ignored the hungering poor about them. In their hauteur the Sodomites decided that they were above the moral law; hence they did "abominable things." So God destroyed them.

Ezekiel does not delineate the sins of Samaria, possibly because Amos did the task so thoroughly (Amos 2:6—8:10). He

16:51   says only that, by contrast with Jerusalem, Samaria looks righteous (Jeremiah 3:11).

Sodom was destroyed. Samaria was destroyed. Speaking to Jerusalem, who will be destroyed, Ezekiel counsels, "Bear your

16:52   disgrace, for you have made your sisters appear righteous." This pithy counsel is a high point in Ezekiel's brutal irony. Yet, paradoxically, this concentrate of wormwood leads directly to the most radiant hope to be found, not only in this prophecy, but in the entire OT. The prophecy of Jonah alone radiates this hope with equal splendor. Samaria and Jerusalem will be

16:53   restored. Other strong men of God had foreseen this. But Ezekiel adds that Sodom will be restored. (Jeremiah 12:14-17 foresees the conversion to Hebrew faith and the restoration of evil neighbors, but he does not name Sodom.) Sodom never had been part of the covenant people. Sodom had despised and rejected God and His righteousness. Hence Sodom was destroyed.

But Sodom will be restored. Christians all believe that God cares even for the people who hate Him. Christians learned this, in large part, from Ezekiel.

For haughty Jerusalem, Ezekiel's hope was tinged with gall. Jerusalem must be dragged through destruction with Samaria 16:55 and Sodom before she can be restored with them. She must 16:57 know the contempt of her neighbors. She must bear the penalty 16:58 of her lewdness. Ezekiel frequently states his points negatively. Christians would say that before one can know the forgiveness of God he must go through the bitterness of repentance. Ezekiel, in a particular historical context, emphasizes the bitterness. His overwhelming vision of glory is yet to come.

c. The Restoration, 16:59-63.

Jerusalem has been unfaithful to the covenant with God. She has despised the "oath," or "curse" pronounced upon those 16:59 who violate it. The nature of this curse is spelled out in Deuteronomy 28:15-68 in terms that almost match Ezekiel's. Jerusalem has sinned and must accept the consequence. This Ezekiel has made abundantly plain. Nevertheless, "I will re-16:60 member my covenant." The "I" is emphatic. In Hebrew the verb form usually expresses the "I," but here God, speaking through Ezekiel, uses the strong word. Man has forgotten. God will remember. He will renew the bond that faithless Jerusalem has broken and the renewed covenant will be everlasting.

When Jerusalem has been restored by God's grace and favor, she will look back in humble repentance upon the sins in her 16:61 lurid past. God will take her two once-scarlet "sisters" and give them to her as "daughters." It is possible, of course, to interpret this gift in crude terms of political aggrandizement, that Jerusalem which was a poor small nation will become a large rich nation. But respect for Ezekiel's message should lead us to see the promise in moral terms, not those of power politics. Jerusalem will be the center from which faith will extend to the surrounding peoples, even those who have been most hostile to God. The phrase "but not on account of the covenant with you" is difficult. Probably it means that when the everlasting covenant is in effect, God will go far beyond the good He has promised.

Ezekiel looks far into the future, to the day when the everlasting covenant is established, and he sings, "You shall know 16:62 that I am the Lord." The words have been a dirge and a death

knell. Now they are a song of hope. Jerusalem will never forget
the gruesome experience of the past, but always will remember
it with profit, "when I forgive you all that you have done." The
verb "forgive" usually means "to make expiation" by some ritual
act of man. But no amount of ceremonial purification can
cleanse Jerusalem's guilt, only God can do that. Ezekiel is not
far from saying, "by grace you have been saved" (Ephesians
2:8).

This passage is the longest sustained expression of hope that
we have yet encountered in Ezekiel's prophecy. It is the first
clear covenant section in the prophecy, though far from being
the last. Here for the first time Ezekiel mentions forgiveness.
Increasingly these are to be the dominant themes of the book,
as judgment is the dominant theme in the earlier chapters.

  2. Zedekiah's Folly, 17:1-24.

The seventeenth chapter, like its predecessor, begins with
an elaborate allegory, follows this with an interpretation, and
concludes with radiant hope. The allegory concerns Zedekiah,
the prince regent, who in 588 B.C. entered into a disastrous
alliance with Egypt and rebelled against Babylon. The chapter
supports and develops the grim message preceding. That one
dealt with the long history of Jerusalem's sin, this with sins of
the immediate present.

  a. The Riddle of the Eagle, 17:1-10.

The Lord commands the prophet to "propound a riddle and
speak an allegory." The dividing line between the two is quite
17:2   thin. A riddle is intentionally puzzling until one has the key
to its solution. An allegory is an extended metaphor in which
many details have a significance contributing to the total meaning. Ezekiel has used puzzling allegories frequently, but he has
not labeled them as "riddles." Since Ezekiel was "dumb" when
he spoke by more conventional means, he attempts here to force
attention by using a different teaching device, the riddle. His
fellow-exiles wanted a prophecy of quick restoration to their
homeland. Zedekiah's rebellion rekindled hopes that such a
return might come soon. Ezekiel's gloomy foreboding was increasingly unpopular; so he attempted a new approach. (See
Judges 14:14; II Samuel 12:1-12).

There is little point in our trying to be puzzled by the riddle.
We know the key only too well. The great "eagle" (possibly

17:3   "vulture") represents Nebuchadnezzar. The bird is a symbol for the monarch whose power extended over incredible distances, and who swooped down relentlessly upon his prey. The many colors probably indicate that the Chaldean empire comprised many different peoples and cultures, or they may indicate the highly colored plumage of the gigantic birds in the Babylonian reliefs and statues. Lebanon suggests the land of Israel. The cedar of Lebanon denotes the house of David. The top of the cedar, of course, is the king himself.

    Nebuchadnezzar carried King Jehoiachin into exile in 597 B.C. (II Kings 24:15). Ezekiel's term translated "land of trade"
17:4   is literally "land of Canaan." This is a play on words of the type that Ezekiel loves. Phonecia, the mercantile center, was the largest and most prosperous part of "Canaan," and so the word became a general term for "trader." Babylon was a great commercial center, hence "the land of Canaan," but definitely not the "land of Canaan" the exiles longed for.

    Now Ezekiel changes the figure of speech. Nebuchadnezzar took the "seed of the land," significantly not the seed of the
17:5   gigantic cedar, and planted it with care beside the waters. The emperor set Zedekiah upon the Judean throne. The soil was "fertile" in that Jerusalem had every opportunity to repent of her sins and to live at peace within the Babylonian Empire. The reference to a willow twig is confusing. JPS wisely para-phrases, "he set it as a slip," meaning that the emperor placed the seedling with the care that one would use to plant a rooted cutting in a land where gardening is, at best, difficult. The ten-
17:6   der plant turned into "low, spreading vine," not a sturdy, independent tree of the forest. The tendrils stretched toward the eagle, but the roots stayed fixed in the soil where they were planted. Ezekiel does not mention fruit.

    Zedekiah was on the throne. He had immeasurable opportu-nity to develop honorable agriculture, trade, and civic right-eousness in his kingdom, while foreign policy remained in Nebuchadnezzar's hands. It is no shame for a plant to be a vine if the vine is fruitful. But under Zedekiah the kingdom of Judah "brought forth branches and put forth foliage."

    The second great eagle is Pharaoh Hophra who ascended the Egyptian throne in 588 B.C. Almost immediately Zedekiah
17:7   asked him for help against Babylon (Jeremiah 37:7; 44:30). Turning to Egypt was both political folly and the violation of

a solemn oath (II Chronicles 36:13). Politically the move was suicidal. Egypt was weak; Babylon was strong. And supposing that Egypt were able to stand up against Nebuchadnezzar's reprisals, what would it benefit Zedekiah to change one taskmaster for another?

With Zedekiah's enthusiastic cooperation, Hophra attempted to transplant the vine from Palestinian to Egyptian soil, in the
17:8   fantastic hope that it might "bear fruit and become a noble vine." Ezekiel predicts, with grim accuracy, that the first eagle
17:9   will pull up the vine by its roots and "cut off its branches." Contemptuously he adds that "it will not take a strong arm."
17:10   When the east wind strikes, the uprooted vine will utterly wither away.

b. Interpretation of the Riddle, 17:11-21.

The interpretation adds only one element to our understanding. Ezekiel emphasizes the violation of Zedekiah's oath, not
17:12   the political folly of trading taskmasters. (For reasons now invisible, this verse is the only place where LXX uses the word
17:13   "king" in speaking of the earthly monarch.) We know little about the oath of allegiance that Zedekiah gave to Nebuchad-
17:14   nezzar, save that the king had sworn by God (II Chronicles 36:13). Ezekiel does absolute justice to Nebuchadnezzar's policy. It was humiliating but not destructive. Nebuchadnezzar wanted the Judean kingdom to prosper in subordination to him.

As soon as Hophra had ascended to the Egyptian throne Zedekiah violated the oath and appealed to him for horses
17:16   and troops. (Hophra's immediate predecessor, Necho, had lost all his Asiatic possessions to Nebuchadnezzar in 605 B.C.
17:17   [II Kings 24:7]. Possibly Zedekiah had appealed to Necho unsuccessfully.) Hophra did send an army to Jerusalem in 588 B.C., and forced the Babylonian troops to suspend their siege. But when Nebuchadnezzar sent his full might against Jerusalem, the Egyptians deserted their allies and fled (Jeremiah
17:18   37:5-11). Ezekiel warns that a political alliance based upon immoral foundations can have only a disastrous outcome. Can a man break the covenant and yet escape? This covenant was made with an alien whom the Hebrews had little reason to love. Still it was an oath, taken in the name of God. Can a man or nation violate a covenant with God and still hope for God's blessing? Ezekiel will not accept the coming destruction as a

mere misreading of the political probabilities. It is one thing
to make an honest mistake. It is a completely different thing
to commit a flagrant moral wrong. Under other circumstances
Jeremiah likewise virulently criticized the breaking of a covenant (Jeremiah 34:8-22).

The political events that brought forth Ezekiel's stern judgment are ancient history, but the principle upon which that
17:19 judgment depends is always new. An oath is sacred. National
morality is just as important as individual morality. God is
the Ruler, both over Judah and Babylon. When the King of
17:20 Judah violates a solemn treaty "I will spread my net over him."
It is not clear why Ezekiel abandons the allegory at this point,
comparing Hezekiah to a bird and Nebuchadnezzar to a hunter.
(See 12:13). Really, it does not concern us nearly so much as
the basic principle that violation of an oath or treaty is "trea-
17:21 son . . . against me." In the harsh judgments of history men
will learn that morality is sacred.

c. The Promise of a New King, 17:22-24.

Ezekiel returns to his allegory of the cedar tree. God Himself
will take a sprig from the lofty top of the cedar and will set it
17:22 out in a high mountain. The "I" is emphatic. This will not be
the work of a human intermediary like Nebuchadnezzar; it
will be God's own work. The lofty mountain upon which He
will plant the new cutting is Zion. Its height is spiritual rather
than geographical. The language is ornate, but the meaning is
inescapable. In the fulness of time, God Himself will select a
17:23 descendant of the house of David to be king over Israel. The
tree will grow to noble height and will bear the fruit that has
been so conspicuously missing in the botanical allegories that
have preceded. The tree will provide shelter and sustenance
17:24 for all manner of beasts and birds. The other trees (nations)
will recognize that God alone is Master of the forest.

Today some critics date this passage in the time of Zerubbabel who led the restoration after the exile, while others believe that it was composed even later.

Long before the time of Jesus, Hebrew commentators thought
this section a prophecy of the coming Messiah. Modern students
quite correctly react against an over-enthusiastic messianism
that reads all sorts of predictions into the Bible. The reaction
has gone too far. Now some claim that the prophets had nothing to say about the coming Messiah. The passage looks into the

future. It foresees a king of the Davidic line. This king would necessarily be an "Anointed One" or "Messiah" or "Christ." (The three terms are identical in meaning. The first is English, the second Hebrew, and the third Greek. Every king was a Christ.) This king will exert a world-wide influence that finally will cause all nations to know that God is the Lord of history. It would be extravagant flattery to describe Zerubbabel, or any other Hebrew king, in such terms. The writer of Ezekiel was not given to flattery. Surely we have noticed that much. Here he tells his contemporaries that, at some date in the future, God will send a Man to give spiritual leadership to His people, both those from a Jewish background and those from other cultures. This prediction was fulfilled when Jesus Christ came. It is difficult to see why the section should not be called a Messianic prophecy.

F. God and the Human Individual, 18:1-32.

The eighteenth chapter is one of the most important, and most puzzling, sections of the book. Some modern critics have grumbled that here Ezekiel reduces morality to an atomistic basis. If the chapter be isolated from the remainder of the prophecy, the charge must stand. But the chapter is a unit in a massive, complex structure. In simple justice one must interpret the chapter in the light of what goes before and what follows. Chapter 16 has made abundantly plain that the individual is part of society. Here the prophet focuses attention upon the individual's responsibility.

The sins of Manasseh were the focal point in Hebrew failure. When sorrow befell the people of Jerusalem, religious leaders said that it was punishment for Manasseh's sin (II Kings 24:3). Ezekiel has conceded that the spiritual nadir came under Manasseh; but he has stressed that past evils continued in slightly disguised form into the present. Even so, many among the exiles had adopted Manasseh as the sole cause of divine judgment. Hence they had a permanent excuse for irresponsible attitudes. Manasseh died half a century before their time. It was hard for them to feel any personal responsibility for his sins.

Many exiles were honestly perplexed by the religious implications of their banishment from Jerusalem. Why were they singled out for punishment while others, less worthy, were allowed to remain? Some decided that the moral struggle is hopeless, that individual righteousness or sin makes little difference in the meaningless cosmic scheme of things; so they came to terms with the materialistic culture about them. They sank into a mood of fatalism (33:10), and to exculpate themselves they bandied about witticisms at the expense of God.

Bewilderment, cynicism, and despair are not the stuff from which heroes are made. Ezekiel is striving to create heroes who will stand up to defend the faith when the Temple lies in ashes. To help in this seemingly hopeless task, the prophet strips morality to the bare bones. A skeleton is necessarily incomplete, but it provides the framework and support necessary for life. Here Ezekiel makes the skeletal claims of moral life, from which he draws a practical conclusion. The claims are:

(1) Each soul is immediately related to God.

(2) The destiny of each soul depends upon the quality of this relationship.

The conclusion is: Turn and live.

After reading several dozen critiques of this chapter, one is constrained to remark that Ezekiel is talking about God to people who know, intellectually at least, that God is merciful and gracious. In the opening verses of the chapter Ezekiel does not re-examine the basic elements of Hebrew faith, he assumes them. He does not think it necessary to say that God holds no man responsible for the circumstances in which he finds himself, but for the use he makes of the opportunities available to him. Ezekiel assumes the reader's understanding that perfect wisdom can cut through the tangle of social involvement, direct to the responsibility of the individual in a particular situation. Human wisdom cannot discern so deeply. This is one of many reasons why we hold to a faith that goes beyond what we can see. Holding this faith, we are responsible to live the moral life that is its expression, even by the river Chebar.

If anything, the problem with which Ezekiel deals is more critical today than it was in his own time. Modern man is part of the mass. Who could deny it? The individual is swept along by currents of history that he did not create and, seemingly, cannot alter. Major philosophies in our time deny that there is any true human freedom, hence there is no responsibility. Not surprisingly, these philosophies have produced cynicism and despair. The church needs as never before the conviction that each individual is directly responsible to almighty God, who calls him to turn Godward and live even when civilization is dying.

1. Individual Responsibility, 18:1-20.

There is a traceable relationship between some kinds of sin and some kinds of pain; and so many have concluded that every pain is a punishment for a particular sin. This idea persists even among Christians who look to the sinless yet suffering Christ. Today's troubles, often enough, can be traced to a cause several generations earlier; for the fathers inevitably leave an inheritance for good or for ill to their children. This is the way the world operates. Does the fact excuse us from moral responsibility? Or does it make ever imperative that the man of faith live his responsibility?

18:2   A cynical proverb circulated through the land of Judah (Jeremiah 31:29), and so it naturally came to the exiles. The children whose teeth were "on edge" saw no justice when told that their suffering was punishment for Manasseh's wrongdoing (II Kings 21:10-15). Deeply as one sympathizes with this feeling, one still must admit that human solidarity is a fact. Yesterday's actions produce results today. Today's actions will produce results tomorrow. Man does not live alone. Each generation carries a crushing load of unfinished business from the past (Exodus 34:7; Numbers 14:18). When the fact of human solidarity becomes an excuse for individual irresponsibility, its truth becomes a half-truth. Here Ezekiel is examining the fact of personal responsibility. Like any other truth concerning the human situation this one may be examined in isolation, but it must be lived amid myriad complexities. When spiritual leaders emphasized one part of the truth at the expense of the other, thinking people in Israel rejected the fatalistic theology that condemned them because of their fathers' sin. Jeremiah has already joined them in protest against a facile, deterministic half-truth (Jeremiah 31:30). Now Ezekiel joins his elder brother in emphasizing the opposite truth, that of individual responsibility. (See also Lamentations 5:7.)

18:4   The key sentence in Ezekiel's prophecy is: "Behold, all souls are mine; the soul of the father as well as the soul of the son is mine: the soul that sins shall die." If only the thought were presented positively instead of negatively, this would be one of the most beloved verses in the entire Bible. Faith, negatively stated, is the avoidance of death. Positively stated, faith is entering eternal life. Ezekiel's message would have meant the same had he said, "The soul that is righteous shall surely live." God created the soul of the father. He created the soul of the son. And he calls each to express an individual love that responds to His. Father or son can ignore the divine call. Experience, Ezekiel, and the rest of the Bible tell us that much. But father or son can likewise respond to the divine call, even in the valley of the shadow, and live. This, positively stated, is the central thought in Ezekiel's prophecy.

God is the Creator of each individual. Hence each individual stands in the same direct, personal, immediate relationship to Him. Those who are bound by the closest physical ties still are separate individuals. Each is responsible for his own destiny. None can pass the responsibility to another. Membership in a family, a tribe, or the chosen people is beside the point. God examines the use the individual makes of his God-given life.

When Ezekiel speaks of the soul dying or living, Christians usually understand it in terms of eternal life or death. The OT lays little emphasis upon the life that follows our years on earth. The idea of eternal life is implicit in the OT as the Pharisees taught in Jesus' time. But the Sadducees, who were biblical literalists, denied that there is any resurrection of the dead. Commentators disagree about Ezekiel's meaning when he says "The soul that sins shall die." Some say that when people lack any belief in life that follows physical death, the only evidence they can have of divine favor is prosperity, good health, and long life. So they say that here Ezekiel is promising these outward blessings to the one who lives his faith. If this be the case, it is a surprisingly obtuse promise from a keen observer like Ezekiel. Others say that the prophet is looking forward to the new age, promising that those who are righteous will survive to see it. Again, if this is the prophet's true meaning, it is less astute than most of Ezekiel's teachings thus far have been. Yet many commentators seem to think that we are bound to a choice between these alternatives, neither of which squares with the elementary facts of experience. Is there no other possible meaning for "life" and "death?"

A person with a clean conscience and the knowledge of God's presence is "alive," even when his earthly surroundings are almost unbearable. A person who has shut himself away from

God may dwell in a palace, but he is "dead." This was the essential message of Ezekiel's first vision, that man can "live" with God even by the river Chebar. This is the essential message in many of the gloomy chapters that we have read, that a person may have every outward spiritual advantage of life in Jerusalem, yet may be spiritually "dead." The present chapter gives no reason to believe that Ezekiel has changed his mind.

Christians sometimes talk as if the OT is concerned with outward conduct and the NT with inward intent. A careful reading of the NT shows deep concern for outward conduct, and a careful reading of the OT shows an ever-present awareness that right conduct is the outgrowth of right faith. In 18:5-9 Ezekiel draws a picture of a righteous man that might profitably be compared with that in Job 31, Psalm 15, Isaiah 58:5-7, or the picture of the righteous woman in Proverbs 31. To Ezekiel right living is the result of loyalty to God. In our zeal to trace out secondary causes we attribute right living to a sunny disposition, or to social pressures, or to fear of the consequences if we do wrong, or to whatever. Sometimes we lose sight of the primary cause altogether.

The picture of a righteous man shows one who is loyal to God. We Christians would say that he is in a "state of grace," and that his outward acts are expressions of divine grace operative in his life. The righteous man's life is marked by piety, purity, and benevolence.

18:5

First of all, the righteous man is faithful to his religious duties. After the sacrifice upon a "high place" there would be a sacrificial meal. The righteous man has shunned any participation in pagan worship, and has fulfilled the letter and spirit of Exodus 20:3-6. (Some believe that a slight change in the Hebrew would give a better reading—"eat with the blood," which corresponds with 33:25.) The description continues with the responsibilities of marriage. The righteous man is guiltless of adultery (Exodus 20:14), and he has respected the code of purity (Leviticus 15:19-30).

18:6

Notice the architectural balance with which Ezekiel describes the righteous man's acts of benevolence. Right acts performed and evil acts shunned are weighed together until three negatives contrasted with three positives lead to the conclusion: "He is righteous, he shall surely live."

The benevolent acts of the righteous man are in the fine OT

tradition of social responsibility, where a God-centered faith
must be expressed in relation to one's neighbor (Leviticus 25:
17). This tradition presupposes widespread poverty. An article
necessary for survival could be given in pledge only on a tem-
porary basis. A money lender must return a cloak, for example,
to the needy borrower so that he could use it as a blanket at
night (Exodus 22:25-27). The righteous man both refrains from
criminal actions (e.g. robbery), and is generous to his brother
in need (Deuteronomy 15:7-11). He does not lend money at interest (Leviticus 25:35-37).

The history of the Christian conscience battling against the
need of the market place is long and complex. In the late
Middle Ages the scholastic theologians finally decided that social and economic conditions had so changed since the days of
Moses that a Christian could, with conscience, accept interest
on a commercial loan. Modern society abhors a person who
takes advantage of his neighbor's poverty to demand exhorbitant
interest. But Ezekiel will not tolerate any interest whatsoever.
The righteous man he describes "does not lend at interest" and, if the grateful borrower voluntarily offers him something, he will not "take any increase." Negatively, the righteous
man "withholds his hand from iniquity." Positively, he "exe-
cutes true justice between man and man."

In summary, the one who is righteous "walks in my statutes."
Walking is the old, familiar biblical metaphor for daily life.
The practice of faith is a daily affair that demands constant
attention to right conduct in all the relationships of life. He
whose daily concern is to practice the righteous implicit in his
faith "shall surely live, says the Lord God." This description of
the one who shall live follows hard upon the lengthy, sordid
discussion of Israel's past. The fathers and the grandfathers have
sinned grievously, yet the sons can live—if they will. God asks
you not what your fathers did but what is the state of your
heart.

The righteous man has an evil son whose life is the exact
opposite of his father's. Ezekiel was aware, as all his noisier
critics are aware, that human personality cannot be accurately
portrayed in such vivid contrasts of black and white. Ezekiel is
like an anatomist who strips the flesh from the bones to expose
the bare skeleton. He does not pretend to give a portrait of
human nature. Rather he portrays the skeletal structure of

moral life. A righteous man has an unrighteous son. This has
happened often enough, God knows. Does the father's righteousness accumulate merit for the son? Many people with distinguished ancestors act as if this were the case. In later years,
John the Baptist excoriated the people, "Do not presume to
18:13   say to yourselves, We have Abraham as our father" (Matthew
3:9). In much the same sense, Ezekiel says that righteousness
is not transferred from person to person. The man who destroys
his bond with God will "surely die."

The third generation brings a change for the better. The son
"sees all the sins which his father has done, and fears." The
18:14   written Hebrew is "fears," but, following a long tradition, the
reader says "considers." And this is the heart of Chapter 18.
Ezekiel is calling upon his fellow-exiles to think, to consider.
They are not chained to the sins of the past. Neither are they
to bask in the glory of the past. They are to think, and thinking to practice their faith where they are. No person chooses
18:17   the circumstances that will surround his life. Within a given
circumstance, each person must choose what kind of person he
will be. The one who practices his faith, however evil his father may have been, "shall surely live." Ezekiel does *not* say,
here or in verse 20, that the actions of the father have no effect
upon the son's outward condition. Such a statement would be
both foolish and false. He is talking about man's essential relationship with God. This cannot be passed from generation
to generation; neither can one generation steal it from the next.

In the center of the chapter Ezekiel repeats the basic question
and gives the answer that he is illustrating in such detail. The
18:19   translation in RSV, though grammatically sound, is hard to
understand. AV perfectly summarizes the case Ezekiel is refut-
ing with the question, "Why? doth not the son bear the iniquity
of the father?" Here is a group of exiles, suffering because of
sins and mistakes that others had made. Can Ezekiel deny that
they are bearing the iniquity of their fathers?

The prophet denies that the exiles' spiritual condition is
doomed by ancestral sins. He states, in clear, concise terms, the
18:20   general principle to which the foregoing discussion has been
leading. He affirms the moral freedom of the individual. This
freedom is implicit in all the OT, and explicit in Jeremiah
(Jeremiah 31:29f.). Historically, Ezekiel was the first to spell it
out in specific detail. He was opposing the popular theology of

his day, which was based upon a wooden interpretation of the Law (Exodus 20:5)and the cruel facts of experience. To people who are suffering, he says, "The son shall not suffer for the iniquity of the father." Taken from context, the statement obviously is untrue. If the father squanders his wealth, the son will be poor. In context, the statement is true and central to moral life. The son shall not suffer (in the essential relation with God) because someone else has erred. The exiles are by the Chebar, far from the home they long for. But even there the bonds with God can be strong or can be shattered. The individual must decide.

2. Freedom to Change, 18:21-29.

The prophet turns to another aspect of the question. He has stated clearly that the individual is not chained to the sins or the righteousness of his father. Now he states that the individual is not chained to his own past. The prophet, up to this point, has said remarkably little about repentance; for he is speaking to people who recognize no need for repentance and see no hope if they do repent. Concisely Ezekiel sums up the essentials. The repentant man "turns away from all his sins" and "keeps all my statutes." True repentance involves more than Godly sorrow for past sins; it is also a renewed life.

Divine forgiveness, like repentance, has not figured largely in the prophecy up to this point, but now Ezekiel reminds the reader of the essential truth that God is gracious and forgiving. He created man free to do right or wrong, and responsible for the consequence. It is God's unchanging desire that man should do right and live. He does not wish to enforce the moral law when man rebels against his Creator, but still He enforces it, for He is morally responsible, and He calls man to moral responsibility. A man's turning from his righteousness to commit iniquity obviously means a complete change in the direction of life, not the occasional slip into misconduct that most right living persons experience. Ezekiel is painting the picture in vivid contrasting colors, illustrating a principle, not examining historical personalities.

The Son of Man points beyond the perishable evidences of divine favor to the imperishable nature of God Himself. Jerusalem will crumble, as Ezekiel tearfully predicts, but God will remain. His mercy endureth forever. His purpose, expressed

18:21

8:22
8:23

124 Ezekiel, Prophecy of Hope

sometimes in thunder, is that men be saved. Christians find an even deeper meaning in salvation than did the exiles by the Chebar.

18:24 The basic principle that Ezekiel is developing here is not strict retributive justice, but the moral freedom and independence of the individual, in a world where God enforces the moral law while He longs for man to turn to Him and live. The message of hope must ever be accompanied by the solemn warning: no man is safe. God cares about the state of man's heart. He does not strike a statistical average of a person's moral career. He examines the intention, the desire, the direction of growth. The Talmud says about the one righteous man who has fallen into evil that this refers to the apostate so vile that he even regrets the good he once did (*Kiddushin* 40a). He is guilty of "treachery," or rebellion against God, and he has willfully adopted a sinful way of life.

Once more Ezekiel anticipates the rebuttal to his argument: "The way of the Lord is not just." "Just" means "equal, ad-
18:25 justed to the standard." Ezekiel faced the old, old longing for a cut-and-dried program of salvation. Put in so many good deeds and pull out the blessings of material prosperity and an easy conscience. Moral life is not like that. The material blessings of life, every observer has noticed, are distributed with little regard for the recipient's piety. The way of perfect righteousness may lead to an earthly crown of thorns and a cross. God's purpose for human life is not to make his devoted followers comfortable, but to fit them, by harsh trial when necessary, to be His sons for eternity.

Possibly some of the exiles, like the elder brother of the Prodigal Son, were unwilling that God should forgive the repentant sinner. Unless God is forgiving, there can be no fellowship with Him. If He is forgiving to all, on equal terms, then His way is just.

A slight grammatical distinction may or may not be significant. "Is my *way* not just? Is it not your *ways* that are not just?" Ezekiel has pointed out, through the symbolism of the charioteers, that God moves "straight forward" (e.g. 1:12). When the eye of flesh sees only turmoil and confusion the eye of faith sees that God is progressing toward His goal. The distinction, if it be valid, lies between our many contradictory human "ways" and God's one eternal "way." Unhappily, this distinction is not observed in 18:29, while the Greek uses the singular in both instances.

3. The Call to Life, 18:30-32.

The conclusion of the whole matter is a call to action: "Repent." Theologians who have examined the eighteenth chap-
8:30 ter of Ezekiel apart from its context have come up with some
startling misinterpretations. In its context—where we are examining it—the chapter is a plea for moral responsibility to
those who are drifting into cynicism and indifference. The chapter does not contradict the Christian doctrines of original sin
and election. It is addressed to those who are part of the covenant, calling them to live their covenant relationship.

The real problem is not God's unwillingness to save us, but
our unwillingness to be saved. "Why will you die, O house of
8:31 Israel?" The need is not for an explanation but for a renewal
of heart. Even this magnificent call to faith can be, and has
been, misconstrued. Taken from context, it sounds as if Ezekiel
is exalting self-improvement as the way to life. He has already
expressed the basic truth, that God alone is the Author of salvation (e.g. 11:19). Here he calls upon man to repent and live.
There is no clash. Divine grace does not exclude human freedom, but enlists it. This controversial, crucial eighteenth chapter is calling men who have almost forgotten their faith to re-
dedicate themselves to God.

G. Lamentations, 19:1-14.

The nineteenth chapter concludes the second cycle of
warnings, chapters 12-19. If you will first read this chapter then briefly review the preceding chapters, you will be
struck by the incredible variety of thought and style that the
prophet has brought to bear upon his work. He has employed
dramatic parables. He has attacked specific abuses. He has
dipped his pen in vitriol. He has developed long, involved allegories. He has presented an extended philosophic discussion.
And here he shows his skill as a poet. The poems are not especially beloved because they deal with subject matter that has
only historical interest for most readers today. But they lack
nothing in beauty or in poetic imagery.

The poems are written in the *quinah* or "lamentation" form,
which was frequently used for Hebrew elegies. (See 27, 28; II

19:1 Samuel 1:19-27; Lamentations 1-5.) Each line contains two
sections. The former has three stresses and the latter two. Even
in translation it is possible to discern the mournful cadence as
the prophet sings the glory and the destruction of the "princes,"
and of Israel.

Notice that Ezekiel is commanded by God to sing these
beautiful, melancholy songs, just as he has earlier been commanded to speak some harsh but necessary truths.

1. Lamentation for the Princes, 19:1-9.

Although some have suggested that the "lioness" represents
Hamutal, wife of Josiah, mother of Jehoahaz and Zedekiah (II
19:2 Kings 23:31; 24:18), the tenor of the passage suggests the nation
rather than any individual. Judah was frequently symbolized
as a lion (Genesis 49:9), as have been many other nations not
particularly notable for their leonine qualities. The picture of
young lions is not sarcastic. Even as he is sketching in the outlines, chiding his fellow-exiles for their absurd dreams of political glory, Ezekiel's own feelings shine through the imagery of
the poem. He shows his love for his people, his hopes for their
ruler, and his bitter grief that these hopes have remained unfulfilled.

The first young lion pictured is obviously Jehoahaz, who was
crowned when he was twenty-three years old, about 608 B.C.,
19:3 following the death of his father Josiah at the Battle of Megiddo (II Kings 23:29f). The bloodthirsty activities attributed
to the young lion should be understood in terms of the allegory,
not literally; for Jehoahaz reigned only three months. Pharaoh
19:4 Necho of Egypt deposed him and put Jehoiakim on the throne.
Then the Pharaoh took Jehoahaz to Egypt where he died (II
Kings 23:30-34). His brief life consisted of opportunities that
never were realized. This is the pathos and the tragedy of the
poem.

The majority of modern Christian students believe that the
second young lion represents Jehoiachin, Ezekiel's contempo-
19:5 rary in exile, but the classical Jewish commentators taught that
he symbolizes Jehoiakim, whose eleven year reign was tragic
enough to fill any heart with pity and fear. He was placed on
the throne by Necho, about 608 B.C. In 605 B.C. Nebuchadnezzar defeated Necho at the Battle of Carchemish, and made
19:7 Jehoiakim a vassal. Three years later he rashly rebelled and

19:9   was carried off to Babylon, but later was reinstated on his throne. Finally, at the instigation of Nebuchadnezzar, he was assassinated, and his body given "the burial of an ass" that is, no burial at all (II Kings 24:1ff.; Jeremiah 22:19; Josephus, *Antiquities*, 10,6,3). The "hooks" and the "cage" may be understood allegorically, but it is quite possible that the Babylonian troops actually used hooks to drag their captives away. It is known that Ashurbanipal, the Assyrian monarch, placed a cage at the east gate of Nineveh in which he kept a captive king.

The Kingdom of Judah was a bit of political flotsam, caught between two conflicting currents, from Egypt and Babylon. Had Jehoiakim been a strong king, he still could not have affected the ebb and flow of military power, but in the maelstrom he might have been able to guide his nation in ways of faith and peace. Instead he reverted to the idolatry that his father had attempted to stamp out. He is remembered today chiefly for his contemptible effort to silence a prophet (Jeremiah 36). His political vacillations showed neither sagacity nor honor. Yet he was the earthly ruler of Israel, a "young lion" for whom Ezekiel grieves.

2. Lamentation for Israel, 19:10-14.

The second poem is far more realistic in its symbolism than the former. Here the symbol would be grotesque, if applied to
9:10   the Queen Mother Hamutal, though it is appropriate and meaningful when applied to the Hebrew nation. Ezekiel reverts to the symbol of the grapevine, without the savage fury that he showed before (15:1-8; 17:3-10). It is no disgrace to be a vine, if the vine is fruitful. In contrast with his earlier symbol of the fruitless vine in the forest, Ezekiel here shows a productive vine in the vineyard. (The reader must keep always in mind that the logical law of contradiction does not apply in a figure of speech with the same force that it has in discursive prose.) The
9:11   "strongest stem" may well represent Jehoiachin, the king in exile, or it may refer to Zedekiah, who was on the throne in Jerusalem busily plotting a rebellion that must fail. In either case, the description "it towered aloft" is somewhat fulsome.

Ezekiel has predicted the destruction of Jerusalem many times, but never with the pathos that he shows here as the vine
9:12   is uprooted, stripped of its fruit, withered, and burned. Of course many critics believe that this poem was written after the

event, when the fires of Babylon had destroyed the city Jerusalem. The critic Gustav Hölscher denies that this poem is Ezekiel's because the imagery is taken from 17:5-10 and is used inconsistently. For how can the vine that has been destroyed be transplanted in the wilderness? The observation is less astute than many of Dr. Hölscher's penetrating insights. This picture of utter destruction, with the similar pictures that have gone before and will follow, is a preparation for the vision to come, as the Lord commands Ezekiel to prophesy, "Come from the four winds, O Breath [Spirit] and breathe upon these slain that they may live" (37:9). How can the withered, charred vine live when transplanted in the wilderness. It cannot, without the life-giving Spirit of God.

For all his grief, Ezekiel remains a prophet. It is his task to call the people to responsibility. We blame the tragedies that
19:14 befall us upon everyone and anyone but ourselves. Ezekiel will not cast the blame for Judah's destruction upon Babylon or Egypt. The fault is Judah's. The destroying fire comes not from Babylon, but "from its stem." If Zedekiah had given heed to the wise counsel of Ezekiel—Yes, if. But he did not. He engaged in a suicidal rebellion. As a consequence, Nebuchadnezzar burned Jerusalem, decimated the surrounding kingdom, and put to death all of Zedekiah's heirs "so that there remains in it no strong stem, no scepter for a ruler."

> The fault, dear Brutus, is not in our stars
> But in ourselves.
> —*Julius Caesar*, Act I, Scene i

V. THE THIRD CYCLE OF WARNINGS, 20:1–24:27.

The third cycle of warnings is largely a restatement and intensification of Ezekiel's basic message. It begins a year after the last date given and covers the period up to the siege against Jerusalem. The warnings fall into two groups. In rough outline, one group consists of renewed indictments against Israel and the exiles (Chapter 20), against Jerusalem (Chapter 22), and against the Hebrew nation in the past (Chapter 23). The other group interprets current history. One chapter describes Nebuchadnezzar's advance against Jerusalem, including the vivid and terrifying "Song of the Sword" (Chapter 21). The last chapter in the section imaginatively pictures the siege (Chapter 24).

In the preceding pages we have traced the development of the hope motif, from its barely recognizable beginnings to the glorious climax that Sodom will be restored (16:55) and the call to life in the valley of the shadow (18:31-32). This section contains few expressions of hope; the doom is too near. But those few expressions are vivid. Here the hope-filled thought is made explicit, that God acts for the sake of His name (20:9, 14, 22). The brief cry of hope (20:40-42) is the clearest statement of God's redemptive purpose in the entire first half of the book.

A. The Fate of Israel, 20:1-44.

The twentieth chapter is divided into three major parts. The first (20:1-32) is a long, despairing picture of Israel's history. The second (20:33-44) looks into the future and predicts the irrevocable harsh judgments of God, culminating in the radiant hope of restoration. The third (20:45-49) belongs properly with the following chapter, and will be considered with it.

Ezekiel's pessimistic view of Israel's morality has been given in 14:1-11 and 16:1-34. It is to be repeated in 22:1-31 and 23:1-21. Here there is no allegory, nothing but the depressing, straightforward recital of a degrading story. Israel has from the beginning been guilty of idolatry and the moral conduct that goes with it. God has been close to destroying Israel, again and again. But for the sake of His name He has spared the people whom He has chosen. Now the evil has reached such an intensity that the destruction of Jerusalem is inevitable. Even so, God's purpose still is redemptive.

There is a marked contrast between Ezekiel's understanding of his nation's history and what might be called the traditional view. Ezekiel's contemporaries, like most Jews or Christians today, thought of the period from the Egyptian captivity to the Babylonian exile as a time of faith marked by frequent lapses into idolatry and social unrighteousness. The prophets see history in a more sober light, and of all the prophets Ezekiel is the most negative about the past. He sees his nation's history as a long period of evil, marked by occasional interludes of faith and righteousness. God has been faithful. His chosen people have not.

1. Israel's History, 20:1-32.

Eleven months after the last dated oracle (8:1), on the tenth day of Ab (July-August) 591 B.C., four years before the actual fall of Jerusalem, certain elders of Israel came before Ezekiel to inquire of the Lord. According to the fairly consistent usage in the prophecy, the "elders of Israel" are the spiritual leaders among the exiles. We shall consider the question they asked in connection with verse 30. It is difficult not to sympathize with these elders. The record shows that when they came before Ezekiel (8:1; 14:1) they received tongue lashings that have never been rivalled in the history of condemnation. Yet they kept coming back. Ezekiel's teaching was not, and is not, pleasant, but it reaches into the depths of the human tragedy where Ezekiel teaches us to discern the controlling purpose of God.

20:1

The Lord refuses to receive the inquiry. Instead He asks the prophet himself to "judge" the elders. His question, "Will you judge them?" has the force of an imperative. Were the speaker human, the repetition would suggest impatience. (See 22:2; 23: 36.) "Judge," in this and the following two chapters, means "outline the case against." It is not Ezekiel's task to impose the sentence but to explain why it is just.

20:4

The "judgment" recapitulates the long, sordid history of Israel. Were this chapter to be examined in isolation, it would seem to contradict the principle of individual responsibility that Ezekiel has so carefully established in Chapter 18. But the whole point of this and the subsequent chapters is that the sins of the past have continued into the present. Ezekiel has never denied the law of continuity. Here he emphasizes it, as in Chapter 18 he emphasized the law of individuality.

"When I chose Israel." There is no contradiction between the idea of human freedom and the idea of divine election, though many people have tried to create one. Ezekiel's primary emphasis is upon human responsibility; so, not surprisingly, he lays little stress upon the complementary truth that God chooses His servants. This is the only place in which he mentions that God chose Israel. Ezekiel's elder contemporary likewise mentions this choice only once (Jeremiah 33:24). The thought of divine election is developed to its full glory in Isaiah 40-56 and the Pauline letters, where it does not imply the slightest diminution of human freedom. As Amos has made abundantly clear,

20:5

God "knows" or "chooses" a person to bear special responsibility (Amos 3:2).

God "chose" Israel in the land of Egypt. Men had known and worshiped God long before the Egyptian captivity. The choice was a specific responsibility to interpret God's nature and will to the surrounding nations by developing a pure faith in the midst of idolatry, and living righteously in the midst of sin. Exodus 6:8 relates the promise made to Abraham, Isaac, and Israel, or Jacob. But Abraham's son Ishmael and Isaac's son Esau were not heirs to the promise; so it is customary to date God's choice of His *people* from the time when Israel's family was enslaved in Egypt, and God made His will known through Moses.

Ezekiel shares the Hebraic view of the mystical connection between God, the chosen people, and the Palestinian soil, even though he was one of God's principal agents to teach that faith is independent of geography. His statement that Palestine is a "land flowing with milk and honey" is literal and exact. The land of Palestine is parched, rocky, and—in much of its extent —barren. But even in the torrid wilderness there is pasture for milch-goats, and Palestinian bees are world famous today. When Ezekiel describes his country as "the most glorious of all lands" no Christian could debate the spiritual accuracy of the description. In any other sense, however, one must decide that the beauty lay in the eye of the beholder.

It is impossible to speak with accuracy about the religious practice of the captives in Egypt. Moses could not well have rallied the slaves in the name of the Lord had they forgotten their faith altogether. But subsequent history shows that, at best, the true faith was sadly diluted with idolatry. What evidence we have shows surprisingly little influence of Egyptian religious practices. Most Hebrew idolatry lay in aping the customs of the other Canaanitish people and in recalling the gods of their fathers back in the land of the Chaldeans.

When Ezekiel says that the enslaved Hebrews "rebelled" against God, he may be referring to an incident unknown to us. Exodus does not mention anything that we would call a rebellion. The mutterings against Moses and Aaron should not be dignified by such a term. But in Ezekiel's overall view of history the word is understandable. Accepting the Lord God of Israel demands the total rejection of other gods and all reli-

20:6

20:7

gious practices that are not specifically His. This total rejection of false gods and cultic practices was not complete in Israel until the post-exilic period. In this sense, then, we can understand that the captives in Egypt "rebelled" against the Lord.

Religious and moral laxity were such that the Egyptian captives deserved to perish. But God acted for the sake of His "name," not in accord with the merits of His chosen people. Ezekiel's argument is: if God had allowed the children of Israel to perish in Egypt, then other nations would have thought that He lacked the power to deliver His own (Numbers 14:16; Deuteronomy 9:28); and so His "name" would be profaned.

20:9

The "name" of course is more than the written or spoken symbol YHWH. (The custom of leaving the sacred name unspoken appears to be later than the time of Ezekiel.) The "name" means the character, that which God is revealing Himself to be. To express much the same thought we would say "essence." Ezekiel is developing a thought quite similar to that in Chapter 16, that God loves Israel, not because Israel is lovable, but because His essential nature is love. (See Jeremiah 14:7, 21.)

The past several chapters have been leading up to the thought here expressed, that God has acted for the sake of His name. This concept is to be explicitly stated several times more (20:14, 22, 44; 36:21, 22, 23; 39:25), but it is far more basic to understanding the prophecy than its comparative infrequency would suggest. In the following pages this thought—however it may be worded—will be summed up under the NT word "grace." The Hebrew *chen* is occasionally translated "grace," but usually as "favor." It means kindness and graciousness in general. LXX translates *charis,* the same pleasant, sociable term that is exalted beyond the stars in NT, particularly in Paul's writings. One could more easily define the universe than the NT meaning of "grace." But perhaps it would be safe to claim as the central meaning that God's merciful actions toward us proceed from His nature and not from our merit. This, of course, is exactly what Ezekiel is saying. The closest OT equivalent is *chesed,* usually translated "loving-kindness" or "steadfast love," a term that is conspicuously rare in Ezekiel. In LXX this is generally *eleos,* or "pity." Rather than using a comparatively weak term, Paul took another that had a social rather than a theological connotation, and suffused it with glory. The *idea* of grace, as distinct from the word, fills the OT. This idea is what binds the prophecy of Ezekiel together.

Three specific acts are mentioned by which God made Himself known. The first, of course, is the physical deliverance from the land of Egypt into the relative safety of the wilderness. The second is the giving of statutes and ordinances, the "Law" that figures so largely in Jewish life. We would consider the third included in the second. God gave His "sabbaths as a sign." The plural indicates not only the weekly day of rest but the other holy days in the Hebrew calendar (e.g. Leviticus 23:24-29). In view of the circumstances this emphasis is not surprising. The Babylonians had laws about killing, stealing, and adultery. They said prayers and sang hymns. But the Sabbath was the distinctive sign of Hebrew faith. It could be observed at any distance from the Temple. It compressed the whole covenant relation into a single observance. It bound the Hebrews together and distinguished them from all other peoples.

Many acts of rebellion in the wilderness are known to us, of which the outstanding is the making of the golden calf. Aaron designated the worship of this idol as "a feast to the Lord," while Moses (and Ezekiel) thought it an act of rebellion against God (Exodus 32).

Once more the children of Israel deserved to perish for their sins. Once more God acted lest His name be "profaned in the sight of the nations." Here we are dealing with anthropomorphic language, which must not be taken so literally as to mean that God acts merely to preserve His reputation. The divine "name" is far more. The reason for divine mercy is found in God, not in man. Yet God was concerned, and is concerned, with what people think about Him. He wants the love even of the Sodomites. Hence he spared the children of Israel.

The second generation in the wilderness repeated all the sins of their fathers. This is the point Ezekiel is making at such length, not that the fathers sinned many centuries ago, but that each generation continued the sins of the past. Again, for the sake of His name, God withheld His hand. The mystery, as Ezekiel sees it, is not why God smites, but why He refrains from smiting. Even while the children of Israel were nomads in the desert God warned them that if they persisted in their idolatry He would scatter them abroad (cf. Deuteronomy 4:27).

After making all possible allowances for anthropomorphic

20:25 language—as one must in reading this chapter—one still faces a genuine difficulty when God says, through His prophet, "I gave them statutes that were not good and ordinances by which they could not have life." The Targum, quite understandably, distorted the text to read, "They made them decrees which were not right, and laws by which you cannot be established." Dr. Bewer claims that here a scribe has jumbled the order of verses, that verse 27 introduces verse 25 rather than verse 28; hence the original reading was, "Your fathers uttered this blasphemy against me—when they dealt treacherously with me—that I had given them statutes that were not good," etc. The suggestion is attractive, perhaps too attractive. It eliminates a verse that makes us shudder. Yet this verse, in all its shuddering awfulness, occurs in LXX, where many divergences from our text of Ezekiel avoid the more difficult anthropomorphisms. Possibly Ezekiel intended for us to shudder at this point. He has not spared our feelings hitherto.

The point of historical fact is clear, that some of the Hebrews did "offer by fire all their first-born." The difficulty lies in God's saying that He commanded it. (The same difficulty was found in 14:9, where God states that He "deceived" the false prophets.) Many Canaanitish peoples engaged in child sacrifice. When the children of Israel went lusting after false gods, they engaged in all the beastly horror that their neighbors practiced (Leviticus 18:21, etc). But Jeremiah and Ezekiel both say that this atrocity sometimes took place when Hebrews were "worshiping" the Lord (Jeremiah 7:30-31). (Most of the children's skeletons found at Gezer are those of infants under a week old. The mute evidence would indicate that these infants did not all die a natural death.) Ezekiel seems to be saying that the practice of child sacrifice had been more or less continuous since the entry into the Promised Land. Ezekiel was not a statistician. He was pointing out an evil that must be cast out—and who could disagree with him? We cannot learn from reading Ezekiel and the other prophets how widespread was the practice, but we must agree that it existed.

How can Ezekiel say that God commanded His people to sacrifice their children "that they might know that I am the Lord?" Actually we have here nothing more than a brutal phrasing of the insoluble mystery of evil in the world that God created good. Faith offers ways to overcome evil. It offers no theoreti-

cal explanation why evil is here to be overcome. The best interpretation of this verse is that given by the Jewish scholar
Rashi: when people reject the discipline of truth and righteousness, God permits the evil desires of their hearts to rule over
them. The children of Israel rejected pure faith and righteous
life. Hence God permitted them to listen to false religious leaders who encouraged child sacrifice and other abominations. The
biblical writers usually attribute to God the inevitable result
of man's free choice. Today we describe everything in terms of
secondary causes. But who created the secondary causes? It is
God's will that man should turn to Him and live. Ezekiel has
stated this. Here, as in many other passages, Ezekiel is pointing
out that quite frequently man wills to turn from God and die.
God allows man to turn away, and to learn through suffering
in order that man may turn back and "know that I am the
Lord."

If one holds that verse 27 belongs before verse 25, then there
is no problem about the verb "blasphemed." "Blasphemy" is a
0:27 Greek word that refers to irreverent speech. Here Ezekiel is
refering to irreverent actions rather than words. His verb has a
basic meaning "to cut off," from which it acquired a figurative
meaning, "to cut off with opprobrious words." But this cutting
off may be done also in act, when men's lives mock God and His
righteousness. Perhaps Ezekiel is telling us that the really important blasphemy is lived rather than spoken.

When the children of Israel entered the Promised Land, they
adopted with gusto the indigenous cultic practices. The original
0:28 inhabitants of the land had shrines on many of the hills. The
Israelites readily took these over (Deuteronomy 12:1-4). Their
worship, conducted in the name of YHWH, often did not differ
materially from that which had been conducted in the name of
0:29 Baal. The question about the meaning of the high places is
asked in contempt. Are these heathen shrines fit places to worship the Almighty? At the same time it is a play on words.
"What (*mah*) is the high place (*bamah*) to which you go (*ba*)?"
The etymology of *bamah* is unknown.

The long historical discussion has grown from the inquiry of
the elders. Now Ezekiel is speaking directly to the elders con-
0:30 cerning the present day, and we are able, finally, to consider
the question they wished to ask of the Lord through Ezekiel.
In view of all that has gone before it seems probable that the

elders wished to establish a "high place" for sacrifice in Babylon. Their intent was to preserve their own faith, free from the Babylonian idolatry. Ezekiel believes their plan to be wrong. Jerusalem is the only place where sacrifice may legitimately be offered. If the exiles erect a high place in Babylon, they will gradually assimilate the Babylonian cultic practices into the worship of God, until the people recognize no real distinction between YHWH and a pagan deity.

During the Babylonian captivity the Hebrew people developed the synagogue. This was a place of instruction, of legal interpretation, and of prayer. But no sacrifice was offered on an altar. Even when the Temple lay in ruins, and no sacrifice could be offered there, the exiles heeded Ezekiel's counsel. They did not erect an altar outside the Promised Land. (The Jews who were in Elephantine [now Aswan] Egypt did build a temple with an altar during the sixth century B.C., and in the second century another was built at Leontopolis.)

If the elders' question has been correctly interpreted, then the Lord's response may be understood as the conclusion of an argument from history. "If you build a high place in Babylon, then you will defile yourselves just as your fathers did, and you will go astray (LXX reads "go a-whoring") after detestable things. If you make the first concession to idolatry, you will finally sink even into the abyss of child sacrifice."

The entire section has been couched in negative terms. It concludes with a promise, likewise expressed as a negation. This **20:32** thing "shall never happen." The chosen people will not be lost in the morass of polytheism. (See Jeremiah 44:15-19.)

2. Israel's Only Hope, the Unchanging Nature of God, 20:33-44.

Ezekiel has dashed to the ground the hopes of the elders, perhaps with more savagery than was strictly necessary. Now, on **20:33** behalf of the Lord, he proclaims the hope that is inseparable from true faith. No one can accuse Ezekiel of the blind optimism that ignores unpleasant facts. Ezekiel's hope is fixed, not in the ever-changing events of history and the fickle counsels of men, but in the unchanging nature of God. "As I live," swears the Lord, in evident contrast to the deities of wood and stone just mentioned, "I will be king over you." The victory will not be lightly won. It will come only after the divine "wrath" is "poured out." But it will come.

It is difficult to discover a better term than "wrath," even with all its possibility of misinterpretation. Certainly it does not mean the surge of adrenalin into the bloodstream with which we are so familiar, followed often by irresponsible action. Rather it means God's unchanging attitude toward evil. In completely colorless terms it means the enforcement of the moral law. But God has revealed Himself to be more like a person than a process. When we speak of Him in personal terms—like wrath—we incur inevitable dangers. But these dangers are less than those encountered when man describes God impersonally as the moral law or the triadic dialectic or any combination of natural forces and processes.

The Lord promises the exiles, "I will . . . gather you out of the countries where you are scattered." That much is clear 20:34 enough. But the picture is not so clear when He adds, "I will 20:35 bring you into the wilderness of the peoples, and there I will enter into judgment with you." Interpretations of the verse differ. The "wilderness of the peoples" may be the desert country between Babylon and Palestine. On their return to the Promised Land, the exiles would skirt the edges of this wilderness almost all the way, and sometimes the road would lead them through the desert. But more probably the wilderness is spiritual. It is a figure of speech for the rigors of Babylon in which the exiles 20:36 came "face to face" with God. This second desert migration will be a sharp contrast with the first (20:10-26), when the fathers continued the sins of the past. The second wilderness journey will be a time of purification.

The figure "I will make you pass under the rod" refers to the shepherd at the annual roundup of his flock. He would drive 20:37 the sheep one by one under his staff (presumably with the help of a narrow defile or a set of fences) and every tenth animal he would dedicate to the Lord (Leviticus 27:32). Anyone who has been around sheep knows the terror they show when being herded about in strange places. The shepherd subjects them to this bewilderment because it is needful that his flock "go in 20:38 by number." If the flock is to endure, he must remove the culls. Likewise, during the second wilderness journey God will remove the "rebels" from His people.

Verse 39 takes up the thought of verse 32 where (if the interpretation above be accepted) Ezekiel has advised the elders 20:39 that building a high place in Babylon can lead only to idolatry and licentiousness. The prophet has given his warning. He has showed how the "wilderness" through which they are passing is God's testing time. Ezekiel can do no more. The elders are free, if they will, to ignore his teaching. If the text as we have it is correct, then the Lord is speaking with heavy irony, followed by an uncompleted threat and a promise. LXX gives a quite different reading that is far more intelligible, "Put away each one of you his evil practices, and hereafter if you hearken to me, then you shall no more profane my holy name by your gifts and evil practices." However lacking in charm the verse may be, it expresses a basic truth. The first condition of religious revival is making up one's mind. A person, or a nation, must decide for or against God. It is useless to offer gifts to God unless the gift-bearer comes with clean hands and a heart lifted up to the Lord.

20:40
The third cycle of warnings is a charnel-house of horrors, but in the midst of the blackest blackness is the brightest light we have yet seen, as in clear, unmistakable language Ezekiel predicts the return of his people to the Promised Land where, on "the mountain height of Israel" (Mount Zion) the altar will rise once more, and the people will serve the Lord throughout the land. Some have charged that other prophets disparage the importance of worship by their emphasis upon righteousness (e.g. Amos 5:21-24). The opposite charge has, with equal inaccuracy, been laid against Ezekiel. He sees right worship inseparable from right living. When the Israelites have returned to the Promised Land, and when the people are living righteously, God—who rejects idolatrous worship and despises a tainted gift—will "accept" His people and "require" their offerings.

20:41
When God has restored His people to their land He will accept them "as a pleasing odor." The allusion is to the smoke of sacrifice. Crude primitive people may well have thought that God "smelled" the sacrifice as a hungry man sniffs roasting meat. The prophets were not crude primitive people, but they sometimes retained the language of an earlier day. As God rejected the impure sacrifice of the fathers (20:31), He will accept the lives of His people as a pure sacrifice, and through their purified lives He will show the nations what is the nature of God. God promises His people that, when they return to the

20:42
Promised Land, "you shall know that I am the Lord." Here

the words that have been a death knell are a peal of joy. Ezekiel is one of few exiles in Babylon who believe that Jerusalem must fall because God is unchanging. But he sees beyond the fall of Jerusalem to the restoration, on exactly the same grounds. God is unchanging. He has made a covenant with His people and He will see it through.

20:43
Contrast the rapturous picture of restoration in Isaiah 40-56 with the brooding melancholy of Ezekiel's picture in which the people who have been saved are filled with remorse as they think of the sins that brought on their downfall. Both pictures are correct. One shows the spiritual significance of the return; the other shows the travail that leads to the glory. As we look at the faint beginnings of the restoration and the harsh insecurity of the early years (Ezra 2-5; Nehemiah 1-6), we must con-

20:44
clude that Ezekiel was an accurate predictor. Yet he sees beyond the remorse. Through their bitter sorrow the returned exiles will "know that I am the Lord." Centuries later another servant of God expressed the same thought: "Do you not know that God's kindness is meant to lead you to repentance?" (Romans 2:4).

God deals with His people for His "name's sake." He will restore them, not because of their merits, but because of His essential nature. He has chosen a people through whom He is revealing Himself to the nations of the world. However that people may turn aside from His ways, He will call them back. God has a plan for the world. The plan will be fulfilled. "By grace you have been saved through faith; and this is not your own doing, it is the gift of God—not because of works, lest any man should boast. For we are His workmanship" (Ephesians 2:8-10).

B. Oracles of Doom, 20:45–21:32.

After the vision of restoration, Ezekiel reverts to his major theme—during the first half of the prophecy—that Jerusalem must be destroyed. Various oracles, poems, and interpretations that doubtless were spoken on different occasions have been gathered together into one section proclaiming the same basic message. God's justice demands that Jerusalem fall.

In this section we have two glimpses of the prophet's personal feeling. First he complains, gently, that his people whom he is trying to help think of him as an entertainer. Then, before he sings the barbaric Song of the Sword, he sighs "with breaking heart and bitter grief." And the people, apparently, think the whole procedure quite funny.

The text of the section is in unusually bad state, particularly in the Song of the Sword.

1. The Forest Fire, 20:45-49.

MT and the Targum begin Chapter 21 with this section. However, the English translators have followed LXX, the Syriac, and the Vulgate, which inexplicably treat these verses as the conclusion of Chapter 20. In every sense they belong with what follows rather than with what precedes.

20:46   The invader would necessarily descend upon Jerusalem from the north, even though it lies almost due west of Babylon. Hence the emphasis upon the south. Two words, both translated "south," are used doubtless for the sake of variety. But the third, "south field" in AV, is correctly translated "Negeb," the "dry land" extending from Beersheba to Kadesh Barnea. The meaning is that not only will populous Jerusalem be destroyed, but even the barren Negeb must burn.

20:47   Ezekiel's unwelcome message is not so much that the Negeb will burn as that God will kindle the fire. The horror to come is not just an accident in a world that is filled with horrors; it is a judgment of God upon His people. Ezekiel has not often mentioned the righteous people in Jerusalem, along with the many sinners. Here he says that the fire will burn both the green trees and the dry trees, a figure for both the righteous and the wicked, and "all faces from south to north shall be scorched by it." The result of the conflagration will be that "all flesh

20:48   shall see that I, the Lord, have kindled it." Ezekiel does not say, here, that God's purpose for "all flesh" is redemptive.

Almost certainly the allegory of the forest fire is not a continuation of the response to the elders. It is a separate oracle, spoken first we know not to whom. We have little record of the immediate reception of Ezekiel's message; but we may infer, with comparative safety, that the dour predictions in Chapter 2 were fulfilled a thousand times over. (See 12:27; 17:2; 33:32.) Apparently the people once more turn a deaf ear to the message God has spoken through Ezekiel, and the prophet complains, softly, that they consider him a skillful composer of allegories, not a spokesman for God. The allegory can be a powerful method of teaching an unwelcome truth. But sometimes the hearer looks at the fanciful details of the allegory rather than to the truth being proclaimed. Ezekiel is conscious, painfully conscious, that his fellow-exiles are not heeding the warning he must give. They consider him an eccentric, perhaps a madman, who composes allegories skillfully enough. They hear the words he speaks, but they do not hear the divine call to repentance and life.

2. Interpretation of the Allegory, 21:1-7.

Since his hearers have not listened to the allegory, Ezekiel says much the same thing in straightforward prose. He ad-
21:2 dresses "Jerusalem . . . the sanctuaries . . . the land of Israel," with a message of unrelieved doom. "I am against you and will
21:3 draw forth my sword." With no figurative fire, green trees and dry trees, the Lord says, I "will cut off from you both righteous and wicked." Many commentators today feel called upon to say that this statement contradicts all that was said in Chapter 18. If one interprets that chapter in literal terms—a dangerous thing to do when reading Ezekiel—then the charge must stand. But if there Ezekiel is speaking in symbolic language, as he does almost everywhere else, no contradiction exists. A man of faith and integrity, whose life is cut off by sword or bullet, has "died" by every possible test of physical death. But spiritually he "lives," in contrast to his faithless neighbor who continues performing all his biological functions. LXX, however, destroys the parallelism with 20:47 by the reading, "I will destroy out of you both the lawless man and the transgressor." Both historical probability and Ezekiel's brutal honesty make it seem almost certain that the original reading was "righteous and wicked." When Jerusalem fell and the Negeb burned, righteous people died—physically.

The land of Judah, itself, lay for a time inert, psysically reduced, its remnants of population bereft of direction and spirit. Recent excavations at such sites as Lachish, Bethshemesh and Tell Beit Mirsim (perhaps Kiriat-sepher) bear eloquent testimony to the devastation wreaked on the rebellious kingdom of Judah by the forces of Chaldea. In 1935 a number of *ostraca*—potsherds used as writing material—were dug up at Lachish. Most of these appear to have been military dispatches written about 588 B.C. and record a determined struggle on the part of the Judean garrisons against the more powerful Babylonian enemy. The writer of Ostracon VI expressed deep concern about rumors of defeatism among the ruling class in Jerusalem: "And behold the words of the (princes) are not good, but to weaken our hands." Significantly, these relics were found buried deep in ashes.

—J. Finegan, "The Lachish Letters,"
Light from the Ancient Past, pp. 160-163

21:5 From the catastrophes of history, both past and future, Ezekiel expects "all flesh" to draw the conclusion that "I the Lord have drawn my sword." Ezekiel's message of divine sovereignty is readily acceptable when things are going pleasantly. Ezekiel's strength is the ability to see that God is sovereign still when every earthly consideration makes it seem that He has failed. Never was this aspect of faith brought into sharper focus than when Jesus was crucified.

21:6 God has given Ezekiel a message to proclaim. God has not asked Ezekiel to like the message. The Lord chose a man of iron self-discipline, who faithfully discharged his duty and kept his emotions out of sight most of the time. But here and there Ezekiel has let us see his own feeling about the tragedy that he must predict. And now, in words that could not be clearer, he speaks of his "breaking heart and bitter grief." Yet some commentators, in describing the Song of the Sword that follows hard after these verses, say that Ezekiel is "exulting." As we have seen repeatedly, Ezekiel did not readily change his mind. We might at least do him the compliment of saying that his essential feelings about his land and his people did not rapidly change either. During the days before Jerusalem fell Ezekiel prophesied with a "breaking heart," and his neighbors, blind and deaf to the signs of the times, asked him, "Why do **21:7** you sigh?"

3. The Song of the Sword, 21:8-17.

It is customary today to say that Ezekiel's Song of the Sword has been roughly handled by scribes and editors. Speaking of this passage, H. L. Ellison, the most conservative of commentators, says, "It would be dangerous to assume that the text is in order." Occasionally one finds a line in the three-two, or *quinah,* measure, but it is difficult to find any arrangement of the lines into strophes. Possibly Ezekiel first sang this song while he was acting out a parable of devastation, where actions would fill in the gaps of meaning. But in the present state of the text it is not possible even to tell, much of the time, whether Ezekiel, the Lord, or the people is speaking. It goes without saying that many ingenious emendations have been made, most of which are quite disappointing.

When all the negations have been carefully noted, we may now look at the Song of the Sword, and what do we find? We find an incredible picture of terrified men, when "every heart will break and all hands will become feeble, and all flesh and every spirit will faint, and all thighs shall be defiled with moisture" (21:7 LXX). Anyone who has been under attack can remember his intensity of emotion—not exultation. He can remember the horrified fascination with which he watched the enemy making preparations for his slaughter. He can remember the disjointedness of it all, as past and future, faith and doubt, fear and sickly gleams of hope swirled through his mind with no logical connection. Unconnected episodes are etched indelibly into his mind. He can remember all these things. Would God he could forget them. Such is the impression one receives from reading the Song of the Sword as it appears today. This is not to deny that hands other than Ezekiel's entered into its composition. But it is to affirm that the editor who finally assembled the prophecy was more skillful than some modern commentators seem to think.

First the Song expresses the feelings of the besieged people in Jerusalem as they watch the enemy whetting his sword. In 21:9 the days when only an arrow's flight separated besieged from the besieger, it would be possible to count the rotations of the 21:10 grindstone. There follows a thought that is elusive at best. Literally it is: "or we will rejoice, the rod of my son despising every tree." LXX gives here a bold chain of imperatives, "slay, set at naught, despise every tree." The terse translation in RSV suggests the sardonic humor with which men seek to break unbearable tension, followed by the grim assurance that the siege is no laughing matter. Israel has jested at the lighter, 21:11 wooden chastisements of God. Now the sword is given by God "into the hand of the slayer."

Once more the Lord calls upon the prophet to cry and wail, and to smite his thigh. Why? "For it is against *my* people." God 21:12 has given the sword into the hands of the slayer for reasons that Ezekiel has been discussing at considerable length. Yet these who face the sword remain God's people. Many have been faithless to Him. He remains faithful, even when exercising His

harshest judgment. Dr. G. A. Cooke, to whom every student of
Ezekiel owes an incalculable debt of gratitude, says: "It is not
likely that any part of the verse belonged to the original poem,
for two reasons: Jahveh is the Speaker; the call to show grief
and mourning does not agree with the fierce satisfaction which
the poem itself expresses." That the poem is fierce is self-evi-
dent. That it expresses satisfaction is debatable. Intensity of
emotion, yes, a thousand times over. But the emotion is not
satisfaction.

Even today, in the near east, when a person wishes to call
his servant he claps his hands; so the prophet is told to summon
21:14 the avenger to brandish the sword. Some Jewish commentators
understand the phrase "twice, yea thrice" to mean that the third
stroke, which will destroy Zedekiah, is to be far worse than the
first and second, by which Jehoiakim and Jehoiachin respectively
were dethroned. Perhaps the wisest comment that has ever been
21:15 made upon the concluding verses of the poem is that of W. F.
Lofthouse, "The prophet's voice rises to a shriek."

Possibly the command, "Cut sharply to right and left" is
spoken to Nebuchadnezzar, as suggested by AV, "Go thee one
21:16 way or other, either on the right hand or on the left." If this
21:17 be the case, then the Lord will clap His hands summoning His
royal servant to carry out His judgment against a sinful people.

The Song of the Sword offers a thousand intriguing puzzles
for the student who is interested in linguistic, historical, textual, and critical studies. The various translations and interpretations mentioned here are but a tiny sampling from the
confusion of tongues awaiting him who wishes to enter deeply
into the subject. However, for us who are concerned primarily
with the message of Ezekiel to the world today, the Song raises
no questions that Ezekiel has not raised a dozen times over.
Chief among these is: why does God use evil agents to accomplish His purposes? With all the faults that existed in Jerusalem,
the soldiers of Babylon were far worse than the Hebrews. Why
did God send Babylonians to punish people who were relatively
better? This is a question that must remain without an answer
until the time when the other Son of Man was nailed to the
Cross by Roman mercenary soldiers. He answered, not in words
but in act, that beyond the Cross is the Resurrection and the
Life.

The reader may find helpful a revision of the Song suggested by Dr. Julius A. Bewer:

> A sword, a sword is sharpened,
>   and also furbished.
> Sharpened for slaughter
>   furbished to flash lightning.
>
> How shall I revoke it?
>   Thou hast despised the rod
>   and every counsel.
>
> So I gave it to one to furbish it
>   that it could be handled.
>
> He sharpened the sword
>   and he furbished it
>   to give it into the hands of a slayer.
>
> Cry and howl, Son of Man.
>   For it is against my people,
>   it is against all the princes of Israel.
>
> They are delivered to the sword
>   with my people.
>
> Smite therefore upon thy thigh.
>   For the test has been made,
>   and why, if thou despisest the rod
>   should it not come?
>   says the Lord.
>
> And thou, Son of Man, prophesy
>   and smite thy hands together
>
> that the sword be doubled, trebled,
>   the sword of mortal wounds
>
> it is the great sword of mortal wounds
>   that penetrates into their innermost parts.
>
> I have set the slaughter
>   against all their gates
>   that the hearts shall melt
>   and the fallen be many.
>
> O sword, made for slaughter
>   furbished for lightning,
>   cut sharply to right and to left
>   wherever thy edge is pointed.

I will also smite my hands together,
and I will wreak my fury.

I the Lord have spoken.

4. Nebuchadnezzar, the Sword of the Lord, 21:18-23.

After the hysterical outburst comes the calm, reasoned analysis. The scattered intimations of destruction take on form and dreadful meaning. This is not to suggest that the Song and the interpretation were given on the same occasion. Ezekiel, or his disciple, has arranged the different teachings to give a growing impression of doom.

Nebuchadnezzar had troubles within his realm. We have already considered Zedekiah's fantastic plot to rebel. We gather from Jeremiah 27:1-3 that the rulers of various other small nations were parties to the same plot. Apparently the king of the Ammonites was among the leaders in this rebellion. Ammon, in Ezekiel's time, was a small kingdom north of Moab, east of the Jordan. Its capital city was Rabbah (or Rabbath) about twenty-five miles northeast from the northern end of the Dead Sea, the modern city Amman. The Ammonites and the Hebrews were enemies of long standing. For example, Uriah the Hittite died in a foray against Rabbah (II Samuel 11:1-25). But the traditional enemies found a common cause in their hatred for the Babylonian oppressor.

When Nebuchadnezzar's troops marched westward, they faced a choice between enemies to subdue. The troops would follow
21:19 the long road through the Fertile Crescent to Damascus, where the trade routes separated. One road went southwest toward Egypt, the other went east of the Jordan valley to Arabia. At God's command, Ezekiel presents another parable, tracing the path that "the sword of the King of Babylon" will follow, until it comes to the dividing of the ways. If the destination is Jerusalem, the army will follow the Egyptian road. If it is Rabbah, the army will travel toward Arabia. Naturally the Hebrews in exile and those in Jerusalem knew that Nebuchadnezzar was on the march. Until his army had reached the crossroads, they could not know whether the initial attack would be against Jerusalem or Rabbah. Since Jerusalem was heavily fortified and Rabbah, apparently, was not, it was understandable that the Hebrews hoped the attack would be directed against the weaker city.

Nebuchadnezzar was less magic-ridden than some of his pred-
ecessors had been. Even so, Ezekiel pictures him turning to the

21:21 arts of divination for the decision he must make. He employs
three different methods to make sure that he has correctly interpreted the will of the gods. The first consists of two arrows in
a quiver, each inscribed with the name of a city. He draws out
one in each hand. That in his right hand reveals the decision of
the god. The second is the use of "teraphim," or household
images. We do not know how these rendered their verdict. The
third method is the inspection of a sheep's liver. This practice
was traditional among the Babylonians. Apparently it was not
widespread among the Hebrews; for this is the only time it is
mentioned in the OT. Plato says of the liver, "The faculty of
prognostication belongs to that part of the soul which is situ-
ated in the liver, because that part has no share in reason or
thought" (*Timaeus* 32). In the British Museum is a Babylonian
clay model of a sheep's liver, divided into sections, with the
occult significance of each section inscribed.

Nebuchadnezzar drew the arrows from their quiver, and that
in his right hand was inscribed "Jerusalem." Besieging the
21:22 Judean capital would require heavy equipment to batter
21:23 through massive defenses. The people of Jerusalem were not
terrified by the divination; for they trusted in the alliance they
had made with the Egyptian Pharaoh. Again Ezekiel reminds
his people that they have violated their solemn pact with the
Babylonian emperor (17:16-18), and says that "he [Nebuchad-
nezzar] brings their guilt to remembrance." That is, Nebuchadnezzar is like the prosecutor who brings the charge before
the judge, as, in due time, he will be the executor who carries
out the sentence.

5. Oracle against Zedekiah, 21:24-27.

From the mood of fascinated horror, Ezekiel reverts to his
mood of frenzy, as he contemplates Zedekiah, the ruler in
21:24 Jerusalem. Never does Ezekiel call him "king." He describes a
21:25 weak man who has woven a net of transgressions in which he
must inevitably be caught. God commands the unhallowed
21:26 princeling to "remove the turban." The turban usually was
worn by the High Priest (Exodus 28:4). Possibly Ezekiel means
that Zedekiah had been trying to encroach upon priestly functions. (See 46:2, etc., where the prince is placed as one of the

worshiping people, not among the officiating priests.) Possibly, of course, the king wore a distinctive turban that is not known today. Ezekiel describes the impending dethronement with two brief proverbs. "Things shall not remain as they are." Literally, the proverb is, "This not this." The second proverb has its echo in the Song of Mary (Luke 1:52). The meaning of the two is inescapable. The established order will be overthrown.

The prince will be cast from his throne, and there will be "Ruin, ruin, ruin . . . until he comes whose right it is." It may 21:27 be, as many commentators think, that here Ezekiel is merely predicting a rightful heir of the Davidic line upon the throne in Jerusalem once more. If this be the case, Ezekiel chose a peculiar way to say it. He is making an obvious reference to a passage that the Hebrews consider a prophecy of the coming Messiah:

> The scepter shall not depart from Judah,
>   nor the ruler's staff from between his feet,
> until he comes to whom it belongs;
>   and to him shall be the obedience of the peoples.
>   —Genesis 49:10

One may reject a zealous messianism that discovers predictions of Christ in unwarranted places. It is quite possible to find meanings in the Bible that are really not there. But it is likewise possible to miss the meanings that genuinely are there. It is difficult to see why one should avoid calling this verse in Ezekiel a messianic prophecy.

6. Oracle against the Ammonites, 21:28-29.

Ezekiel has pictured Nebuchadnezzar at the crossroads, deciding to attack Jerusalem rather than Rabbah. From the scraps of evidence available it seems that the traditional hostility between the Hebrews and the Ammonites had continued with little interruption until the uneasy alliance against Nebuchadnezzar. When the Babylonian army captured King Jehoiakim, the Ammonites were hostile to Judea (II Kings 24:2). The Ammonites reverted to enmity when the attack was directed against Zedekiah (25:1-7). They took advantage of Judah's misery to encroach upon Hebrew territory (Zephaniah 2:8). Ezekiel's message has been that God is Lord over the entire world. He has said that Jerusalem must perish for her sins. What shall he say of Ammon, likewise a sinner?

Again Ezekiel sees the sword, honed to the finest edge. The sword of the Lord that is directed against Jerusalem will likewise be directed against Rabbah. The soothsayers in Ammon will see "false visions" and will "divine lies." But the sword will be "laid on the necks of the unhallowed wicked."

21:28
21:29

We have no record that Nebuchadnezzar made a direct attack upon Rabbah. Quite possibly the king of Ammon diverted the attack by grovelling submission. Five years later, Josephus tells us, Ammon and Moab were brought "under subjection" (*Antiquities*, 10, 9, 7).

Many modern commentators believe that the "sword" in 21:28-30 is Ammon's rather than Nebuchadnezzar's, thus the section 21:28-32 is one oracle rather than two. If this be the case, then the section does not belong with the rest of the chapter. It is a hideous anticlimax, as if a man about to be devoured by a lion were warned of a puppy yapping at his heels. As interpreted here, the chapter is about God's lordship over history, only incidentally is it about Ammon, Babylon, or even Jerusalem.

7. Oracle against Nebuchadnezzar, 21:30-32.

The chapter has raised a question that will not be stifled. Why does God use morally unworthy agents to carry out His judgments? Here Ezekiel answers that Babylon, like Ammon and Jerusalem, lies under the judgment of God. He cannot say this directly, for reasons of physical survival. Centuries later, his disciple on Patmos followed a similar course, writing "Babylon" when he meant "Rome" (e.g. Revelation 18:2). So Ezekiel shows the warrior commanded to return his sword to the sheath. The Babylonian security police would find nothing subversive in such a verse. It would not add greatly to their bewilderment, which must already have been considerable. Who is the warrior? Who but Nebuchadnezzar? When the siege is over he will march back to the land of his birth, and there, says God, "I will judge you." The same standards of judgment that hold for Jerusalem and Rabbah will be applied against Babylon.

21:30

21:32

And how was this prediction carried out? Nebuchadnezzar was a strong, capable monarch. He was followed by weaklings on the throne, two of whom were assassinated. In 539 B.C. Cyrus, King of Persia, conquered Babylon and established a new dynasty. Once Cyrus was on the throne, it was possible for the

Hebrew exiles to return to the Promised Land. Ezekiel's prediction was fulfilled.

C.   The Indictment against Jerusalem, 22:1-31.

The third cycle of warnings continues with unabated savagery, as Ezekiel condemns not only the rulers, but the people of Jerusalem. He is thinking of sins in the present, not in Jerusalem's past. The indictment is divided into three oracles, each beginning, "The word of the Lord came to me." In the indictment Ezekiel adds little to what he has previously charged. The expression of hope is scarcely discernible as hope. The purpose of the chapter is to demonstrate beyond all possibility of doubt that Jerusalem is irrevocably doomed.

1.   The Bloody City, 22:1-16.

Once more the Lord asks the prophet a question with the force of an imperative, "Will you judge the bloody city?" (See
22:2   20:4.) In this section the word "blood" occurs seven times. It would be hazardous to assume that the crimes of murder and manslaughter were unusually prevalent in Jerusalem. Ezekiel links bloodshed to idolatry, contempt for parents, injustice to the helpless, irreverence, Sabbath breaking, lascivious conduct, and extortion. The shedding of blood may be symbolic for any action that tends to destroy the life of another. In Hebrew thought the life is the blood (Leviticus 17:11, 14) or the blood is the life (Deuteronomy 12:23). So every sin against a fellow man that threatens the structure of society is, symbolically, "bloodshed."

The first illustration of "bloodshed" is not a symbol but a grisly reality. Sometimes in the worship of idols Hebrews sacri-
22:3   ficed their children. Idolatry will lead directly to the city's downfall. The first commandment tells man to give first place in his life to God. The city that ignores this commandment is
22:4   begging that her time may come. Since Jerusalem is guilty, she will become a "reproach" and a "mocking to all the countries."

The general indictment now breaks down into particulars. "The princes of Israel" are the ruling class. Ezekiel charges that
22:6   they have sought the privileges of rank, each "according to his power," rather than the responsibilities. Then he charges that they have violated the basic Hebrew virtues: respect for parents, respect for the "sojourner," and respect for the helpless. The

22:8   "princes" had set the example of "contempt" that the people of Jerusalem had followed. "You had despised my holy things" means that the religious leaders had ignored the laws governing the sacredness of the Temple and its sacrifices, perhaps in offering blemished animals for sacrifice. The rulers had, in a thousand ways, "profaned my Sabbaths."

Other iniquities follow. Ezekiel lists together three cardinal sins: false witness, idolatry, and unchastity. "Slander to shed

22:9   blood" probably means bearing false witness against one accused of a capital crime (Leviticus 19:16). Again the fact and the symbol are one. Ezekiel has spoken many times about those who "eat upon the mountains." The charge of "lewdness" introduces the revolting particulars that follow. To "uncover"

22:10   one's father's "nakedness" means to contract a marriage with one's stepmother (Leviticus 18:7f.). The rules about menstrual

22:11   purity were scoffed at (Leviticus 18:19). Adultery was rampant (Exodus 20:14), and incest was not unknown (Leviticus

22:12   18:9, 15). From sexual sins Ezekiel turns to financial sins. He charges that judges will accept bribery, even when a man's life is at stake (Deuteronomy 16:19). He charges that business men will go to any lengths to make a profit at the expense of a neighbor (Leviticus 25:36f.).

The summary of it all is: "you have forgotten me, says the Lord God." The picture above shows a city where the rulers are despotic and corrupt; where the people show little respect for the family or for the helpless; where false religion is prevalent; where sexual license is widespread; and where greed is the ruling passion in many lives. One finds much the same nauseating picture in the writings of Ezekiel's fellow prophet (Jeremiah 5:7ff.; 6:13; 7:5f.; 22:3).

The sins that have been described in such profusion must inevitably produce a result. The Lord says, "I strike my hands

22:13   together." The obvious meaning of the gesture is despair. The point would scarcely be worth noting were it not that on other occasions when God, or Ezekiel, is represented as clapping his hands (e.g. 21:14, 17), some commentators say that this signifies "exulting." It is a sign of strong emotion. Here the emotion anthropomorphically attributed to God can be nothing but despair. God does not want to inflict His harsh judgment upon

22:14   Jerusalem. He asks those who have weakened themselves if

22:15   they will be able to endure the inevitable result of their actions when they are dispersed among the nations. Yet, even while He pronounces sentence upon the guilt of Jerusalem, God shows His redemptive purpose. "I will consume your filthiness out of you." This is the message of Ezekiel, that in the madness of history God is working out His purpose. Amid the black storm cloud He moves "straight-forward."

God knows the danger. The short-term result of His judgment upon His people will be disastrous, not only to them but 22:16 to the whole cause of faith upon earth. "I shall be profaned through you in the sight of the nations." But the long-term result will be a blessing. "You shall know that I am the Lord."

2. The Hope beyond the Judgment, 22:17-22.

In the second oracle Ezekiel pictures a refiner's fire to expand the thought, "I will consume your filthiness." His words 22:18 contain not one iota of sympathy or one suggestion of hope. But the reader knows that the only reason for melting dross is to derive pure metal from a worthless mixture. Ezekiel will not speak of gold in Jerusalem (Zechariah 13:9), but he does admit the presence of silver among the baser metals. Jerusalem will become a refiner's furnace, fanned not with leather bellows, but with the wrath of God.

Many commentators treat this figure as if Ezekiel were describing the production of metal from the ore, but the picture 22:20 is rather that of a metalsmith who sweeps up from the floor of his shop fragments of "silver and bronze and iron and lead and tin." The scraps are worthless until they have been purified. The first step in recovering silver was to melt down all the metal. The second step was to place the alloy in a crucible made of bone-ash, which was heated until the bone-ash absorbed the base metals. In his figure of speech here Ezekiel does not describe the second step, as he pictured the second wilderness journey in 20:33-38. But he does describe the first step. Therein 22:21 is the hope. Gloomy and horrible as this oracle is, Jeremiah 6:27-30, employing the same figure, is even gloomier.

3. The Widespread Corruption, 22:23-31.

The final indictment is addressed to the entire land of Judah, "a land that is not cleansed or rained upon in the day of in- 22:24 dignation." The "day" probably refers not to the forthcoming siege but to the long process of moral corruption that now is coming to its inevitable end. The "cleansing" and the "rain" are separate yet related blessings. Rain-fall usually suggests fertility; so the phrase means, "the land that is barren and filthy." Ezekiel examines all the social classes except the utterly helpless, and finds them equally corrupt.

The "princes" Ezekiel compares with a "roaring lion." (Almost certainly RSV is correct in following LXX rather than

22:25 reading "prophets" with M.T. "Prophets" is *nebi'im,* while "princes" is *nesi'im.* Ezekiel deals scornfully with the prophets in another verse.) "Prince" is an unfortunate translation in that it implies royal blood. The same word frequently is translated "captain," and in a dozen other ways. The ruler would, of course, be a "prince," but so would the other leaders in government and commerce. Ezekiel accuses the princes of judicial murder and extortion.

As is his custom, Ezekiel places the moral and the ritual on the same footing. Right living is inseparable from right wor-

22:26 ship. He is not urging, here or elsewhere, that the priests correct their liturgical errors without regard for their private or public morality. Christians sometimes think of "my law" as a set of meaningless ritual acts, thoroughly divorced from human character. The Law was the way of life that Jeremiah and Ezekiel and Jesus followed. The priests were the guardians and interpreters of the Law, when they were faithful to their duty (Deuteronomy 17:8ff.). But these in Judah held their responsibilities lightly. (AV translates literally that the priests "have hid their eyes from my Sabbaths." RSV loses color with no appreciable gain in understanding by the translation "disregarded.") So gross has been the laxity of the priests, both in their ritual duties and in their work as instructors of the people, that "I am profaned." This, if possible, is even more serious than the profanation of God's "name" (20:9).

Another class of "princes" is dealt with. Here Ezekiel uses a different word, *sarim.* Possibly this means the magistrates, as

22:27 distinct from the "princes" mentioned above. These are comparable to wolves. A lion is more powerful than a wolf, but there is really little to choose between being devoured by one

22:28 or the other. The former bitter charges against the prophets are concisely summarized (13:1-16).

The phrase "people of the land" went through many changes of meaning during the course of the centuries. Here probably

22:29 it means the landholding farmers (II Kings 23:35). These peo-

ple were the backbone of the nation. As the reader may gather
by reading II Kings, they were not docile sheep, to be led about
by the "princes." When they united their forces they could
overthrow kings. Although they suffered often enough from the
ruling classes in Jerusalem, Ezekiel says that they faithfully
imitated all the bad examples set before them. The "people of
the land" were not poor. They were among the oppressors.

    If only there had been a leader strong enough to correct the
abuses in the land . . . Yes, if. But there was not. Zedekiah was
22:30   on the throne, caught in the web he had woven. Looking back
on the centuries before Ezekiel, we find two strong, godly mon-
archs, Hezekiah and Josiah, who carried through noteworthy
and important reforms, but their successors were much weaker
men who could not, or would not, continue the process of bet-
terment. Even these valiant saints had not been able to change
the course of history. And in Ezekiel's time there was no one of
comparable strength to "stand in the breach."

    The conclusion is inevitable. Ezekiel speaks in the "prophetic
perfect," describing a future event as if it had already taken
22:31   place. "Their ways have I requited upon their heads, says the
Lord God."

D. The Allegory of the Two Sisters, 23:1-49.

    Chapter 23 develops the allegory that began in Chapter 16,
but with a different emphasis. There the downfall of Judah
was traced to idolatry, here the ruin of Judah and Israel is
traced to political alliances. Actually the two emphases were
not so far apart as they seem today. Many people, even among
the Hebrews, believed that wars and dynastic upsets on earth
reflected quarrels and reconciliations among the gods. So when
a Hebrew monarch sought protection from Egypt, it meant to
some that the Lord was turning to the sun-god Amon-Re for
aid. This helps to explain why the prophets show such marked
antipathy to foreign alliances, especially those with major
powers. Such alliances betrayed lack of trust in God. In terms
of the allegory, they were sheer harlotry.

1. The Two Sisters, 23:1-4.

    Centuries before Ezekiel's time, the Kingdom of Israel and
the Kingdom of Judah were one country. Hence they are de-
23:2   scribed as the daughters of one mother. Yet before the kingdom

divided there was a cleavage between the tribe of Ephraim and the tribe of Judah, extending back to the Egyptian captivity. Under the strong leadership of David the division was patched over and the tribes were united into a kingdom that shortly

23:3 afterward fell apart. So Ezekiel can describe his people as two wanton sisters, even while they were enslaved in Egypt.

The names of the sisters are puzzling. According to the older Jewish commentators, "Oholah" means "her tent," or the sanc-

23:4 tuary in the northern Kingdom; whereas Jerusalem is "Oholibah" or "my tent in her." Today few students accept this distinction. Most believe that the "tent" in each case refers to the booths on the high places, rather than to the Temple in Jerusalem or that in Samaria. The similarity in name and destiny is the whole point of the allegory that follows. While the children of Israel were in Egypt they were wedded to the Lord, and they bore Him sons and daughters. The relationship between God and His people is so close that it can best be described in terms of family love. Yet these who were so close to God rejected Him.

2. Samaria's Alliances, 23:5-10.

Oholah is the elder daughter. The kingdom of Israel was in every respect larger and more prosperous than the kingdom of

23:5 Judah. While wedded to the Lord Oholah played the harlot
23:6 with the Assyrians. The Assyrian cavalry was the envy or terror
23:7 of other nations. Just as a foolish country girl might give herself to a handsome cavalryman, Oholah bestowed her harlotries. The first biblical record of an Assyrian alliance is that contracted by Menahem (c. 744-735 B.C.) with Tiglath Pileser (II

23:8 Kings 15:19). An obelisk in the British museum shows that a century earlier Jehu (c. 842-814 B.C.) voluntarily paid tribute to Shalmaneser III. But Ezekiel speaks of foreign alliance as if it had been a process uninterrupted from the beginning.

Oholah turned from God, who loved her, to earthly infatuations, forgetting that God is Lord over Assyria as well as Sa-

23:9 maria. The Lord delivered His faithless bride into the hands of her "lovers," who ravished and slew her. These things were

3:10 not done in secret. The fate of Oholah was "a byword among women," that is, everyone was in a position to read the moral.

Shalmaneser V sent an army against Samaria and conducted a siege that endured for three horrible years. The resistance was

so determined that victory did not come until his commander in chief became his successor, Sargon II. Sargon considered the defeat of Samaria one of his major victories. He reports:

> At the beginning of my royal rule, I besieged and conquered Samaria, led away as booty 27,290 inhabitants of it. I formed from them a contingent of 50 chariots and made the remaining [inhabitants] assume their [social] positions. I installed over them an officer of mine and imposed upon them the tribute of the former king.
> —The Annals of Sargon II, translated by A. Leo Oppenheim, in *Ancient Near Eastern Texts*, edited by J. B. Pritchard (Princeton, 1950), pp. 284-285.

3. Jerusalem's Alliances, 23:11-21.

Judah, of all nations, was the one most able to profit from the mistakes of Samaria. Instead, Oholibah outdid her elder 23:11 sister in profligacy. Not only did she dote upon the Assyrians; 23:12 she was also enraptured by pictures of the Chaldeans. (It is 23:14 difficult today for the reader who is not a historian to keep straight the political changes in biblical times. The Chaldeans lived in the marsh country at the head of the Persian Gulf. From time to time, they gained power and seized control of Babylon. Nebuchadnezzar's father, Nabopolasser, was a Chaldean who overcame the Assyrians, destroyed their capital city Nineveh, and founded the neo-Babylonian Empire. So, depending upon the date of reference, the Chaldeans may be called Babylonians or distinguished from them. Nebuchadnezzar's Chaldeo-Babylonian Army included Assyrian contingents.)

Babylonian mosaic murals still express the vigor that Ezekiel briefly describes. The predominant motif is strength, exactly 23:15 what Judah lacked. We gather from the phrase "Babylonians whose native land was Chaldea" that Ezekiel is overlooking foreign alliances in the remote past (II Kings 16:7-10; 20:12-19), and is referring to some incident in comparatively recent 23:16 times. Foolish Oholibah "sent messengers" to those who would destroy her. Possibly this means Jehoiakim's submission to Nebuchadnezzar after the Battle of Carchemish in 605 B.C. 23:17 After a brief bout of lust, Oholibah grew sick of her new lover, as Jehoiakim rebelled against Nebuchadnezzar after three years (II Kings 24:1).

The Lord turned in disgust from Oholibah, as He had turned

from her sister. The Chaldeans, with Syrian, Moabite, and Ammonite assistance, overthrew Jehoiakim (II Kings 24:2), as the Assyrians had overthrown Hoshea, king of Samaria (II Kings 17:4). Instead of turning back to her "husband," Oholibah turned to Egypt for further dalliance. Presumably we are now up to Ezekiel's time. He refers with evident loathing to Zedekiah's appeal for Egyptian help against Nebuchadnezzar. While Ezekiel could scarce be accused of admiring the Babylonians, he has described them as virile (23:15), but he can describe the Egyptians only as beasts. Probably he is using some popular epithets to express his contempt for a decadent empire.

4. Jerusalem's Punishment, 23:22-35.

Just as the Lord did with Oholah He will do with Oholibah. He will bring her rejected "lovers" against her. Nebuchadnezzar's Babylonian army would include Chaldeans, Assyrians, and three smaller ethnic groups from east of the Tigris better known to Ezekiel's hearers than to us. These will come, not to engage in further harlotry, but for war, "and I will commit the judgment to them, and they shall judge you according to their judgments." As the following verses indicate, their judgments were harsh.

Ezekiel describes crisply the "fury" of the invading army. The phrase "cut off your nose and your ears" probably is more than a figure of speech. Ramases III quelled a palace conspiracy centering in the harem, and wrote laconically, "sentence was carried out by cutting off their noses and their ears." The Babylonians on a punitive expedition may have done much the same thing. The sons and daughters would be valuable as slaves. The soldiers would loot Jerusalem before applying the torch. And "thus I will put an end to your lewdness."

The conclusion of the whole matter is, "You have gone the way of your sister, therefore I will give her cup into your hand." Ezekiel vividly pictures the cup of wrath. The road from license through harlotry to alcoholism was traveled in ancient times just as it is today. Drunkenness is not among the sins that Ezekiel stresses; so it should be understood here as a continuation of the allegory. The aged harlot, no longer wanted, drinks to forget herself while those standing about hoot and jeer at her. But she finds no release in her drunkenness, only

further horror and desolation, and the sodden wretch mutilates
herself in the agony of her self-loathing.

For sheer vividness there are few passages in literature to
compare with the vignette of the drunken hag. Had Ezekiel directed his massive talent toward savory topics, he would be
esteemed today as one of the world's greatest poets. But God
called him to service by the river Chebar to deliver a message
that few were willing to hear. God called and Ezekiel served.

5. The Judgment of the Sisters, 23:36-49.

The conclusion of the chapter is a new oracle continuing the
allegory. Here the emphasis lies upon both religious sins and
political. The section is confusing for three reasons. First, it is
largely a recapitulation of what has already been said, sometimes in the same words and phrases. Apparently the oracle was
delivered on a separate occasion, and later attached to the
longer allegory. Second, the pronouns are shifted about with
startling abandon. For a few verses the subject is "they," then
"you" (singular), then the prophet speaks of "her," and finally
of "them." Probably the "you" section is a parenthesis, directed
to Jerusalem. Third, and most puzzling, earlier in the chapter
the sisters were judged separately. Here they are judged together, as if the punishment of Samaria had not taken place
almost a century and a half before. Certainly this coupling of
the living with the dead has great dramatic impact. Even so,
the difficulty is such that some believe Ezekiel has abandoned
his allegory, and now is speaking of two typical women known
to his hearers. The interpretation followed here is that the allegory continues. Ezekiel still speaks about Jerusalem and Samaria by the names of Oholibah and Oholah.

Again the Lord asks a question with the force of an imperative, as He orders the Son of Man to "declare" their "abominable deeds" to the two scarlet sisters. Ezekiel has made the
charges often enough, but if they have not been heard, they
must be made once more. The first charge is idolatry, expressed
in two different ways: first as adultery, continuing the allegory,
then more literally, as shedding blood. The latter Ezekiel makes
hideously explicit by saying, "they have even offered up to them
[the idols] for food the sons whom they had borne to me." Evidently muddled religious thinking is nothing new in the world.

23:38   The prophet shows that the sisters who have done this ghastly

thing and who have "profaned my sabbaths" by idolatrous worship still come to the Lord's sanctuary, where their very pres-
:39 ence is a defilement. He shows them offering a child sacrifice
to an idol in the morning, and on the same day coming to God's
Temple.

As if the sin of idolatry were not enough, the sisters have
also engaged in "harlotry." (In this allegory Ezekiel distin-
:40 guishes between "adultery" or idol worship and "harlotry" or
political alliance. The distinction was not observed in Chapter
16.) Most vividly Ezekiel pictures a harlot adorning herself to
attract men, and sending a panderer to bring them to her. Notice the change, *"they* even sent for men," "for them *you* bathed
yourself." This section apparently deals with a specific Judean
political alliance, possibly to the league with Edom, Moab,
Ammon, Tyre and Sidon (Jeremiah 27:3) by which the smaller
powers hoped to wrest independence from Nebuchadnezzar.

To entice her lovers the harlot used gifts she had received
from her husband, "my incense and oil." At best she succeeded
:41 in luring in a crew of ruffians, "drunkards . . . from the wil-
:42 derness." Instead of "drunkards" AV reads "Sabaeans," a nomadic desert people. The two words are quite similar. In either
case, the meaning is that Judah has fallen so low that she con-
sorts with the dregs of the population, and will do anything to
appeal even to these.

Verse 43, as it stands in the Hebrew, is obscure. RSV has followed LXX. If this translation be accepted, the verse means
:43 that "harlotry" or political alliance is actually the equivalent
of "adultery" or idol worship. However JPS translates the
verse, "Then said I of her that was worn out by adulteries:
Still they commit harlotries with her, even her." Earth offers
few more hideous sights than that of a harlot who has lost her
beauty. Only drunkards will take any interest in her.

The "righteous men" who will judge the sisters are difficult to
define. The older Jewish commentators said that they were the
45 Babylonian host, coming to execute God's judgment. In contrast with Judah, they appeared "righteous." However many
today believe that they represent "the moral sense of the community . . . There is still enough conscience left in the nation
to condemn the national guilt" (G. A. Cooke). If this interpretation be followed, then Ezekiel is saying that the best among

the Hebrews recognize that political alliance is infidelity to God, and that child sacrifice is murder.

The punishment of the sisters will be grim and swift. Ezekiel combines phrases from 23:25 and 16:41, showing the harlots **23:47** judged, condemned, and executed. The Babylonian troops carried out against Jerusalem something remarkably similar to the traditional punishment for an adulteress. But this destruction is not just blind fury or the soldiers' greed for spoil. The **23:48** final result will be cleansing, "Thus will I put an end to lewdness in the land." More important, even in their judgment and condemnation the chosen people will be God's messengers to the world, "that all women may take warning and not commit lewdness as you have done."

In a time of crisis twenty centuries after Ezekiel, another embattled saint of God turned to this passage for light and hope and political guidance, and he said, "Out of the blindness and stubbornness of the people of God the goodness of the Most High had to be made plain to the world" (Thomas Muntser, *Sermon before the Princes,* July 13, 1524).

E. The End of Jerusalem, 24:1-27.

The condemnation against Jerusalem is finished. Now Ezekiel learns that the judgment has taken effect. As is his custom, he expresses an unwelcome truth by means of a dramatic parable. The reader has been tempted, quite frequently, to forget that delivering all these elaborate and distressing parables, allegories, oracles, poems, and sermons was a man, with his full quota of human feeling. The man has kept himself almost completely out of sight. Occasionally he has allowed us to see the broken heart that he brought to his unsavory task. But now, as Jerusalem is falling, Ezekiel gives us our only glimpse of his personal life. (The mention of Buzi, Ezekiel's father, in 1:3, tells us nothing beyond the bare name, and that either Ezekiel or Buzi was priest.) The prophet's own wife dies. His private, personal grief is overwhelmed in the deeper grief he feels because Jerusalem is lost. He shows none of the usual signs of mourning. Rather, he faces the loss in his own life and the loss to the entire Hebrew community with a strange calm. He has issued warnings with frantic intensity while there was time for Jerusalem to repent. Now that the unchangeable event has come, he looks toward the future. The message of hope, that has been doled out so sparingly, is to be the dominant theme of the book from this point on.

1. The Parable of the Boiling Pot, 24:1-5.

The tenth month (Tebeth) corresponds with January in our calendar. The ninth year of exile was 588 B.C. on our calendar. On the tenth day of ill omen, Nebuchadnezzar began his siege against Jerusalem (II Kings 25:1; Jeremiah 39:1; 52:4). A completely unavoidable question arises. The whole book has pictured Ezekiel in Babylon hurling some of his thunderbolts at distant Jerusalem, but concentrating his efforts upon Israel in captivity. How could he know, in a time of slow communication, that the attack was taking place? Some say that the section was written months or years after the event. Some say that Ezekiel was in Jerusalem when the siege began. Some say that God revealed the date to his prophet. (One who believes that the entire prophecy is revealed still must notice that the revelation concerns God's purpose in history. Ezekiel works with the historical materials at his hand. In the opening vision, God did not reveal the storm cloud to Ezekiel. It was visible to any observer. God revealed *Himself* in the storm cloud. So he who seeks a naturalistic answer to a puzzling question may still be taking the fact of revelation seriously. As has been mentioned, Ezekiel was a "clear seer" but he was not a "clairvoyant"). It is likewise possible that when Nebuchadnezzar stood at the crossroads seeking guidance by divination (21:18-23), he was told not only which city to attack, but the propitious date to commence hostilities, and that this information got back to the exiles. The Hebrews in Babylon believed still that Jerusalem was inviolable, Ezekiel believed the contrary. The city was besieged for one and one-half years, during which time no further word from God came to Ezekiel.

Again the unanswerable question arises, whether or not Ezekiel acted out his parable. He pictures a cook setting a pot on the fire and carving up a lamb to make a stew. It is scarcely probable that the vision came to him while engaged in a household task, if for no other reason, because there would have been no one to witness. He expressed the vision in poetry so vivid that it would not be greatly enhanced by physical enactment. So we may picture Ezekiel chanting his poem to the neighbors who refuse to take him seriously. We need not picture him chopping up the lamb as he chants.

The symbol of the bubbling pot on the stove is not one of terror—though it strikes the modern reader that way—it is one 24:4 of confidence, the false confidence displayed by those in Jerusalem and in Babylon (11:3). The parable must be interpreted from the viewpoint of the eater, not that of the lamb. The pot represents the protective walls of Jerusalem. The fires of the siege will but enable the "flesh" of Jerusalem to achieve its true destiny. Such is the confidence that Ezekiel here summarizes, only to shatter it.

2. Interpretation of the Parable, 24:6-14.

A bubbling cauldron on the stove is a symbol of contentment. But if the pot itself is filthy, the resulting stew will be a revolt- 24:6 ing mess. As Ezekiel has said, Jerusalem is a filthy city. He draws an analogy between the "blood" with which Jerusalem is stained and the "rust" that corrodes the inside of a cauldron. (Students of Hebrew differ vigorously whether *chel'ah* means "scum" [AV], or "filth" [JPS], or metallic corrosion. LXX uses *ios* which means either "poison" or "rust." Determining the right translation will make no difference to the correct interpretation of the parable. The "pot" itself will ruin the stew.)

Ezekiel's horror of cooking with the blood is both actual and symbolic. The legal prohibition (Genesis 9:4; Leviticus 7:26) 24:7 was based upon the thought that the blood is the life (Leviticus 17:14). The Hebrew aversion to eating the blood amounts to nausea. This suggests a reaction against some pagan practice. The blood that was shed in Jerusalem is "still in the midst of her." Even a hunter was required to cover the blood of his prey (Leviticus 17:13), while human blood left on the ground cried aloud for vengeance (Genesis 4:10). But Jerusalem shamelessly 24:8 has left the blood "on the bare rock." Once more Ezekiel reverts to his theme that actions have consequences. "I have set on the bare rock the blood she has shed." Because Jerusalem has cared 24:9 so little, God will preserve the bloodstains. The time for expiation has passed. God Himself will build up the destroying fire.

The parable grows intense. Instead of the tranquil domestic scene where the cook finishes the stew, Ezekiel shows the cook 24:10 leaving the pot on the fire, as the flames grow higher and higher, until the broth is boiled away, the meat is charred, and the very bones burned. (JPS supports this interpretation better than RSV. "I also will make the pile great, heaping on the

wood, kindling the fire, that the flesh may be consumed; and
preparing the mixture, that the bones also may be burned.")
Then the pot itself begins to melt. This last dramatic symbol
would have been quite expensive to act out.

(The reader surely has noticed the confusion between 24:6
and 24:10. In the earlier verse the meat was removed from the
pot. In the latter it is consumed. Possibly there was a scribal
error in which 6a and 6b were transposed; so 6b concludes the
parable of confidence, and 6a introduces the grim rebuttal.)

Although the translation of 24:12 is conjectural, it represents
the best possible sense of an obscure verse. God has toiled till
He is weary, trying to cleanse His chosen vessel, but without
success. Since even fire will not burn out the rust, there remains
nothing to do but melt down the copper in the cauldron and
begin again. This God has determined to do. In one brief verse
the Lord expresses His determination in seven different ways:
I the Lord have spoken—it shall come to pass—I will do it—I
will not go back—I will not spare—I will not repent—I will
judge you. In the Hebrew these reiterated judgments reverber-
ate with the ominous intensity of a war drum summoning the
troops to destroy.

3. The End, 24:15-27.

One has the feeling, as he reads of Ezekiel's loss, that the
word about his personal bereavement came to him on the same
day the attack against Jerusalem began. A careful reading shows
that this is only a feeling. It reads more meaning into "also"
than the word usually carries. The prophet learns that his wife,
the delight of his eyes, is about to die. He is forbidden to show
any of the usual signs of mourning. He may "sigh, but not
aloud." So, as was his custom, Ezekiel obeyed the Lord.

Quite naturally the question arises whether the death of
Ezekiel's wife was an actual occurrence or if it is another symbol.
It is no argument one way or the other to say that Ezekiel uses
the event to symbolize the destruction of Jerusalem. Perhaps it
is relevant that LXX omits the clause "at evening my wife
died," perhaps not. Again one is left with only a feeling that
such massive restraint, in one who was usually so expressive,
cloaks the unspeakable grief of a loving husband who has endured a loss almost too great for him to bear.

The neighbors crowd around with an uneasy presentiment

that the prophet's strange calm has a meaning for them, rather
24:19 than for Ezekiel alone, asking "what these things mean *for us,*
that you are acting thus?" For the last time Ezekiel says that
24:21 Jerusalem "the delight of your eyes" must fall. Friends and
close relatives, even sons and daughters, will die during the
24:22 siege. And the prophet issues the Lord's strange commandment
that the exiles shall not mourn their loss when it comes. They
24:23 shall continue to dress and act in the normal fashion—in public. Only in private may they "groan to one another." They
must restrain the customary, extravagant, outward signs of the
grief that, inevitably, they will know.

The modern explanations of the ban against mourning are
even stranger than the ban itself. Most say that the blow will
so stun the people that they will be unable to grieve in the normal manner. A far more intelligible explanation was advanced
by Rashi, the medieval Jewish commentator. The Hebrew community in exile would, quite naturally, be under suspicion because of the rebellion in Jerusalem. The Babylonians would
interpret any public demonstration of grief, following the fall
of Jerusalem, as sympathy with the rebels. So, for the sake of
their own survival, the exiles must cloak their grief when it
comes.

The Lord promises that when Jerusalem has fallen a refugee
will bring the bitter news to Babylon. When that happens,
24:26 then finally Ezekiel's blight of "dumbness" will be lifted. The
prophet's mouth will be opened "together with him that is
24:27 escaped" (JPS). I have interpreted Ezekiel's "dumbness" as a
symbol for his inability to convince others, not a physical or
neurotic disturbance, nor even, as many understand it, a refusal
to speak in public. One need go back no farther than 24:20
to read, "Then I said to them." Ezekiel has been speaking to the
public during all these years, begging, pleading, threatening,
and crying aloud in terror. He has spoken, by every physiologi-
cal test of speech, but his thoughts have not penetrated to the
exiles' hearts. When finally the refugee comes with the sad word,
the exiles will "hear" him, and then they will "hear" Ezekiel. At
last Ezekiel's mission will be vindicated. Then he will be a
watchman whose voice is heard. Then he will be able to devote
his massive talents to the building of a new Jerusalem. Then
"they will know that there has been a prophet among them"
(2:5). More important, "they will know that I am the Lord."

II. THE PROPHECY OF HOPE, 25:1—48:35

II. The Prophecy of Hope, 25:1–48:35

I. PROPHECIES AGAINST FOREIGN NATIONS, 25:1–32:32.

The Book of Ezekiel is divided with mathematical precision into two almost equal parts. The first we have finished examining with its message of "lamentation and mourning and woe" (2:10). As the siege against Jerusalem begins the bitter prophecy of doom comes to an end. Now the Son of Man begins his message of hope. Hitherto the prophet has expressed judgment with carefully measured expressions of hope. Henceforth he speaks hope with a dark coloration of judgment. Faith, then as now, must swim against the current.

[The concrete form of Ezekiel's hope is that the exiles will be restored to Jerusalem. This restoration is a vast symbol of God's universal rule. But the symbol must take place in the world now filled with tensions and strife.] Before the exiles can return, it must be politically possible for them to do so. So the opening section in the prophecy of hope concerns foreign nations, seven in number. The seven symbolizes completeness. Ezekiel need not discuss every nation to make it clear that God is Lord over the entire world [The general message of this section is that God will subdue the nations that are hostile to His people, so that Israel may dwell in peace. Amos 1-2, Isaiah 13-27, and Jeremiah 46-51 likewise show God's lordship over the nations] (In LXX Jeremiah's oracles against the surrounding nations precede the prophecy of restoration, just as they do in the other major prophets.)

The first section consists of prose oracles concerning four small nations; the second and third contain magnificent poems that deal with Tyre and Egypt. It is impossible today to say when many of the oracles were composed. 29:1 is earlier than 26:1, while 29:1 and 29:17 show a gap of seventeen years. This should be sufficient evidence that the present arrangement is logical rather than chronological.

167

A. Against Ammon, Moab, Edom, and Philistia, 25:1-17.

The oracles against the four small nations presuppose the destruction of Jerusalem. Standing—imaginatively—in the rubble, the prophet faces toward the northeast, and hurls a charge against Ammon. Turning almost due east, he rebukes the land of Moab. Turning south, he speaks to Edom; and turning west, to Philistia. Thus he has described almost a complete circle, and faced a traditional enemy in every direction.

The Interpreter's Bible suggests that this chapter offers a startling parallel to the principle varieties of anti-semitism in the world today. Ammon represents the unreasoning type. Moab is the rationalistic type, that which refuses to see any special value in the Jewish tradition, and would reduce all nations and all religions to one level. Edom represents the anti-semitism that is rooted in blood relationship, like that of the Christian who hates the Jew; while Philistia shows the open and violent variety.

1. Against Ammon, 25:1-7.

The Ammonites were a people living northeast of the Dead Sea. They were racially akin to the Hebrews (Genesis 19:38), but relationships between the two nations were almost always strained, and warfare was frequent. When the kingdom of Israel was decimated in 722 B.C., the Ammonites repossessed what once had been their land (Jeremiah 49:1; Zephaniah 2:8). While Judah was having her death-struggle with Babylon the Ammonites joined in a coalition against Jerusalem (II Kings 24:2). When Jerusalem had fallen the king of Ammon sent an assassin to kill Gedaliah, whom Nebuchadnezzar had appointed governor of the territory (Jeremiah 40:13—41:2). For several centuries after Ezekiel's time the hostility continued.

The particular charge Ezekiel brings against the Ammonites is that they showed malicious joy, first over the destruction of
25:3 Israel, then over that of Judah. For this the Lord will turn them over to "the people of the East," desert nomads, rather
25:4 than the Babylonians.

The identical judgment against Ammon is repeated in quite different language. Notice the play on words, "because you have
25:6 clapped your hands" (in malicious joy) "I have stretched out
25:7 my hand against you." Jeremiah 49:6 foretells the restoration of Ammon. Ezekiel does not mention it here, though he has already foretold the restoration of Sodom (16:53).

2. Against Moab, 25:8-11.

The Moabites were a Semitic people whose boundaries—constantly shifting—were east of the Dead Sea. The tribe of Reuben occupied the territory immediately to the north. Inscriptions indicate that Reuben's occupation was more theoretical than actual until the time of David who subdued the Moabites. During the Hebrew monarchy they made repeated, sometimes successful, efforts to be independent. The Moabites joined with the Ammonites and others to help in the destruction of Jerusalem.

Ezekiel charges that Moab has said, "Behold the house of Judah is like all the other nations." It is hard not to sympa-
25:8 thize with the Moabites. The only superiority Judah possessed was in the knowledge of God. Since many Hebrews understood this knowledge to be a lucky talisman that would deliver them from the consequences of their acts, it is not surprising that their neighbors made the same mistake. When Jerusalem fell the Moabites concluded that the Lord of the Hebrews was no more powerful than any other local deity. They did not see—how could they see?—the power of God who triumphs through a Cross. It is not for us to decide, but for God alone, how far a person is responsible to break the bonds of his own cultural environment and to recognize the truth embodied in an alien culture (John 18:37).

Ezekiel warns that the Lord will "open the flank of Moab."
The Moabites had a line of fortresses, often within sight of one
25:9 another, on hilltops at the extreme edge of the Moabite plateau. The three named were presumably the most important among the defending cities. Beth-jeshimoth (Tell el Aseimeh) is about two and one-half miles north of the Dead Sea; Baal-meon (Ma'in) is about nine miles east of the Dead Sea, and about ten miles south of Baal-meon is Keriathaim (el Qereiyat).

According to Josephus, Nebuchadnezzar overcame Ammon and Moab five years after his conquering Jerusalem (*Antiquities* 10, 9, 7).

3. Against Edom, 25:12-14.

Edom was the land south of the Dead Sea, with a long and colorful history of hostility against Judah. David conquered Edom, but a rebellion against Jehoram won independence. Amaziah and Uzziah reconquered Edom, but a rebellion against Ahaz was again successful. The specific charge is that

25:12   Edom "acted revengefully against the house of Judah." This
charge is developed, with distressing detail, in Obadiah 10-14.
The emotional impact upon the Hebrews is well expressed in
Psalm 137:7ff., possibly the least Christ-like verses in the entire
OT.

Teman was a district in the northern part of Edom. Dedan
probably is the name of a tribe bordering Edom on the south.
25:13   It is not the same as Dedan in Arabia (27:20; 38:13). The two
words together encompass the entire land. God will carry out
25:14   His judgment against the vengeful Edomites "by the hand of
my people Israel." During the Maccabean Wars the Edomites
finally were defeated and were taken into the Jewish state.

4. Against Philistia, 25:15-17.

The Philistines, unlike the other peoples mentioned, were
not Semites, but were originally settlers from the island of
25:15   Crete who entered Palestine about 1200 B.C. and gave their
name to the entire country. (The biblical "Philistia" is roughly
the equivalent of modern "Palestine.") The blood soaked pages
of Judges and the Books of Samuel show vividly an age-old and
bitter enmity between the Philistines and the Hebrews. Even so,
there is no biblical record, other than the present passage, that
the Philistines took any unusual part in the siege of Jerusalem.
(In Joel 3:4 the Philistines are linked with Tyre and Sidon.)

The "Cherethites" are called "Cretans" in LXX. The traditional view is that they were a Philistine tribe who provided
25:16   mercenary troops for David's bodyguard (II Samuel 8:18).
However, recent discoveries make it appear likely that they
were a group of Phonecians who lived amicably with the Philistines. In any case, Ezekiel makes a grim play on words. "Cherethites" is *CeReThim*. "I will cut off" is *hiCRaTti*. (In Hebrew
a root, usually of three letters, goes through a gamut of meanings by the addition of prefixes and suffixes and by vowel
changes. Here the root in each case is CRT.)

B. Against Tyre, 26:1—28:26.

Tyre (a rock) and Sidon (a fishery) were the great cities of
the Phonecians. Although Sidon was for many years the more
important, by Ezekiel's time Tyre was the dominant city. Here
it serves as a symbol for the entire Phonecian civilization. Phonecia was a narrow strip of land bounded on the east by the
Mediterranean and on the west by a ridge of the Lebanon

range. The northern limit was Arvad. The southern limit was only a few miles south of Tyre. Despite its insignificant size, Phonecia was one of the most influential civilizations in the ancient world. The coast line provided excellent harbors, and the Lebanons provided a wonderful supply of timber; so the Phonecians became shipbuilders, navigators, traders, and colonists. Phonecian traders went through the Pillars of Hercules and south along the African coast at least as far as modern Liberia. Northward they reached the British Isles. Only a few years before the Hebrew exile, Pharaoh Necho commissioned a group of Phonecian explorers who successfully circumnavigated the African continent (Herodotus *Persian Wars,* 4,2). The Phonecians were called "Canaanites" (traders) by the Hebrews (Genesis 10:15; Isaiah 23:11).

Relationships between the Phonecians and the Hebrews were friendly most of the time. David and Solomon looked to Tyre for building materials, craftsmen, and architectural models (I Kings 5-9). During the great period of expansion no attempt was made to incorporate Phonecian territory into the Hebrew kingdom. Ahab, king of Israel, married Jezebel, princess of Sidon (I Kings 16:31), for political and economic reasons. Spiritual considerations, apparently, were not important. The biblical references to Tyre and Sidon show a civilization with great technical skill and vast wealth, where the rich, successful people demonstrated little regard for the human cost of their profits.

Except for the brief poem in Isaiah 23:1-12, the other prophets pay little or no attention to Tyre, yet almost one seventh of Ezekiel is devoted to this kingdom. There are two reasons, possibly three. The one closer at hand lies in the political struggle of the day. In 594-3 B.C. the kings of Tyre and Sidon joined in the futile alliance of small nations against Nebuchadnezzar (Jeremiah 27:1-7). In 588 B.C. Pharaoh Hophra of Egypt overcame Tyre and Sidon. However, Ithobaal II, King of Tyre, threw off the Egyptians and then planned to attack Babylon. As soon as Nebuchadnezzar had conquered Jerusalem he turned his attention to Tyre, and laid a siege that continued for thirteen years (585-573 B.C.). Ezekiel writes shortly after the fall of Jerusalem. The whole purpose of his prophecy is to show that God is Lord over the entire world. God has destroyed Jerusalem. Will He pass by proud Tyre? The second reason for Ezekiel's stress upon the Phonecian city is more immediately relevant to us. Here the prophet examines in depth the temptations and pitfalls that go with success and prosperity. H. L. Ellison suggests another possible reason. Tyre may be a symbol for Babylon. Babylon, like Tyre, was a trading center filled with wealth from a score of different nations. Ezekiel could not very well predict that Babylon would be overthrown. Such a message in time of tension would bring destruction to the prophet and to his fellow exiles. But he could, and did, examine the destiny of a commercial civilization that ranks profit ahead of righteousness.

There are many knotty technical problems in the section about Tyre, beginning with the disputed date in 26:1. But these are small when compared with the unescapable spiritual problem that students of prophecy cannot ignore. Here Ezekiel predicts that Nebuchadnezzar will utterly destroy Tyre, and that it will never rise again. He made the prediction when the siege of Tyre was beginning. After thirteen long years, Nebuchadnezzar finally lifted the siege. Ezekiel—brutally honest as always—admits that his prediction was not fulfilled (29:18).

Some people think they are defending the inerrancy of the Scripture when they claim that Ezekiel predicted the destruction of old Tyre, the city on the shore. There was a mainland settlement at the time, and doubtless Nebuchadnezzar demolished it quite capably, but that is not what Ezekiel is talking about. Others would defend the Bible by showing that Alexander the Great captured Tyre in 332 B.C. But the city was rebuilt in short order, and it continued to be a trading center until the time of the Crusades. The Bible does not need any defense. Those who think to defend it by spurious exegesis and clever juggling can but defeat their own purpose.

The Bible has some clear words to say about prophetic prediction and fulfillment:

> If at any time I declare concerning a nation or a kingdom, that I will pluck up and break down and destroy it, and if that nation, concerning which I have spoken, turns from its evil, I will repent of the evil that I intended to do to it. And if at any time I declare concerning a nation or a kingdom that I will build and plant it, and if it does evil in my sight, not listening to my voice, then I will repent of the good which I had intended to do to it. Now, therefore, say to the men of Judah and the inhabitants of Jerusalem: "Thus says the Lord, Behold, I am shaping evil

against you and devising a plan against you. Return, every one from his evil way, and amend your ways and your doings" (Jeremiah 18:7-11).

While there was yet time for Jerusalem to repent Ezekiel said much the same thing.

God's warnings are issued in order that they may not be fulfilled. God keeps His promises, though sometimes He must delay because conditions are not right for their completion. God's nature is unchanging. The human condition changes constantly. When a man or a nation is plunging blindly into disaster God warns, sometimes through a prophet, that the man or nation may turn aside and live.

I have said before that the predictive element is a small part of Ezekiel's prophecy. Ezekiel calls man to recognize the eternal verities and to guide his life by them. He warns man to turn away from destruction. He has transmitted to us a burning question from God:

> Have I any pleasure in the death of the wicked, says the Lord God, and not rather that he should turn from his way and live? (18:23).

The basic principle applies even when the sinner lives in Tyre.

1. The Fall of Tyre, 26:1-21.

"The word of the Lord" comes to Ezekiel, foretelling the doom of Tyre. The chapter is divided into four sections, one of which, "The Lament of the Princes," is filled with rare poetic beauty.

a. Tyre's Guilt, 26:1-2.

26:1 The date is incomplete and filled with difficulty. We are not told what month, hence some have concluded that it is probably the fifth month, in which Jerusalem fell. From the scraps of contradictory evidence, we gather that before the messenger brought the bitter news (33:21), Ezekiel received a vision from the Lord in which he saw that the same principles governing Jerusalem likewise governed Tyre.

26:2 The Hebrew name for Tyre is *sor*, "a rock." The city was built on a rocky island, about half a mile from the Phonecian coast. Its position made it all but invulnerable to a land-based attack.

Tyre's sin is not that of the lion attacking its prey, but that of the hyena, gorging itself on the prey that another has slaughtered. With Jerusalem destroyed the greedy Tyrians expect to benefit from increased trading opportunities. They describe Jerusalem, cryptically, as "the gate of the peoples." The Hebrew means "the closed door" (with two leaves). Jerusalem was not nearly so important a trading center as was Tyre. None the less, Jerusalem lay on the route from Tyre to Petra, the mines at Ezion-Geber, Palmyra, and other places where merchants could buy and sell goods. The city through which the caravans must pass could make a profit both by trading with the merchants and by imposing transit taxes. Although, in the long run, Jerusalem's fall could but increase Babylon's power, and give Nebuchadnezzar a strangle hold on Tyre's traffic to the south, greed could see only the short-term advantage. A rival eliminated. A chance to profit. "The gate of the peoples is broken, it has swung open to me." What matter that Jerusalem and Tyre had a long tradition of friendship? What matters anything but the chance to make money?

  b. Tyre's Punishment, 26:3-14.

Ezekiel vividly shows a clash between the trading civilization of Tyre and the armed might of Babylon. Many people today think that economic power and military power are the determining forces in civilization. They disdainfully sniff at the spiritual force symbolized, however imperfectly, by Jerusalem. Today the armies of Babylon are all valiant dust returned to dust; the fleets of Tyre no longer sail the oceans of the world, but the "river" still flows from the Temple in Jerusalem. Ezekiel sees deeper than the outward clash between economic power and military power. Controlling both is moral power— God. "Behold, I am against you, O Tyre, and will bring up many nations against you." The Babylonian army was a heterogeneous collection. Quite possibly soldiers from neighboring states participated in the Tyrian siege, just as they did in that against Jerusalem (II Kings 24:2).

Ezekiel pictures the attacking army as a hurricane that topples the massive buildings and washes the island clean of its soil; so that it is fit only for spreading fish nets to dry. Tyre, the mistress of the seas, shall be a spoil for the nations. The "daughters," of course, are the smaller settlements on the mainland, dependent upon Tyre for their sustenance and defense. From their ruin the Tyrians will "know that I am the Lord." Ezekiel

26:3

26:4

26:5
26:6

had used this phrase often enough about the people of Jerusalem, who must know God in judgment before they can know him in mercy. Will any one claim that Ezekiel was blind to the fact that God made the Tyrians, and that He wanted their love responding to His?

The warning was not carried out in the manner that Ezekiel foresaw. He shows the conquering monarch as Nebuchadrezzar.

26:7 (Notice the change in spelling. Hitherto Ezekiel has spelled the name with an "n." The spelling henceforth is closer to the Babylonian *Nabu-kudurri-usur,* "Nebo protect my labor.") The king descends upon Tyre from the north, presumably from Riblah. He slays the "daughters on the mainland." All these things

26:8 were done, just as predicted. However, the next horrors did not
26:9 take place until the time of Alexander the Great, who built a vast mole out on the island, and proceeded methodically to destroy the city. Even on the fantastic assumption that Ezekiel

26:14 foresaw Alexander's campaign, his prediction still breaks down, for he says, "you shall never be rebuilt." Within a few years after Alexander destroyed it the city was rebuilt. The Babylonian siege ended after thirteen years, when Ithobaal II, king of Tyre made some relatively minor concessions to Nebuchadnezzar, and saved his city from destruction.

Rather than defending the inerrancy of the Scripture by compounding our own errors, it is better to agree with Ezekiel that this conditional warning was not fulfilled (29:17-18), and then to seek the real meaning of the prophecy for today. What are the foundations upon which our civilization is built? This is the profitable question to ask.

c. Lament of the Princes of the Sea, 26:15-18.

Ezekiel pictures the earth trembling as Tyre falls, the groans of her wounded echoing through the nations. The "princes of

26:15 the sea" are the rulers of merchant-states who have done busi-
26:16 ness with Tyre, including, of course, the rulers of Tyrian colonies in Greece, Italy, North Africa, and Spain. When they hear the crash of the island-city's fall, they step down from their thrones, remove their royal garments, and—note this incredibly vivid phrase—"clothe themselves with trembling."

Why does Ezekiel write the lament? He knew that if man is to live on earth there must be commerce. He knew that if the merchant fails to make a profit he cannot continue to perform his necessary function. (Almost certainly Ezekiel had to earn his living by some form of trade or labor. One cannot picture the exiles offering him even the most meager financial support.) Ezekiel knew that Tyre and the princes of the sea were doing something necessary for man's continued existence on earth. But he writes for his fellow exiles and for us that man shall not live by bread alone. The horror of Tyre's fall is actually increased by the blindness of the princes. While they chant their grief in beauteous elegiac (*quinah*) poetry, the princes actually are confessing their own spiritual poverty. For what do they la-

26:18 ment? Tyre, my most successful competitor, has fallen. Therefore my kingdom is likewise in danger. Peril does not lead the merchant-princes to ask the right questions: Am I trading to serve God, or am I making a god out of trade?

d. Tyre's Descent into the Pit, 26:19-21.

Tyre is punished because she has lacked even the elementary decency to sympathize with Jerusalem's fall, but has gloated

26:19 over the chance for greater profits as her rival is eliminated. With one of the savage twists that Ezekiel employs so effectively, he shows Tyre going down into the depths, never to rise again, as a prelude to Jerusalem's restoration. Ezekiel personifies Tyre as a drowning woman. The waters of the sea close

26:20 over her. She descends "to the Pit . . . to dwell in the nether world among primeval ruins . . . so that you will not . . . have a place in the land of the living."

Ezekiel draws a dimly lit picture of a shadowy half-world where dead people dwell. Contrast this with the vision Ezekiel's disciple saw (Revelation 21 and 22). John was living under conditions of physical and mental duress comparable to those Ezekiel endured. He clothed his thought in symbols taken from Ezekiel. His concept of God's final triumph on earth is similar to Ezekiel's. But John's picture of the life following this differs in almost every particular. Ezekiel sees "the Pit." John sees the dazzling, blinding glory of a life where the Lamb is the Light. He sees the kings of the earth bringing their glory into the eternal city, whose gates will never be shut by day, and where there is no night. The difference between Ezekiel and John lies not in intellectual capacity or depth of suffering. Here they are equals. The difference lies in Christ.

2. Lament for Tyre, 27:1-36.

The twenty-seventh is one of few beautiful chapters in the

prophecy of Ezekiel. It is a poem in the *quinah* meter, in which
Ezekiel compares Tyre with a ship that is lost at sea. The poem
is interrupted by a vivid prose description of the varied commerce in which Tyre engaged. To the geographer and the historian the chapter is a priceless addition to knowledge of commerce
in the ancient world. The less specialized reader is bewildered
by allusions to places and articles of trade no longer identifi-
able. Happily our appreciation, either of the poetic beauty or
the theological message, does not depend upon correct geographical or commercial interpretations. Tyre traded with the
whole world known to Ezekiel. She carried every type of cargo
that might earn a profit. In the process she gained the whole
world and lost her own soul. The last thought will be developed
in the following chapter.

a. The Noble Ship, 27:1-9a.

At the Lord's command Ezekiel joins the princes of the sea
in a poetic lament for Tyre's downfall. (Such extended poems
as The Lament for the Princess in 19 and the Song of the Sword
in 21 are not "prophecies" in the usual sense, but they are attributed to God's inspiration.) Unlike the princes, Ezekiel looks
beyond the effect of Tyre's downfall upon his personal for-
tunes. He looks to the eternal Cause. In the light of God he
examines, sympathetically yet critically, the meaning of a commercial civilization.

27:1

To a dweller in Palestine or Babylon, Tyre would be "the
entrance to the sea." The Hebrew reads "entries," possibly signifying the two sections of the harbor, known respectively as
the Sidonian, on the north, and the Egyptian, on the south.
Through these harbors passed much of the sea-borne commerce
that entered or left the Fertile Crescent. Tyrian ships carried
the world's trade to "the peoples on many coastlands." Above
the island city towered two massive "pillars" (26:11), built to
honor the national deity, Melkarth. These inevitably suggested
the masts rising above the ships at the quay. So it was natural
for Ezekiel to describe Tyre as a ship, "perfect in beauty." (The
Hebrew "I" is *ani;* "ship" is likewise *ani,* with a slight difference
in the pronunciation. Since the following poem treats Tyre as a
ship, I believe that the line should be translated "a ship, perfect in beauty.")

27:3

The ship is not a mere coasting vessel, always hugging the
shore, her "borders are in the heart of the seas." Ezekiel's in-

27:4   terest in sound craftsmanship will become increasingly evident.
Here he shows a craftsman's appreciation for the difficult arts
of shipbuilding and navigation. The reader today should remember that Ezekiel lived twenty-two centuries before Linnaeus
27:5   introduced the system of plant classification that we follow.
"Fir," "cedar," "oak," and "pine" have meanings in contemporary English that may not closely agree with those Ezekiel had
in mind. An "oaken" oar, *quercus alba*, for example, would be
unconscionably heavy, and a "pine" deck, *pinus strobus*,
would rot to nothingness in salt air. We may be sure that the
Phonecian craftsmen selected materials fit for their purpose, and
that Ezekiel described these materials correctly in terms of his
day. The ivory inlay in the deck is so puzzling that one may
well follow LXX, "your sacred utensils they made of ivory."
    Phonecian ships usually had one mast and one sail. Rowers
propelled the ship in close quarters and in heavy weather. The
27:7   sail's color and design would serve as an "ensign" to identify
the ship at a great distance. Ezekiel's word translated "linen"
means "something white." Again we may assume that the Tyrian sail makers chose suitable materials for their task. Linen was
too costly for the use of any but high officials and persons of
wealth. It would have been prohibitively expensive for sailcloth.
This may be what Ezekiel wished to convey, a picture of osten-
tatious luxury, where even the sails were made of the most
costly materials. LXX gives a completely different interpretation: "Fine linens with embroidery from Egypt supplied your
couch."
    There may be a suggestion of an ancient malice in the vari-
ous tasks assigned to the crew. Rowing a ship was, obviously,
27:8   an unpleasant job. Sidon had long been the chief Phonecian
city, but in the sixth century Tyre came to the fore; so the proud
Sidonian sailors are consigned to the oars. Arvad (now Ruwad)
lies a little more than a hundred miles north of Tyre. Its inhabitants were reputed brave, competent seamen. The subtle
suggestion is that Tyre employs the finest sailors to perform the
most menial work. The translation "skilled men of Zemer" is
based on conjecture. Zemer lay a little to the south of Arvad.
If the conjecture be accepted, then the passage means that Tyrians do not perform the actual work of seamanship, but employ
experts from other nations. Dr. Cooke supports this conjecture
with the astonishing argument, "The senators of Tyre could

hardly be sailors in the ship which represents Tyre!" That is the whole point of the analogy. Tyrians are the masters. Others do the rowing and caulking. JPS translates literally, "Thy wise men, O Tyre, . . . were thy pilots." As the pilot skillfully guides the ship; so the senators of Tyre are proudly steering the ship of state into destruction. Gebal (modern Jebel) lies midway between Tripoli and Beirut. The leading citizens of Gebal are called to the dirty, sometimes dangerous work of caulking (literally "strengtheners of your breach") the ship of Tyre.

b. Tyre's Trade, 27:9b-25a.

RSV unaccountably continues the poem to 9b. 9a represents the ship. The caulkers are "in you." But in 9b the "ships of the sea" are "in you." "You" has evidently undergone a considerable shift in meaning. Now it refers to the city of Tyre, where merchants come from every direction to barter their wares. Since the Phonecians were few, and their energies were directed toward commerce, they employed mercenary soldiers from Persia, Lydia (in western Asia Minor), the African coast of the Red Sea, from Arvad, already mentioned, from Helech and Gamad. The last two are unidentifiable today. According to LXX they should not be considered as cities or regions at all: "The sons of the Aradians and your army were upon your walls; there were guards in your towers; they hung their quivers on your battlements round about." Though there is room for debate about the translation of "Persia" and "Lydia," the passage means simply that Tyre had enough power and wealth to recruit her army from distant places.

There are so many geographical unknowns in the fascinating list of cities and merchandise that we cannot be sure what trade routes Ezekiel imaginatively is following. Tarshish was a Phonecian colony in southern Spain. Does the presence of tin and lead in the merchandise point to established commercial connections with England? Javan means the Ionian Greeks of Asia Minor. Joel 3:6 comments acidly that the Tyrians sold Hebrews as slaves to Javan. Slavery was the economic basis of civilization in the ancient world; still Ezekiel bitterly describes the slave trade as traffic in "the soul of man," colorlessly translated "persons of men." Tubal and Meshech are usually identified with some peoples in eastern Asia Minor, on either side of the Anti-Taurus range. Bethtogarmah is probably a part of Armenia, the

27:9

27:10

27:11

27:12

27:13

27:14

extreme northern limit of the world known to Ezekiel. The
same people appear in the army of Gog, along with others from
the ends of the earth (38:6).

Thus far the geographic sweep has been from west to east.
However Rhodes plunges us back into the Mediterranean. RSV
27:15 follows LXX. The Hebrew is *Dedan*. In Hebrew R and D are
quite similar in shape, and easily mistaken for one another.
Dedan is mentioned in verse 20 among the cities of Arabia. In
25:13 the region immediately south of Edom was called Dedan.
This would fit in well with the next trade route described,
through Edom, Judah, and Israel, but it seems an odd way to
bring "ivory tusks and ebony" to Tyre. Probably RSV is right
in reading "Rhodes," but JPS gives a better interpretation of
the verb, "the men of Dedan were thy traffickers." That is,
Tyrian merchants employed sailors from Rhodes to go to far
distant places in pursuit of luxury goods.

The trade route through Edom, Judah, and Israel has been
mentioned (26:2.) Is it just an accident that when Ezekiel
27:17 speaks of commerce with other nations he mentions the luxury
items, but when he describes trade with his own land he
stresses the necessities of life? Was it economic geography that
made Judah and Israel exporters of "wheat, olives, and early
figs" or did a basic conviction that the "earth is the Lord's"
lead them to emphasize the essentials rather than the luxuries?
Much the same cruel economic geography worked upon Judah
and Edom, but Ezekiel shows one catering to man's vanity,
while the other serves man's need.

Next Ezekiel describes trade with Damascus to the northeast
of Tyre. The vineyards of Helbon, north of Damascus, still are
27:18 producing superb grapes. In MT the following verse treats of
27:19 commerce with "Vedan and Javan." If this is the correct reading, we do not know enough about ancient times and cultures
to explain the meaning. RSV, following LXX, reads Uzal, pos-
27:21 sibly the ancient name for San'a, the modern capital of Yemen.
Arabia and Kedar are names for nomadic Bedouin peoples of
the desert who traded their livestock for the merchandise of
Tyre. Sheba and Raamah were districts in southwest Arabia
27:22 that distributed their spices, precious stones and gold through
the Tyrian wholesalers to the peoples of the world.

Next the prophet pictures Tyre's trade with the cities of
Mesopotamia. Haran is best known to biblical students as the

27:23 city where Terah, Abraham's father, stopped rather than take the long journey into the land of Canaan (Genesis 11:31). Haran today is a small village on the Belikh, an affluent of the Euphrates. In Ezekiel's time it was one of the principal trading centers in the world, at the junction of the routes from Carchemish, Nineveh, Damascus, and Babylon. The other locations are conjectural. Presumably they are all Mesopotamian commercial cities or regions. The spelling of "Eden" differs slightly from that of the biblical paradise (Genesis 2:15). If one accepts the conjectural translation, "Asshur" is not the Assyrian empire, but a town on the Tigris. Finally Ezekiel turns our attention from the dusty camels plodding toward Tyre with the world's wealth on their backs to the Spanish ships, approaching the
27:25 same city from the opposite direction, likewise burdened with the necessities and luxuries that brought fortune to the Tyrian merchants.

c. The Loss of the Ship, 27:25b-36.

The poem resumes. Again we are reading about Tyre figuratively described as a ship. The ship with its skillful crew
27:26 aboard is loaded at the pier, then the rowers work it away from the dock, through the crowded harbor, out away from the shore, and into the "heart of the seas." There the "east wind" wrecks the ship. The east wind is, symbolically, any force beyond human control (Genesis 41:23; Psalm 48:7; Jeremiah 18:17). Here, of course, the east wind represents Nebuchad-
27:27 rezzar. Ezekiel speaks in the "prophetic perfect," describing a future event as if it had already taken place, as cargo, crew, passengers, and armed guard "sink into the heart of the seas."

The "heart of the sea" is not necessarily far distant from land. Most shipwrecks occur when gale and current or human
27:28 error drive the vessel upon a reef or into shoal water, where the action of wind and wave break it apart. So Ezekiel pictures the
27:29 terrified cries of the pilots reaching the shore, while the sailors from other ships gather to look with helpless horror at the swirling waters where once the good ship had floated. Their
27:30 outward demonstrations of grief for a commercial rival, some-
27:31 times even an enemy, are a grim contrast with the massive restraint the exiles must show when their own sons and daughters die in the fall of Jerusalem (24:22f). In their lament the pilots underscore a point that Ezekiel has implicitly been making throughout this poem. The Tyrian merchants, with all their

faults, were serving as God's agents to meet human need. "When
27:33 your wares came from the seas, you satisfied many peoples."
Like the "princes of the sea," the mariners and the pilots
express sympathetic grief at the loss of their fellow-sailors. The
27:34 Tyrians had made their livelihood by the seas, and "by the
seas" they were destroyed. In their lament the mariners show
27:35 the reaction of various classes. The people of the coastlands
are "appalled," the kings are "horribly afraid, their faces are
convulsed," and the merchants "hiss." This last has almost completely changed its meaning. Today it is a sign of shame and
disapproval. Then it was a sign of amazement and dismay.

The mariners, like the princes, fail to relate their natural,
human grief to God. When the storm blows Ezekiel has taught
us to look unblinking into the blackness and to see the light of
God. Here he shows us a negative example. The mariners look
into the storm and see the sinking ship. They do not look for,
or find, the living God in the midst of human tragedy. And so
their thoughts can but end on a note of despair:

27:36   You have come to a dreadful end
                    and shall be no more for ever.

3. The Prince of Tyre, 28:1-19.
The mariners have keened their despair. And now Ezekiel
shows the difference that faith makes in life. He looks—in
imagination—at exactly the same event (here described with a
different figure of speech), and comes to exactly the same earth-
bound conclusion, "you have come to a dreadful end and shall
be no more for ever"; but the mariners have been unable to
see beyond their grief, while Ezekiel looks beyond grief to God.
He sees the spiritual reason for Tyre's fall. If any think this
meager consolation for the prince who is going down to his
doom, he should remember that a cure usually requires a correct diagnosis. It is almost unthinkable that Ezekiel's prophecy
reached Tyre during the siege, yet something happened that
averted the impending destruction. Nebuchadrezzar lifted the
frightful siege. Why? As Ezekiel has been telling us, God was
in charge of Nebuchadrezzar. The Tyrians themselves may well
have re-examined the false goals they had been pursuing.

The prophet looks at the Tyrian civilization as embodied in
the prince. Neither in this chapter nor in the following chapters
concerning Pharaoh does he consider the ruler's private char-

acter. In each case the ruler stands, by simple metonymy, as a symbol for his people. A casual reading of the chapter, particularly of verse 16, might convince one that Ezekiel is hostile to commerce. A more careful reading shows that Ezekiel is exposing the danger inherent in any type of success, "your heart has become proud in your wealth."

To a strict literalist, the chapter raises a theological problem that defies solution, as Ezekiel shows the prince in the Garden of Eden, blameless in all his ways. When one considers the symbolic nature of the entire prophecy, the pseudo-problem vanishes.

a. The Prince's Sin, 28:1-5.

The prince of Tyre was Ithobaal II (574-564 B.C.). Here he stands as a symbol for the Tyrian civilization, previously symbolized as a ship. He is guilty of the original sin, pride. Pride is the original sin because all other sins originate from a proud disposition. With superb theological penetration, Ezekiel shows the nature of pride in perhaps the clearest statement to be found in the entire Bible. "You have said, 'I am a god, I sit in the seat of the gods'." When man makes a god of himself, the sin is pride and the result is disaster. Though many have suggested that this phrase implies a Tyrian belief in the divinity of kings, that is not Ezekiel's emphasis. Rather he shows a man, endowed by God with superb talents and opportunities, who takes credit to himself for using the gifts God has given to him. He may continue to worship God with his lips; with his life he deifies himself. Recent history has demonstrated that when man tears God from the throne, shortly thereafter man attempts to climb upon the throne himself. However, as Ezekiel points out, "you are a man, and no god." The various men and states that have deified themselves in the twentieth century have invariably disclosed their full share of mortal weakness.

Ezekiel lauds the skill and daring that built a world power on a tiny island. He compares the prince with Daniel. The spelling differs from that of the prophet Daniel, as it did in 14:14. There Daniel was praised for his piety, here for his wisdom. Probably Ezekiel refers again to Daniel (justice of God), the Phonecian folk hero of 1400 B.C., who "renders justice to the widow and orphan." Building the vast commercial empire required "wisdom" and "understanding." But he who showed such sagacity in the lesser affairs of life lost sight of

28:2

28:3

28:4

28:5   man's true goal. He successfully amassed riches until his heart
became proud in his wealth.

b. The Prince's Judgment, 28:6-10.

In terms that Ezekiel has made painfully familiar to us, he
describes God's judgment upon the prince of Tyre. The Baby-
28:7   lonian troops will descend, destroying the "beauty" of the
prince's "wisdom." Since the prince has used his wisdom for
28:8   material gain, its beauty can be destroyed by a sword. Soldiers
will slaughter the man who thought himself to be among the
28:9   immortal gods. Although the language and the figures of speech
differ considerably, Ezekiel's message is exactly that of Jesus in
His parable of the rich fool, to whom God said, "This night
your soul is required of you; and the things you have prepared,
whose will they be?" (Luke 12:20). The Tyrian prince has used
his talents to enrich himself. He has made a life-goal of his
own desires. He has chosen profits rather than justice. He has
loved wealth more than mercy. He has sought luxury rather
than the humble walk with God. And so, in the presence of his
executioner, the prince must finally realize that he is a man,
hence mortal. Man's true destiny is to serve God, not himself.

c. Lament for the Prince, 28:11-19.

As has been mentioned, Ezekiel's lament for the prince differs
from the previous laments by exploring the theological implications of an earthly tragedy. It has likewise been mentioned that
the lament raises a theological problem, when Ezekiel likens
the prince to paradisic man in Eden, the Garden of God. The
several versions contain many different readings that do little
to clarify the issue. The passage bears many obvious resem-
blances to the account of man's creation and fall in Genesis 1-3.
There are likewise differences between Ezekiel's account and
that in Genesis; for example, Ezekiel's Garden is located on a
mountain.

Interpretations of the passage differ almost fantastically from
one another. Some of the early church fathers taught that the
picture of creation and fall describes Lucifer, prince of the
angels, who fell and became Satan, the prince of hell (Isaiah
14:12-21). This interpretation grows from the puzzling reference
to the "cherub" in verse 14. The Hebrew is quite obscure. AV
translates, "Thou art the anointed cherub." So it is grammatically possible that Ezekiel has suddenly intruded the war in
heaven into a close-knit allegory about a commercial civiliza-

tion. Few hold this belief today. Ezekiel is the most consistent of books. It is unthinkable that the author should so abruptly change the subject, only to change it back again. Ezekiel still is discussing a commercial civilization as symbolized by the prince of Tyre.

Most modern commentators agree that there were many creation myths in the Babylonian world. "A select few are to be found in Genesis, purged by the genius of Hebrew religion; in Ezekiel the purifying process has not gone so far" (G. A. Cooke). However, as Dr. Cooke concedes, "The myth of a divine garden, an abode of bliss, has not been found in Babylonian sources." A curious variation on this theme is offered by Dr. Ellison, who suggests that Ezekiel is summarizing the creation-beliefs of the Tyrians, thus the whole lament is ironic. If this be the case, "irony" is much too gentle a term; Ezekiel's "lament" is the cruelest sarcasm ever written.

If any of the above suggestions be adopted, the passage has little or nothing to say to us today. Another interpretation is possible. Assume for a moment that the Genesis account rightly belongs in God's message to man. In other words, it expresses a profound, important truth. This truth, obviously, is not the sort of thing that a cultural anthropologist could discover. The Genesis account omits almost everything that a cultural anthropologist would wish included in an analysis of human origins. What then is the truth expressed?

In Genesis we read that God created man. The Hebrew *adam* means "man" in the sense of "mankind." Only secondarily is it a proper name for an individual man. (RSV, quite correctly, does not translate "Adam," but rather "man.") God placed man in a world filled with both present and potential blessing. When created, man was free from any actual evil. But he dared to substitute his judgment for God's. Thus his proud disposition led directly to the sin of disobedience. The result was disaster.

Now turn to Ezekiel's account, which does not discuss man in general, but a particular man, the king of Tyre, who is a symbol 28:12 for a particular kind of man, the merchant. Ezekiel's tendency to elaborate could explain any divergence from the Genesis account. Ezekiel shows a man "full of wisdom and perfect in beauty," to whom God entrusts every imaginable blessing, 28:13 as suggested by the catalogue of jewels. (LXX gives the full list of twelve precious stones on the breastplate of the High Priest

[Exodus 28:17-20]. The list as given in the Hebrew symbolizes God's lavish endowment.) This man lived under the protection of a "guardian cherub"—the Hebrew here is quite uncertain—

28:14 on "the holy mountain of God," where he walked "in the midst of the stones of fire." (Probably this obscure expression refers to the iridescent jewels, so abundant that the prince trod them under foot.) The prince, like the first man, was created innocent

28:15 of any actual evil. (The reader who finds this verse in conflict with the Pauline teachings about original sin should remember that here Ezekiel is presenting an allegory, not a tract in systematic theology.) The point of the allegory thus far—if my minority report be accepted—is that commerce in itself is good. The

28:16 people whom God has created cannot live without the labors of transportation and trade. But "the cares of the world and the delight in riches" can, and do, "choke the word" (Matthew 13:22). In the restless activity of trade the prince forgot about God. He sinned, and, like man in Genesis, was expelled from the Garden.

The entire prophecy of Ezekiel contains no more pertinent words today than the analysis of the prince's sin. "Your heart

28:17 was proud because of your beauty. You corrupted your wisdom for the sake of your splendor." God gave man the gifts of beauty and wisdom to be used in the Lord's service, chiefly by meeting human needs. The prince "corrupted" his endowments, using

28:18 them for selfish luxury. Under these circumstances, trade became unrighteous, and the prince's worship a profane thing. Like the uprooted vine that generated the self-consuming fire (19:14), a culture that worships commercial success will strike the sparks that ultimately will burn it to ashes.

Ezekiel concludes his lament with words that we have read before (27:36). Formerly the words expressed sympathetic human grief. They were a cry of despair. Here they express sym-

28:19 pathetic human grief plus the catalyst of faith. And so they are a prelude to hope.

The prophet was no narrow nationalist. Tyre as well as Jerusalem came within his provenience. Nor did his interest in religion silence him in affairs of business. He believed the shortsighted economic practices of Tyre must be radically punished by a God of Justice. He saw clearly that national decadence and international ill will were probably more deeply rooted in economic causes than in any other.   —I. G. Matthews

4. Oracle against Sidon, 28:20-23.

The warning to Sidon belongs in this place because Sidon was an integral part of the Phonecian civilization. We do not
8:21 know when the oracle was composed. If it was before the siege against Tyre, when Sidon was comparatively unimportant, then it means that God is judging both small and great by the same standard. During the siege Sidon regained its former supremacy, which it retained for some years after. So, if the oracle is late it has the same meaning, but the relative positions of the two states are reversed.

The warning ends with the words "they will know that I am the Lord." The majority of commentators today believe that
8:23 "they" refers to Israel. The reader's first impression is that "they" are the Sidonians. The reader may be right. Ezekiel has already told us that Jerusalem must learn to know God in judgment before knowing Him in redemption. Is it too much to say that here he uses the same words to express the same hope about Sidon?

5. God's Mercy within His Judgment, 28:24-26.

Ezekiel has expressed the thought that Israel is God's messenger to other nations (5:15), and that even Sodom will be re-
8:24 stored (16:53). Here he looks into the future when Israel will be freed from the briars and thorns so liberally supplied by the neighboring states, freed to fulfill his true destiny, making God known to all. When this time comes, "They will know that I am the Lord." Who are "they"? Israel, obviously. But Israel
8:25 is God's messenger to others. The Lord promises that when He has gathered His people back from the lands in which they have been scattered, He will manifest His holiness in Israel "in the sight of the nations." After God has subdued the peoples who
8:26 once treated Israel with contempt, there will be a physical return to a given geographic location where Israel will enjoy political peace and economic abundance. But these are not the goal. These are means through which Israel can discharge his spiritual mission.

C. Against Egypt, 29:1–32:32.

The seventh nation to be examined is Egypt. There are seven oracles, most of which are dated. The first was given to Ezekiel shortly before the fall of Jerusalem, in 587 B.C. The second is

the last dated oracle in the entire book, almost seventeen years
later. The section concerning Egypt is now divided into four
chapters that end with a funeral dirge for Pharaoh as he descends into Sheol. Thus dramatically Ezekiel concludes his examination of other nations, that he may turn to the message of
restoration and hope for Israel.

Unlike the petty kingdoms around Judah, or Tyre (unless
Tyre symbolizes Babylon), Egypt was a power with intermittent
aspirations for world domination, with a tradition of might that
stretched back into the immemorial past. By Ezekiel's time
Egypt was a decadent power, though still a force to be reckoned
with. We have noticed the way in which weak princes almost
instinctively turned to Egypt for help against Babylon. We
know, as did the astute prophets, that this was political, military, and religious folly. But Ezekiel's audience, the house of
Israel, without our hindsight to guide them, scoffed at the
prophets and thought of Egypt as the strongest nation on earth.
Hence Ezekiel places this land in the climactic position to show
that God is Lord over the entire world. (See Jeremiah 37:5-10;
46:1-26.)

1. Pharaoh's Sin, 29:1-16.

The tenth month of the tenth year is January, 587 B.C., about
seven months before Jerusalem fell. The date is earlier than
29:1 the unnamed month of the eleventh year mentionel in 26:1.
This fact, coupled with the date almost seventeen years later in
29:17, gives us a brief glimpse of the way in which the entire
prophecy was composed. The individual oracles, visions, laments, or other prophecies came to Ezekiel as God used the
needs and events of the day to lay different matters on the
prophet's heart. Long afterward someone, Ezekiel or one of his
disciples, arranged the disconnected elements into the logical
pattern that we see today. The book has suffered many things
at the hands of the scribes who copied its puzzling message, and
sometimes added to its difficulty. So we cannot be sure that we
have the exact word Ezekiel proclaimed. But the evidence is
clear before us that we have in the Book of Ezekiel today a massive, consistent, carefully thought-through philosophy of history, that teaches us always to open our eyes to the light of God
in the midst of storm.

The Lord directs the Son of Man to prophesy against Phar-

aoh, as the representative of "all Egypt." At the time, Hophra
29:2 (588-569 B.C.) was Pharaoh. Ezekiel, however, is not concerned
with Hophra's private character. Just as he did with Ithobaal II,
he treats the ruler as a symbol for the nation's strength and
weakness. In the first of many word pictures, Ezekiel calls Phar-
29:3 aoh (Egypt) "the great dragon that lies in the midst of his
streams." "Dragon" is an unfortunate translation, because it
suggests a mythological, fire-breathing monster. Weird monsters
abounded in ancient myth, but Ezekiel here refers to the crocodile, a beast that is fearsome enough in its own right. The
Roman Emperor Augustus depicted Egypt as a crocodile on his
memorial coins. The Arabs today still call the crocodile "Pharaoh." So this long, sinister reptile, lying motionless in the
water, only to dash into a savage fury of action, was a fitting
symbol for Egypt in the days of her pomp and power. At the
time of writing Judah was under siege. Pharaoh, after discover-
ing that an attempt to aid his ally might prove costly, was sun-
ning himself by the Nile. A crocodile aroused is a fearsome
beast. A crocodile at rest resembles a log.

Egypt's sin differs only in detail from Tyre's. It is the same
basic pride. Egypt has said—in act if not in word—"My Nile is
my own; I made it." God created the Nile with its majestic
rhythm of flood and ebb that makes Egypt even today an important agricultural nation. Egypt accepted God's gift, used it
intelligently, and then took credit for making what God created.
RSV follows the versions. But MT has an even bolder affirma-
tion, "I have made myself." If this was Ezekiel's meaning—the
majority believe it was not—then the prophet alludes to the belief that the sun-god Re begot himself. In any case, the vast
monuments from ancient Egypt that remain by the sides of the
Nile are impressive evidence of a highly developed but arrogant
civilization. Imagine the human cost of building a pyramid.
Imagine the pride that would drain a nation to erect such a
monument for the ruler's corpse.

Herodotus tells how the Egyptians captured crocodiles with
a baited hook. Job 41:1 suggests that such hunting called for
29:4 immeasurable skill and daring. The Lord warns that He will
capture Pharaoh as a hunter snags the crocodile and drags him
up on the river bank to rot. The allusion to fish is so puzzling
and it so interrupts the poetic metre, that many believe this a
scribal insertion to symbolize the people of Egypt. (The He-

brew word for "fish" is *dag,* which comes from a verb meaning—among other things—"to be prolific." Though fish other than the remora could not, there are many prolific water-animals that could cling to the scales of a crocodile. If the word is Ezekiel's, possibly he refers to such "fish" that are not of the class *pisces.*)

Egypt is a country almost without rainfall. As far as the life-giving Nile waters extend, it is the most fertile land on
29:5 earth, today as in Ezekiel's time. Where the waters do not reach, suddenly, dramatically, the luxuriant garden ends and the bleak hostile desert begins. A crocodile cast into the "wilderness" (better "desert") could survive but for a time. Shortly it would be prey for the buzzards and the jackals. So it will be with Pharaoh. Through their harsh judgment, the Egyptians will
29:6 "know that I am the Lord." It is not apparent why the division into verses makes this phrase introduce the next thought, rather than conclude the previous, as it usually does.

Ezekiel gives a second example of Egyptian pride. The Egyptians have used Israel—and presumably other nations—to
29:7 forward their own ends without regard for the consequences to the others. Egypt has repeatedly made alliances and lightly broken them. Ezekiel alludes to Rabshakeh's bitter words, comparing Egypt to a staff of reed, weak and unreliable (II Kings 18:21; Isaiah 36:6). Rabshakeh said that the staff would break and pierce Israel's hand. Ezekiel, less probably, shows it wounding his shoulder.

The prophet drops all metaphors. He says that the "sword" will smite, and the "land of Egypt shall be a desolation and a
29:8 waste. Then they will know that I am the Lord." Again Ezekiel
29:9 makes a prediction that was not literally fulfilled. He warns that
29:10 the Lord will withhold the life-giving floods of the Nile from the northern to the southern limits of the nation (near modern
29:11 Aswan), that the land will be desert like the surrounding sands, and the Egyptians will be scattered among the nations for forty
29:12 years, just as the Hebrews have been (4:6). Amid the desolated countries, Egypt will be the outstanding desolation.

Although Egypt has been invaded many times, and the Nile has had many droughts, total wastage has never taken place.
29:13 Rather than complaining that Ezekiel fails to give the headlines of tomorrow's newspaper, we ought to read his message. The same Lord who judges lowly Israel is Judge over mighty Egypt. The same standards of judgment that hold for the one

hold for the other. The same God who will restore Israel will restore Egypt. Israel will return to his land to fulfill his true destiny, that of proclaiming God to the nations. Egypt will return, to what? Ezekiel states this destiny negatively. Egypt will not return to its former size, but will occupy only Pathros, the "south land," or "Upper Egypt." Egypt will not return to its former pomp and power, it will be "lowly," no longer the ruler over other nations. And Egypt will never again be "the reliance" of Israel. Thus, negatively, "they will know that I am the Lord God." Egypt's obvious destiny is to be an agricultural nation, to provide the food and fibre necessary for man's life on earth. Ezekiel has not spelled this out, but surely, underlying his prophecy of restoration, is an echo of the thought, "Blessed be Egypt my people, and Assyria the work of my hands, and Israel my heritage" (Isaiah 19:25).

2. God's Judgment on Egypt, 29:17—30:19.
a. Nebuchadrezzar, God's Agent of Judgment, 29:17-21.

On New Year's Day of 571 B.C. (during our month of April), Ezekiel received his last dated oracle from God. This oracle raises many questions, but it settles at least one. It is simply unthinkable that anyone other than Ezekiel composed this oracle, or the earlier oracles about Egypt and Tyre. Editorial revisions and additions there may well have been. But no disciple in later ages would be quite so inept as to "predict" Tyre's destruction by Nebuchadrezzar, and then try to cover his mistake by making another "prediction" that likewise was not fulfilled. If another than Ezekiel assembled the prophecy into its present form, then he shared his master's fierce honesty. He was determined to save every word that Ezekiel wrote, even when that word seems to present the prophet in an unfavorable light. The light is unfavorable only to those who misunderstand the author's purpose.

After thirteen years of warfare Nebuchadrezzar lifted the siege. During this time his troops were exhausted by their labors. Presumably they attempted to build a mole out to the island, hence "every head was made bald and every shoulder was rubbed bare" by the head-straps on the packs with which the soldiers carried rocks and soil, under fire, out to the end of the mole. In those days troops frequently were paid by the plunder they could extract from the cities they conquered.

Ithobaal II came to some sort of terms with Nebuchadrezzar. Apparently he admitted the suzerainty of Babylon. At least subsequent documents bear the date of the Babylonian monarch. An inscription has been found showing the Tyrian king as a Babylonian official, and a business document dated 564 B.C. reveals that there was a Babylonian high commissioner in Tyre. There is no hint of evidence that the city fell. The troops who carried out the dirty labor were unrewarded.

29:19 Since Nebuchadrezzar had served as God's agent in attacking Tyre, Ezekiel shows God giving him the land to the south, that he may reward his troops with plunder from Egypt, Israel's perfidious ally. Three years after this oracle, in 568 B.C., Nebuchadrezzar did send an expedition against Egypt, as Jeremiah had predicted (Jeremiah 44:30). In 569 B.C. Amasis had overthrown Hophra and seized the throne. Nebuchadrezzar tried to take advantage of the confusion before the new ruler could consolidate his power. Our evidence is extremely sketchy. It seems clear that Nebuchadrezzar did penetrate into Egyptian territory, but he did not devastate the entire land. According to Herodotus (*Persian Wars*, 2, 172), Egypt was fairly prosperous during Amasis' reign.

In the longer perspective of history, Ezekiel was proved right, both about Tyre and Egypt. Tyre today is a ruin. Egypt is stripped of its former might. In 525 B.C. the Persian, Cambyses, overwhelmed Egypt. In 332 B.C. Alexander the Macedonian conquered it. In 30 B.C. the Romans seized power. Since then a dizzying succession of aliens have ruled. Egypt today is not a world conquering power, but is an important agricultural nation, still nourished by the flood and ebb of the Nile.

29:21 "On that day," like so many expressions in Ezekiel, is cryptic. Christian commentators generally believe that it refers to the overthrow of Egypt. But the medieval Jewish scholars thought that it referred to Israel's restoration. The verse echoes 24:27, where the news of Jerusalem's fall will give Ezekiel credence among the exiles. The "horn" is a usual symbol for power and prosperity. Opening the lips is analagous to lifting the blight of "dumbness." So possibly the verse reflects a continued unwillingness of the exiles to believe and trust Ezekiel. He is writing sixteen years after the fall of Jerusalem. The people have begun to hear him. But they do not see how God possibly can deliver them from captivity. Only when Israel at last is secure in his own land will the people "know that there has been a prophet among them" (2:5).

b. The Day of the Lord, 30:1-19.

"The day of the Lord" is a prophetic term to describe the
victory of God. Although "a day of clouds, a time of doom for
30:3 the nations," it is more than brute carnage, it is God's judgment
upon evil and His vindication of good. God gave the prophets
the unwelcome message that "the day" would fall upon the
wicked in Zion (Isaiah 2:12; Amos 5:18; Zephaniah 1:12). Here
30:4 Ezekiel anticipates that "the day" is close at hand for Egypt
and her provinces and allies. Ethiopia is the territory south of
30:5 the rapids at modern Aswan. Put lay on the western coast of the
Red Sea. Lud was probably a district near Put. "The people of
the land that is in league," is literally "the children of the land
of the covenant." Normally this expression would refer to Is-
30:6 rael, but here it probably refers to the political alliances bind-
ing Egypt to her allies, all of whom will fall when Egypt
crumbles.

The description of conquest repeats what has been said before, but there is an added dimension of judgment, "I will
0:13 destroy the idols, and put an end to the images, in Memphis."
"Images" is literally "things of nought," the "not-gods" frequently mentioned in Isaiah, but only here in Ezekiel. The
eight principal cities of Egypt are mentioned by name, in no
discernible geographic order. Three belong to Lower Egypt
and five to Upper Egypt. Religious centers, political capitals
and military fortresses alike will fall. Egypt's "proud might
0:18 shall come to an end . . . Then will they know that I am
0:19 the Lord."

c. Pharaoh's Defeat, 30:20-26.

About four months before Jerusalem fell Ezekiel received
another message from the Lord who said, "I have broken the
0:20 arm of Pharaoh." Probably this refers to Hophra's languid
0:21 attempt to succor Jerusalem, which Nebuchadrezzar easily re-
pulsed (Jeremiah 37:5-8). The reference to a disaster, to be fol-
0:22 lowed shortly by another, certainly suggests that here Ezekiel
is dealing with a historical event that would be known to his
0:25 hearers, coupled with a prediction: Babylon will be the dominant military power in the future, the force of Egypt no longer
0:26 need be reckoned with. But all this is more than shrewd reading of the military probabilities. Ezekiel's message is not that

194   *Ezekiel, Prophecy of Hope*

this or that tyrant will reign for a while, but that God is in charge of all history. Even the disasters—from our human viewpoint—are means of working His final triumph.

d. The Allegory of the Cedar, 31:1-18.

In this section, for reasons given below, I am following the interpretation in AV, though continuing to quote from RSV.

An allegory describing an empire as a gigantic tree is dated about two months after the oracle discussed above. When biblical writers wish to describe a stately tree, they frequently picture the cedar of Lebanon (*cedrus libani*). For once we can be almost sure that we correctly understand one of Ezekiel's botanical allusions. Today the cedar of Lebanon is widely used in lawns and parks; for it is majestic, rising in maturity to a height of eighty feet, with a dense crown of foliage. When grown silviculturally the cedar is a valuable timber tree, as Hiram, king of Tyre, demonstrated long ago by using it in the building of Solomon's Temple (I Kings 5:6). This beautiful and useful tree is being widely used today to reforest the parched, eroded lands of the near east.

RSV follows a conjecture that is accepted by most contemporary students of Ezekiel: the original word was *te'ashshur*, a 31:3   rare term meaning a tall tree. AV, following MT, reads, "Behold, the Assyrian [*ashshur*] was a cedar in Lebanon." It makes no theological difference which interpretation one follows; for it matters little whether one learns the lesson from Assyria or from Egypt. It matters much that one learn the lesson. The linguistic arguments for the conjecture are strong, but the traditional interpretation seems preferable for geographic and botanical reasons. A tree of the mountains would be a most unusual symbol for the palm-studded kingdom by the Nile, though quite understandable for mountainous Assyria. The interpretation followed here is that Ezekiel is addressing Pharaoh, showing him the example of Assyria, only a few years before the most powerful military nation on earth, but reduced to humble submission (in 612 B.C.) by Nabopolasser of Babylon and Cyaxeres, king of the Medes.

The tree rose up with "its top among the clouds," nourished by the waters that God provided. Assyria, like Egypt, had a 31:4   vast irrigation program that sustained its agriculture. Thus bountifully supplied, the tree grew. As it increased in size, the 31:6   cedar offered shelter to "birds," "beasts," and finally to "all

31:7   great nations." This growth and development were not acci-
dental; they formed part of God's plan for the world. In 28:11-
19 Ezekiel likens the prince of Tyre to paradisic man in Eden.
Here the comparison is, if possible, even more bold. Assyria,
31:8   under the figure of a cedar, is called fairer than the trees in
31:9   the Garden of God. The Lord made it so beautiful that "all the
trees of Eden envied it." The "cedar" was guilty of the original
:10   sin, "its heart was proud of its height." The same bitter result
that always eventually follows pride, followed for Assyria. God
:11   "cast it out." "Foreigners" cut down the massive tree, leaving it
:12   to rot in the valley. No longer do "peoples of the earth" rest in
its shadow, but small birds and animals pull away the decaying
:13   bark in their endless search for grubs. (RSV, following a different interpretation, translates the verbs in these and the following verses, as "perfects of certainty," that is, as future tenses. If
the translators are right with their conjecture *te'ashshur*, that
is the correct interpretation of the verbs.)

God asks the men and nations of the world to learn a lesson
from history. He has demonstrated again and again that "pride
:14   goes before destruction, and a haughty spirit before a fall"
(Proverbs 16:18). With the glaring example of Assyria and a
thousand other empires before their eyes, tyrants still seem
unwilling to recognize that man is mortal, "they are all given
over to death." Ezekiel describes man's creaturely, dependent
nature in a strange yet extremely effective manner, calling men
or nations "trees that drink water." Successful, powerful, ty-
rannical men still depend upon the bounty of God for their
survival.

Foreshadowing Pharaoh's descent into the nether world in
the following chapter, the prophet shows that as the "cedar"
:15   went down into Sheol, all the forces of nature mourned, and
the other "trees" grew faint. When the "cedar" fell, the nations
shook at the sound, and all the "trees of Eden" were "com-
:16   forted" in the nether-world. This odd expression—the translation is quite uncertain—probably means that those who had
already experienced God's judgment were "comforted" when
they realized that all, even the most powerful, are judged by
the same God, and brought finally to the same justice. As the
:17   "cedar" was under God's judgment, so are all the nations that
lived under its shadow."

Now the Lord speaks directly to Pharaoh, asking him with

31:18 which of the great past empires he wishes to compare his own, and promising that he too, with all his multitude, will be "brought down with the trees of Eden to the nether world." (The prophet uses a future tense.)

3. Lament for Pharaoh, 32:1-32.

The concluding prophecies against Pharaoh are called a lament (*quinah*). Here this elastic term is used in the sense of a doom song rather than an elegy. The lament is dated almost two years after the preceding chapter. If the date is correct, one can understand the prophet's fierce anger; for Egypt had failed to offer more than a token resistance to Nebuchadrezzar's siege, and Jerusalem had fallen. Of the three sections in the chapter, the first two recapitulate what has already been said, but the third, which is dated earlier, pictures Pharaoh's descent into Sheol. A. B. Davidson accurately describes this section as "one of the most weird passages in literature."

a. The Crocodile Slain, 32:1-8.

The date given in MT falls at the end of February, 585 B.C. The Targum and the Vulgate agree, but the other versions do

32:1 not support this date. The Greek and the Syriac read "the eleventh year," while Jerome notes that Aquila gives "the tenth year." Probably MT is right in the date. When he knew that Jerusalem had fallen, Ezekiel proclaimed that Egypt too lay under the judgment of God. Ezekiel was not a man of stone— as many of his writings would seem to indicate—he had a full supply of human feelings. And here he demonstrates amply his feeling of betrayal. Egypt had made an alliance with Judah, and Hophra had tossed it aside when he saw that keeping the alliance would be costly.

Pharaoh has been wont to think of himself as a "lion," the king of beasts, stalking where he will through jungle or desert.

32:2 Rather, he is like a "crocodile," a beast that is savage enough, but limited to the water for his sphere of real activity. (In biblical usage, "sea" does not necessarily refer to the ocean. The "Sea of Galilee" is what we would call a lake, about thirteen miles in length. In the Temple was a sacrificial vessel some eighteen feet in diameter. Even this was called the "sea" [I Kings 7:23].) A crocodile is not a fragrant reptile. Its presence

32:3 will "foul" the waters. The crocodile is large and fierce, but it

32:4 can be captured. The Lord warns that He will snare the monster, and drag it up onto the bank of the river where the buzzards and jackals will feast on its flesh. The reference to mountains and valleys is perfectly understandable. Egypt has attempted to be an empire, dominating other lands distant from the Nile. The extent of destruction goes even beyond that pictured in 31:15; for even the stars and the sun will be blotted out and darkness will cover the land that was Egypt.

b. Babylon the Destroyer, 32:9-16.

When Egypt falls, many nations will be "appalled," and the kings will "shudder." Again Ezekiel shows the kings trembling for the wrong reasons. (See 26:17f.) They are not looking to the moral cause for Egypt's fall, but are convulsed with an animal terror, lest they fall next. The king of Babylon will descend upon the land, destroying both man and beast; so that neither the foot of man nor the hoof of cattle can roil the waters. The Nile is turbid, for geological reasons that we clearly understand today. This muddiness of the water suggests Egypt's foreign policy to Ezekiel. In a picturesque figure of speech he says that, when the perfidious Egyptians no longer trouble the waters, the Nile will run clear and as smooth as a river of oil.

c. Pharaoh's Descent into Sheol, 32:17-32.

The prophecies of doom against Tyre (Babylon?) and Egypt come to a close with an eerie vision of Egypt's descent into Sheol to join the other defeated nations. During the century and a half before Ezekiel's time, all of the world-shaking powers in the middle east had been overthrown, save Tyre and Egypt alone. Here the prophet foretells Egypt's overthrow and humiliation. For dramatic power, the section is unsurpassed. However it has produced more than its share of theological difficulties, since various sects appeal to its weird imagery to support their views of life after death. In Sheol, Ezekiel shows the several nations gathered together as units, with no hint of individual immortality. This fact alone should suggest that the passage is symbolic rather than doctrinal.

In other OT passages Sheol is a vague, shadowy sort of half-life, where no significant relationship with God is possible (Isaiah 38:18; Psalm 115:17, etc.). Later passages show the beginnings of a faith that the most meaningful bond in life cannot be destroyed by mere physical death (Job 19:27; Daniel 12:2). Even so, when Jesus came, the biblical literalists, or Sadducees, denied the possibility of any resurrection, because the

Torah does not justify such a belief (Matthew 22:23). Jesus joined with the Pharisees, who, in this regard, accepted the spirit rather than the letter of the Law. The imagery of heaven that has seized the Christian imagination is that used by Ezekiel's disciple John, on Patmos, who employed the prophet's concepts and word pictures to portray a life where "the glory of God is its light, and its lamp is the Lamb" (Revelation 21:23). In a book like Ezekiel that is filled with symbolic representation, one should use caution about giving a literal, doctrinal interpretation to details concerning which the NT is far more explicit.

32:17   RSV follows LXX, reading "in the first month," where the Hebrew omits the month. It would be more natural to assume the twelfth month, making this lamentation two weeks after the date in 32:1, though, as we have noticed, the oracles are not always in chronological order. In this lament Ezekiel personifies Egypt as a woman. Occasionally he varies the figure of speech,

32:18   depicting Pharaoh as the embodiment of his empire. Egypt descends to the nether world with the other "daughters of majestic nations." Three different terms are used, "the nether world," "the Pit," and two verses later, "Sheol." There is little apparent difference in the meaning of the terms. Alike they are synonyms for death.

With surprisingly gentle irony, Ezekiel asks the queen who is to die, "Whom do you surpass in beauty?" Either the last half

32:19   of the verse is addressed to Pharaoh or one should accept its emotional rather than its literal content. Dr. Moffatt has well expressed the meaning by his translation, "a shameful death."

32:20   The changing pronouns are confusing. "They" probably refers to the Egyptian soldiers who failed to defend Jerusalem and will fail to defend their own land. "Her multitudes" presumably

32:21   are the civilians of Egypt. "The mighty chiefs" of defeated empires extend to the newcomers their ghostly welcome.

First among the "mighty chiefs" is Assyria, only a quarter-century before the dominant power in the world. With the

32:22   graves of their victims round about them, the conquerors from
32:23   Nineveh lie now in the grave "all of them slain, fallen by the sword, who spread terror in the land of the living."

Elam ("highlands") was a region east of the Tigris. In the time of Abraham, Elam was the regnant power in Mesopotamia,

2:24   with a dominion that extended even to Palestine (Genesis 14: 1-11). During the eighth and seventh centuries B.C., as Assyria was growing more and more powerful, the Elamites provided strong opposition, but gradually the Assyrians won out until, in 645 B.C., they conquered Shushan, the capital city of Elam. With the fall of Nineveh, Elam sprang back as a military force.

2:25   Even so, here Ezekiel pictures the dead warriors of the past, "placed among the slain."

Meshech was a region in the mountains north of Assyria, bounded by Tubal on the west. These peoples have already

2:26   been mentioned in connection with the Phonecian trade (27: 13), and they are to be mentioned again among the warriors of Gog (38:2). Evidently the mountaineers were a brutal, warlike folk who had been brutally conquered.

Possibly we have in a difficult verse an early recognition of distinctions among the dead. Apparently the warriors of Me-

2:27   shech and Tubal lie in a less honored place than the soldiers from other nations, with their "iniquities" (see footnote in RSV) "upon their bones." The distinctions in Sheol lie between the circumcised and the uncircumcised, between those who received an honorable burial and those left unburied, and here, apparently, a place of reproach is reserved for those who have abused military power.

In 25:12-14 and 35:2-15 Edom's destruction lies in the future. It seems odd to find such a tiny kingdom listed among the

2:29   world-shaking military powers. But this is a matter of perspective. A mad dog nearby can be far more dangerous than a distant lion. To a dweller in Jerusalem Edom was a force to be reckoned with. Here Ezekiel consigns this force to Sheol.

Sidon, like Edom, was a petty state. The siege against Tyre gave Sidon a chance to surge back toward her ancient promi-

2:30   nence. This oracle, dated the second year of that siege, shows Sidon as leader among the "princes of the north," a collective term for the Syrian principalities.

When Pharaoh sees the militant host of past ages assembled in the vasty halls of death, "he will comfort himself for all his

2:31   multitude." In the solemn grandeur of Ezekiel's thought, we should not interpret this "comfort" in such glib terms as "mis-

2:32   ery loves company." Rather the prophet shows even Pharaoh, the blindest of the blind, coming finally to realize that God's

goal is just. Pharaoh has chosen the life of conquest rather than
the life of the spirit. In due season he will receive the inevitable
consequence of his choice.

II. PROPHECIES OF ISRAEL'S RESTORATION, 33:1–37:28.

After thirty-two blood-soaked chapters, we come finally to
the positive message. There is only one date given in this section of five chapters, and there are reasons for questioning that.
But the general situation is clear enough. Jerusalem has fallen.
No longer need the prophet issue his grave warnings. Now he
must teach his people to hope. In former days, when Israel in
exile was making a comfortable adjustment to life in Babylon
and only Ezekiel looked into the future with dread, the people
gave him little heed. Now they are crushed with despair, and
only he is able to look ahead with confidence. It is Ezekiel's task
to communicate this confidence to a grief-stricken, cynical
people.

In his message of hope, Ezekiel gives some of the deepest
theological insights to be found in the entire prophecy, particularly in Chapter 33, where he examines in unparalleled depth
the meaning of individual responsibility, in Chapter 36 where
he shows that salvation is by grace alone, and in Chapter 37
where the OT gives its finest teaching about the Holy Spirit.
Chapter 37 contains the best-known symbol in the book, the
valley of dry bones brought to life and usefulness by the Spirit
of God. This chapter ends with a description of Israel returned
to his land, the old division of the kingdom ended, the people
cleansed from their former superstitions, living in the light of
God's law, and worshiping in His sanctuary.

Needless to say, Ezekiel sings his song of hope in a minor key,
with strong dissonances and jarring rhythms. We have come to
expect all sorts of difficulty in reading Ezekiel. This section ful-
fills our expectation to abundance. Even so, as we read through
the five chapters, we see, however dimly, what the prophet is
telling the world. Through the lowering storm cloud shines the
eternal, unquenchable light.

A. From Judgment to Hope, 33:1-33.

Chapter 33 forms a transition from the preceding negative

message to the song of triumph. In this chapter Ezekiel takes up and re-examines the prophet's task as watchman and the doctrine of individual responsibility from a viewpoint different from that expressed in earlier chapters. When Jerusalem finally has fallen, the prophet no longer is "dumb." But still he records bitterly that, while the people gather to hear him, and while they talk with each other about his messages, and while they express love for the prophet who has chastised them, their minds are set on material gain. Still they do not take Ezekiel seriously.

We know what Ezekiel did not know. Some of the people actually listened. Out of horror piled upon horror in exile Israel salvaged a faith, a culture, and a nation from inevitable destruction. Never before in human history had such a thing happened. Statistically the restoration of Israel was impossible. More than any other individual, Ezekiel made it possible.

1. The Prophet's Responsibility, 33:1-9.

This passage uses the figure of speech in 3:16-21 to express the basic principles expounded in 14:1-11 and 18:1-32. Ezekiel has tried—only God and Ezekiel know how he has tried—to warn Israel. Israel has failed to repent, but the prophet's conscience is clean. It was suggested in the earlier chapters that "life" should be understood as communion with God, "death" as alienation from God. Almost certainly Ezekiel is not talking about heaven and hell as understood by Christians. Even a person with quite limited powers of observation has noticed that righteous people die, physically, and wicked people sometimes live to an advanced age. But spiritual "life," or communion with God, is possible for exiles by the Chebar whose capital city is ashes, if they will repent of their sins.

God has appointed some men to be prophets. One of these elect men describes his prophetic task by picturing a military
33:2 sentinel. If the watchman is alert and issues the needful warn-
33:3 ing, then each citizen is responsible for taking the necessary
33:4 steps to save his life and the city. But if the watchman fails to
33:5 do his duty, then he must bear the moral responsibility for the
33:6 carnage that follows. This much was common ground to Ezekiel and his hearers. They could agree about the responsibility of a military sentinel.

The application of the principle to Ezekiel as the prophet was the point of disagreement. The prophet affirms again his

33:7 God-given responsibility to warn Israel. In the maze of political involvements through which we have been trying to find our way, we may have lost sight of the real enemy. Here Ezekiel tells us firmly, clearly, that the real enemy is not Babylon, not Egypt, not Tyre or Edom, or any other kingdom, but sin. On earth man lives in a "political" environment that deeply influences his "spiritual" life, as Ezekiel has abundantly demonstrated.

33:8 The prophet's unpopular duty, whatever the political context, is to warn the sinner, "O wicked man, you shall surely die." If the prophet fails to warn, then he and the sinner alike will

33:9 "die." If the prophet does his duty and the sinner fails to repent, then the man who has chosen to live on in his iniquity will "die," but the prophet who issued the warning will "live."

2. The Hearer's Responsibility, 33:10-20.

The exiles around Ezekiel believed fatalistically that they were doomed to suffer and die in Babylon because Manasseh sinned a century before. Under these circumstances, they saw little profit in individual righteousness. If individuals are not striving to be righteous, there can be no community righteousness. To his despairing compatriots, Ezekiel makes four fundamental points of moral life. He has said these things before, and will say them again, but here they are presented in their sharpest outline. (1) God desires that men shall live. (2) Life must be an individual choice. (3) The way to life is repentance. (4) Man, who is free to sin, is free to repent.

> These principles of the worth and freedom of the individual man, though latent in many parts of the Old Testament, had never been stated so explicitly before. . . . If pressed indeed and regarded as exhaustive (as everything in this prophet is pressed to his disadvantage), they might seem to ascribe more power to man than he possesses. But in subsequent chapters the prophet lays sufficient emphasis upon the operation of God in regenerating the individual mind and in founding the new kingdom.
>
> —A. B. Davidson

Again Ezekiel sums up the thoughts of the exiles in one brief, cynical sentence. They felt that God had chosen to punish them

33:10 for another's sin. They could see no use in repenting. Even if this sentence was written before the exiles had confirmation that Jerusalem had fallen, still they knew that the siege was long continued, and that the hope of Egyptian relief had failed.

Before them lay nothing but the continued horrors of existence in Babylon.

33:11 The Lord swears an oath by His own Life. This oath recurs thirteen times in Ezekiel, far more frequently than in any other prophecy. It is God's pleasure that man shall live. A man may punish an enemy for the sake of revenge, but when God punishes a sinner it is that he may repent and know the Lord. And now Ezekiel addresses the bleak despair that has overcome Israel in exile, proclaiming that man is not chained to his

33:12 past, whether for good or for evil. In the world where the light of God shines among the storm clouds, no man is so bad that he is totally beyond hope, while no man is so good that he can afford to be complacent.

Again Ezekiel strips morality to the bare bones, and presents some ideal case studies that lack the complexity of all human

33:13 conduct. These are not historical examples of faith, but concrete ways of illustrating abstract principles, warnings against complacency, urgings to repent. A "righteous" man "trusts in his righteousness" rather than looking to God for daily strength. He sins and "dies." Ezekiel is *not* saying that God pays no attention to a man's previous life, nor is he talking about a good person who dies (biologically) in an evil moment. He is talking about the whole course of a man's life, announcing the principle that man is free to change it if he will. Of far more practical

33:14 importance, the "wicked" man can repent and live. Repentance
33:15 must be more than lip-service to God. The sinner "restores the pledge, gives back what he has taken by robbery, and walks in

33:16 the statutes of life." The one who sincerely repents can know the healing of God's forgiveness. "He shall surely live."

An early church father, alluding to the passage above, both sheds light upon its meaning and illustrates the elusive nature of certainty in all studies about Ezekiel.

The Master of the universe Himself spoke of repentance with an oath: "For as I live, says the Lord, I do not desire the death of the sinner but his repentance." He added, too, this generous consideration: "Repent, O House of Israel, of your iniquity. Say to the sons of my people, 'Should your sins reach from earth to heaven, and be redder than scarlet and blacker than sackcloth, and should you turn to me with your whole heart and say "Father," I will heed you as though you were a holy people.'"
—Clement's First Letter,
Early Christian Fathers, p. 47

The citation resembles yet differs from the passage in Ezekiel. Although this may be explained by Clement's practice of making a rather free rendering rather than a direct quotation, many believe that Clement was following a text of Ezekiel that differs markedly from ours.

3. The Prophet Vindicated, 33:21-33.

The date when the prophet finally received word that Jerusalem had fallen has given rise to immeasurable discussion because of the discrepancy with Jeremiah 39:2; 52:5-7, and II Kings 25:3, where the fall of Jerusalem is dated the fourth month of the eleventh year. This seems to give a time lag of eighteen months for transmitting the news. After making every possible allowance for the snail-pace of travel in other days, the delay still is incredible. Some Hebrew manuscripts, some Greek manuscripts, and the Syriac have a different date in Ezekiel that reads "the eleventh year," thereby making a gap of six months, which is more reasonable. It is now generally agreed that by the calendar used in Jeremiah and Kings the year began in the autumn, while Ezekiel followed the Babylonian custom, beginning the year in the spring. Nebuchadrezzar took the city in July 586 B.C.; the bitter news reached Ezekiel in January 585. Possibly jeering Babylonians had told the exiles, who refused to believe until confirmation came from a brother Hebrew. They must wait for a fugitive who perhaps had taken work as a camel driver with a caravan making the interminable journey to bring his brothers in faith the unbearable news.

The night before the fugitive brought his news, "the hand of the Lord" fell upon Ezekiel. This term here means, as throughout the prophecy, a state of prophetic rapture. Such states had come upon Ezekiel frequently. There is no suggestion that this time he had any special premonition of the messenger's arrival. (Some commentators make light of the divine visitation immediately before the earthly event. They might profitably answer one question: Did God know that the messenger would arrive the following day?)

In these pages, Ezekiel's "dumbness" has been considered as inability to persuade others that he had a message from God. The foregoing chapters have shown Ezekiel speaking and others listening, but there has been little evidence that the exiles took to heart what the prophet said. Now the word comes. Jerusalem

33:21

33:22

has fallen. Ezekiel is proved right. Whether they will or no, the people must listen. No longer is Ezekiel "dumb"; he speaks as a spokesman for God.

We recognize that the oracles in our Book of Ezekiel do not fall in the same order that the prophet received them. As re-
33:24 corded here, the first message following Jerusalem's fall serves to identify the true Israel. Jerusalem is destroyed, yet there are Hebrews living in the "waste places" about Judea. These, quite naturally, expect to carry on the Hebrew tradition, a tradition
33:25 inseparably bound to the Promised Land. Ezekiel shatters this complacency. Those who persistently wallow in sin, the same
33:26 sin that has destroyed Jerusalem, shall not "possess the land."
33:27 Instead, these residents of Palestine will be subject to the same devastation that has destroyed the city. Thus negatively Ezekiel prepares the way for the message that has been implicit, and henceforth will be explicit. The future of Israel is in the hands of the exiles. The promise is linked to a particular land, but mere physical residence in that land is not enough to make one heir to the promise. That requires repentance, righteousness, and personal commitment to the Lord. Ezekiel must prepare his people to be Abraham's worthy heirs.

Ezekiel's status is changed. No longer do his neighbors refer to him as that madman who thinks he is a prophet. Now they
33:30 say, "Come, and hear what the word is that comes forth *from the Lord.*" Instead of briers and thorns, "with their lips they
33:31 show much love." Yes, Ezekiel's status in the community has changed radically, but the transformation he has sought among the exiles is slow to take place. Still "their heart is set on their gain." At last Ezekiel has a hearing, but he is not satisfied. He has an audience, not a congregation. His neighbors listen
33:32 to him, but they do not hear. The Lord warns that for the immediate future he must expect to be "like one who sings love songs." This does not mean that the Lord, or Ezekiel, thinks the songs hitherto have been lovely. Rather, the prophet has an attentive audience, but the people in it give him no more serious heed than they would give a skillful entertainer.

The concluding verse is puzzling. "When this comes . . ." When what comes? The usual explanation is the fulfillment of
33:33 all Ezekiel's predictions, of which one has been fulfilled. If this were his meaning, it would be far more natural for the prophet to say, "When these things come." As we have noticed, Ezekiel

does not always do what we would think natural. We must remain in doubt about the prophet's exact meaning. Even so, a
clause naturally and normally refers to what has been said
before. The people "hear what you say but they will not do it.
When this comes . . ." When the people actually do what Ezekiel has been urging them to do, then they will recognize that
in fact he was a spokesman for God, just as was promised in 2:5.

B. The Shepherds and the Flock, 34:1-31.

Ezekiel is realistic. He teaches consistently that "spiritual" life
takes place in what we call a "political" context. So the prophecy of hope, that begins by examining the prophet's role in
society, and ends with an extended vision of the coming temple,
here looks at the earthly monarch.

Ezekiel sees the many failures in Israel's political past. The
prophet Samuel looked forward to monarchy with justified fear
(I Samuel 8:11-18). King Saul proved a meager blessing to his
people (I Samuel 14-31). Even David, with all his good work,
still employed the system of forced labor (II Samuel 20:24). Under Solomon the kingdom prospered, at a tragic cost in human
welfare (I Kings 12:4). Though later kings were less prosperous
than Solomon, many continued to chastise the people with
whips, some with scorpions (I Kings 12:11). Prophets before
Ezekiel had examined the monarchy and found it sadly want-
ing (e.g., Micah 2:1-11; 3:1-12; and Jeremiah 23:1-6, upon
which this section is based).

Ezekiel examines the monarch under the figure of a shepherd.
He reaches the conclusion that a king, as such, is not needful
for the public welfare, that only God is Shepherd over Israel.
His words foreshadow the parable of Christ as the Good Shepherd in John 10:1-16; hence Christians can, without reading
meanings into the passage, find here another prophecy of the
coming Messiah.

Ezekiel's words carried great weight in following generations. Israel stands as one of the few nations before Christ that
survived over centuries without a king. Naturally some form
of government was needful. From the time of Moses until the
time of Saul, for which our information is quite incomplete,
"judges" ruled over Israel. Eli, by virtue of his office as high
priest, served as "judge" (I Samuel 4:18). Samuel acted in this
capacity because he was a prophet of the Lord (I Samuel 7:15).
Undoubtedly many others judged whose names are lost to us.

Then for approximately four centuries kings ruled the land. Despite an occasional Hezekiah or Josiah, and despite his personal loyalty to Zedekiah, Ezekiel looks back and sees that monarchy has failed just as Samuel had predicted. Following the return from the exile, the Jews survived centuries more without a king. The high priest acted as official head of the nation. In 140 B.C. the people entrusted all the functions of king to Simon the Hashmonean, but they carefully withheld from him the title (I Maccabees 14:41ff.). Simon's son, John Hyrcanus, called himself king, at the cost of a bitter rupture with the religious leaders. The Hashmonean dynasty fell in 63 B.C., to be followed by the Herodian puppets. Thus, from the days of Ezekiel, Israel knew no king of the Davidic line until a small minority accepted Him whose Kingdom is not of this world.

1. The Evil Shepherds, 34:1-10.

As the prophet is a watchman, so the king is, or ought to be, a shepherd. With his keen sense of social responsibility, Ezekiel
34:2 asks bitingly, "Should not shepherds feed the sheep?" Looking back upon the past four centuries of monarchy, he says that rather the shepherds of Israel have fed themselves, at the ex-
34:3 pense of the flock. Negatively, and yet beautifully, Ezekiel describes the task of a king: to strengthen the weak, to heal the sick,
33:4 to bind up the crippled, to bring back the strayed, and to seek the lost. Israel's nominal shepherds have fallen far below these
34:5 high standards of social justice. The result of the shepherds' failure lay stark before Ezekiel. Jerusalem was in ashes, the Temple was destroyed, and the future lay in the hands of a pathetic little group of exiles. In terms of the metaphor, the people of Israel "became food for all the wild beasts."

Now we find something that has been conspicuously missing from the prophecy of Ezekiel, a note of tenderness, "My sheep."
34:6 The people whom earthly shepherds have buffeted about are God's people. They have no earthly reason left for hope. The sheep are "scattered over all the face of the earth, with none to search or seek for them." Political institutions have failed to save Israel. But God has not forgotten. The people of the covenant are still "My sheep." This is the basis for the prophecy of hope that follows, a prophecy that was fulfilled in the turmoil of history.

As spokesman for God, Ezekiel addresses the shepherds. Again

he uses the personal pronoun, "My shepherds." But this time
34:8   the effect is not tender, rather it is terrifying. If Israel stands
in a special relationship with God, then clearly those who bear
responsibility for Israel bear a special responsibility to God.
34:10   Since the shepherds have abused their privilege, God Himself
will rescue the sheep from the shepherds.

2. God, the True Shepherd, 34:11-22.

The monarchy as an institution must end. God alone will be
King over Israel. The ideal of a theocracy is frequently ex-
34:11   pressed in the Old Testament (Judges 8:23; I Samuel 8:7;
10:19; 12:12,17; Hosea 8:4,10; 10:3; 13:10f.). Nowhere is the
ideal more clearly expressed than in this passage. Now speaking
positively, Ezekiel cries that God will do what the shepherds
have failed to do. He foretells that the Lord will rescue His
34:12   sheep from the places to which they have been scattered, and
34:13   that He will bring them back "into their own land," where
34:14   they will enjoy material abundance, but far more important,
34:15   where they will know that God is watching over them constantly. RSV follows the Greek, "the fat and the strong I will
34:16   watch over." MT reads, "I will destroy." The Hebrew ties in
closely with the following verses, where God serves as Judge
over the flock, restraining the strong from their impositions
upon the weak, but the reading in the Greek is superior by
every moral criterion; for strength is not evil in itself, strength
abused is evil. Even in the ideal kingdom, some people will be
stronger than others. God will feed both the strong and the
weak, in justice.

This passage more closely approaches Jesus' basic teaching
about the nature of God than any other in the OT, even the
beloved Psalm 23. (See especially Luke 15:3-7.) Jesus drew on it,
both for the figure of speech, and more important, for the
thought of God as seeking lost man. Another prophet said, with
more beauty than Ezekiel could command, "Seek the Lord while
he may be found, call upon him while he is near" (Isaiah 55:6).
And this is man's usual picture of deity: One whom we can, by
much searching, discover. Jesus, like Ezekiel, heavily emphasizes man's responsibility to seek, but He goes far beyond. Like
Ezekiel, He teaches us to think of God as the compassionate
Shepherd who hunts through the wilderness to rescue the strays.
Then Jesus goes beyond Ezekiel. He shows us in act the Shep-

herd in whom God is embodied laying down His life for the
sheep.

The Shepherd who is merciful must likewise be stern when
the occasion demands. He will "judge between sheep and sheep,
4:17 rams and he-goats." This figure foreshadows the parable of the
Last Judgment in Matthew 25:31ff., but there is a different
usage. Here the Lord is not dividing the sheep from the goats,
4:18 but judging between those sheep, rams, and goats that have
4:19 abused their strength and those that have suffered from this
4:20 abuse. Always the realist, Ezekiel shows the dangers inherent in
power, any kind of power, as the Lord sternly addresses the
4:21 "fat sheep." Yet, despite human abuses of power within Israel,
4:22 God promises, "I will save my flock."

3. The Ideal Shepherd to Come, 34:23-31.

When Israel is restored "I will set up over them one shepherd,
my servant David." The phrase, quite naturally, has occasioned
4:23 considerable discussion. The bare minimum of meaning is that
there will be no further unhappy division of the people into
two kingdoms, Judah and Israel. Some have found here a prediction of the regency when Zerubbabel was appointed by
Cyrus as political ruler over the returning exiles (Ezra 1-3).
Some think this is a contradiction with 34:15, where God promises, "I myself will be the shepherd," though that promise comes
before the restoration, while this concerns the period after. But
most believe this passage a foretelling of the Messiah who is to
come. Christians and Jews alike find this meaning here. The
disagreement lies in the question of historical fact, whether or
not Jesus of Nazareth is the promised Shepherd. Without attempting to claim that Ezekiel teaches the doctrine of the Holy
Trinity, one may yet mention that the Shepherd-Prince is not
He whom Christians call God the Father, yet He bears the same
title and does the same work.

Ezekiel promises further that the Shepherd-Prince will be
"my servant David." The phrase, taken in isolation, might seem
4:24 to give some biblical support to the Hindu teaching of reincar-
nation. This teaching, which offers such a fascination to the
modern mind, is the direct antithesis of the belief that God is
Savior. Similar expressions in the Bible are to be understood as
figures of speech, not as denials of the basic message. The great
Hebrew commentator Kimchi said of this passage: David is
"the Messiah who will rise from his [David's] seed in the time

of salvation." Ezekiel has castigated the monarchy as an institution, yet he recognizes that there must be leadership, and he recognizes the house and lineage of David as the only legitimate royalty in Israel.

The ideal "David" to come will be "my servant," who will, like his predecessor, be a man after God's own heart (I Samuel 13:14). Contemporary Christians sometimes find it difficult to understand the high esteem in which biblical writers hold King David. The Bible describes David's noble attributes and actions, but the same Bible tells about the hideous affair with Uriah's wife (II Samuel 11:2-27), and it shows David as less than a successful father (II Samuel 13-18). It must be said to David's credit that he brought peace and unity to a land that long had known nothing but internal and external strife. In most of the surrounding kingdoms it would have caused little public comment if the king had taken the wife of a brave soldier. It is no credit to David that he acted like a near-eastern monarch of his time. But it is to his eternal credit that, when he had sinned, he repented. Christians today who look to David's sin forgetting his repentance might profitably re-examine their whole concept of what is important in spiritual life.

God's servant David is to be a "prince." (In 37:22, 24, where the David-concept reappears, he is called "king," though LXX reads "prince.") The distinction between God, the Shepherd-King, and His servant David, the Shepherd-Prince, is quite consistent with the Christian doctrine of the Holy Trinity—God the Father is not God the Son, yet each is God. Ezekiel does not look forward to the restoration of monarchy as the Hebrews, unhappily, had known it. But he is looking forward to an earthly ruler who will fully exemplify the noblest qualities of the king who came closest to the ideal during four long centuries of history.

34:25   At the end of its most savage condemnation, the prophecy foretells "I will establish with you an everlasting covenant" (16:60). Here Ezekiel picks up the loose thread and weaves it back into the tapestry. God promises "to make [literally "cut"] with them a covenant of peace." The peculiar verb alludes to a Semitic practice. When two men made a solemn compact, they would slay an animal and cut it in half. The two would stand between the halves and thus figuratively unite their lives in the life of the victim. (See W. R. Smith, *Religion of the Semites,*

p. 481.) The beauty of the covenant is symbolized by safety in
the wilderness, where a man will be able to sleep even in the
depth of the forest without fear of wild beasts. (See Leviticus
26:6; Hosea 2:18.)

The Lord promises to make "the places round about my hill
a blessing." Probably this means the "high places" liberally
34:26 scattered through the land, to which the prophet has often
referred (e.g., 20:28). The Hebrew noun is different, but the
context leads us to think that the very locations which once
were a curse upon Israel will be turned into blessings. In an
arid land like Palestine men look with gratitude to God for the
blessing of rainfall. The Lord promises that in the days to come
the rains will come "in their season; they shall be showers of
blessings." This last phrase is one of few expressions from Ezekiel that have entered the language of popular piety. The
phrase is the heart of this passage about the restoration. Showers
in season are good, in what we would call a material sense.
These showers are likewise symbolic of blessedness, in what we
would call a spiritual sense. Similarly we should understand the
freedom from wild beasts in the verse preceding, and the abundant harvest in the verse following.

The phrase "they shall know that I am the Lord" has sounded
through the prophecy like a trump of doom. But now it rever-
34:27 berates with joy, as the Lord promises to "break the bars of
their yoke." A Palestinian ox yoke consisted of a heavy timber,
roughly hewn to fit the necks of the oxen. In this timber were
bored four holes, through which were fitted bars that enclosed
the necks of the oxen. The Lord promises to break these "bars,"
and to deliver his people "from the hand of those who enslaved
them." This passage is Ezekiel's bitterest overt criticism of
Babylon. He has wept and prayed that his people might not
rebel against the Babylonian yoke. He has recognized the Babylonian captivity as God's instrument for purifying His people
from their many sins. But he has consistently maintained that
the Lord's goal during this enslavement is to set His people
free, physically free, spiritually free. Instead of a meager sub-
34:29 sistence level Israel will enjoy "prosperous plantations." (By a
slight rearrangement of the Hebrew Letters, LXX translates "a
plant of peace." But MT is far more probable.) There will be
no more tragic droughts, like that described in 14:13f. In an
agricultural catalogue of blessings, fertility is the blessing that

34:30 follows the gentle rain and man's freedom to till the soil, untroubled by "beasts of the land." But Ezekiel is using agriculture as a symbol. The symbolized blessing is "they shall know that I, the Lord their God, am with them, and that they, the house of Israel, are my people."

"My people." "My sheep." Again the note of tenderness, as the prophet concludes the picture of the ideal Shepherd-Prince
34:31 to come. Ezekiel is not teaching the Christian doctrine of the Holy Trinity; still Christians must see something significant in the relationship between the Shepherd-Prince and the Shepherd-King. Christians have sometimes contrasted the mercy and forgiveness of Christ with the just severity of the Father. Such division of purpose is totally alien to the truth. God's purpose, the purpose of the Father and of the Son and of the Holy Ghost, is redemptive. God the Father works through agents, including the Shepherd-Prince, but always His people remain "My sheep."

C. Israel's Restoration, 35:1—37:28.

Ezekiel has never pictured the Babylonian collapse, unless the doom of Tyre (26-28) is such a picture. Under the circumstances, it would have been most inexpedient for him to foretell the overthrow of Babylon, which must be a prelude to Israel's liberation. But here, in a brief chapter, he clears away the final obstacle to the exiles' return. Edom was Israel's "perpetual" enemy, hence a symbol for all other enemies. Ezekiel's contemporaries would realize that the fall of Edom could make little difference to the exiles unless there had been some other major cataclysms.

Chapter 36, which describes the restoration, is the brightest passage in the entire book. It begins with the cleansing of the land. Christian thinkers finally are beginning to realize that this is not a figure of speech; for God who created man likewise created the good earth by which man lives. We are in spiritual peril when we abuse the land that God has entrusted to us. Our faith is deeply and properly concerned with food, clothing, and shelter, all products of the earth, which is the Lord's. Christians are in danger of "spiritualizing" the faith to the point of complete irrelevance to our earthly needs. The chapter concludes with a renewed emphasis upon man's creaturely nature, as the Lord promises to take away "the heart of stone" and to give His people "a heart of flesh." In this section Ezekiel reaffirms his basic message that—in NT terms—salvation is by grace alone.

The vision of the valley of dry bones in Chapter 37 is deservedly the best known passage in Ezekiel. Other parts of the prophecy sometimes require from us an effort of imagination to understand their present relevance, but no one who is engaged in church work today is alien either to the despair or to the hope that fill this vision.

The section about the restoration ends with a vision of the old hostility ended, the two kingdoms united, and the people gladly serving God under the leadership of their Shepherd-Prince. Perhaps it would be more pertinent to stress the present application of this thought than its political ramifications in the fourth or third century B.C. Today this passage cries aloud that it is never God's will for His people to remain separated from one another.

1. The Final Obstacle Removed, 35:1-15.

Since Ezekiel has already predicted the downfall of Edom (25:12-14), some commentators find this chapter superfluous; so

35:2 they suggest a date for its composition years or centuries after the time of the prophet, reflecting a set of political conditions quite different from those immediately following the fall of Jerusalem. However, as Dr. Ellison suggests, "Since it is Ezekiel we are studying, we cannot go far wrong, if we look for a symbolic meaning." He suggests further that the reader examine

35:3 the most unusual designation for Edom, "Mount Seir." This was the mountain range in Edom. The name occurs elsewhere in the OT simply as a geographical expression. Esau, the man who greedily despised his birthright, went to dwell on Mount Seir, or, as sometimes it is called, "Mount Esau." Thus the chapter may be aimed, not at a tiny little near-eastern kingdom, but at every people in every clime whose greed blinds them to moral value. Edom became "a desolation and a waste." But the people today are many who turn aside from God's way and cloak their spiritual hollowness by hating those who are loyal to their Lord. Does the future belong to the forces leagued against God or to those who remain faithful to Him? This is the question answered in Chapter 35, not the destiny of one small country.

Edom—the kingdom, not the symbol—"cherished perpetual enmity" against Israel. The enmity goes back to Esau's hatred

35:5 for Jacob (Genesis 27:41). Moses sought permission to lead the children of Israel through the land of Edom on the way to the Promised Land. The King of Edom refused to allow this (Numbers 20:14-21). Even so, the Edomites were considered closer akin to Israel than were other neighboring people (Deuteronomy 23:7f.). The kinship that should have united the two nations served rather to divide them. The balance of power seesawed back and forth over the centuries, as the reader may learn by reading the books of Kings and Chronicles. Ezekiel implies that the Edomites aided the Chaldaean forces in the destruction of Jerusalem. This is quite probable. Nebuchadrezzar augmented his army with local troops when undertaking a major siege (e.g., II Kings 24:2).

Today we would rephrase one of Ezekiel's essential messages by saying abstractly that this is a moral universe in which ac-

35:6 tions have consequences. The prophet says the same thing concretely, "blood shall pursue you because you are guilty of blood." He amplifies the statement in more detail than modern

35:9 taste considers desirable. But he concludes, at the end of his catalogue of horrors, "Then you will know that I am the Lord."

After the fall of Jerusalem, Edomites began to move into the former kingdom of Judah. Ezekiel intimates that they likewise

35:10 aspired to occupy the former kingdom of Israel, where doubtless they met counter pressures from other land hungry people. The tide of immigration was not reversed until the time of John Hyrcanus in 126 B.C. (I Maccabees 5:3,65). The prophet attacks not so much Edom's greed for land as Edom's blindness to the spiritual values attached to that land. Again he raises without answering the question: how far is a person, or a nation, responsible to see and embrace the truth embodied in an alien culture? The Edomites did not see or else they ignored the glory of God being revealed through Israel.

The Edomites, whose hills will become a desolation and a waste, have said of the Judean hills, "they are laid desolate, they

35:12 are given us to devour." So doing, Edom attacks not only the Hebrews, but God Himself. Hence the Lord promises to make

35:13 Edom desolate "for the rejoicing of the whole earth." The

35:14 passage is a wry expression of redemptive hope. The present human state is such that Edom's avarice looks normal and natural. The destruction of greed in one little kingdom could scarcely bring joy to the world without a profound change in human hearts. This change will take place, slowly perhaps, but certainly. Such acts as God's judgment upon Edom will lead men and nations to cleanse their hearts of moral evil, as they realize that the divine purpose in history is redemptive, not vindictive. With cleansed hearts, men can look at history through eyes of faith, and then they will rejoice because greed is being stamped out, and far more important, because God is Lord.

2. Prophecy to the Mountains of Israel, 36:1-15.

Chapter 6 is a grim warning to the mountains of Israel that was, with the Chaldean conquest, fulfilled to the last grisly 36:1 detail. Now, following the warning to Mount Seir, Ezekiel speaks once more to the mountains of Israel, but this time his words are a benediction. "Israel" embraces the entire country, not just the part that formerly comprised the Northern King- 36:2 dom. The enemy has greedily seized the "ancient heights." Ezekiel uses the word *bamoth,* usually translated "high places," or shrines for idolatrous worship, but here it refers simply to the hilltops, the predominant feature of the Palestinian landscape. (LXX reads "the old waste places.")

The entire land has become a "prey and derision" to other nations. The Hebrews and their God are objects of contempt 36:4 to all nations, especially to the Edomites who hold the southern hills. Again comes Ezekiel's message, apparently so obvious, 36:5 but then as now ever forgotten. Actions have consequences. Moral actions have moral consequences. Sometimes these con- 36:6 sequences are delayed, but God's "jealous wrath" is a factor in the world that neither His friends nor His enemies can afford to ignore. Some Christians today find this language offensively anthropomorphic. It may be presumed that the biblical writers knew they were using inadequate human terms to describe Him 36:7 who is indescribable. In this case Ezekiel means that the greed and spiritual blindness of "the nations that are round about" will, in due time, bring "reproach" upon these nations.

Now, at last, Ezekiel sings a joyous song, a song in which his hearers can take pure delight. The man who has predicted 36:8 "lamentation and mourning and woe" (2:10) to a huddled group of exiles predicts that "they will soon come home." He

sings to the hills which God promised Abraham, the hills for
which the lonely exiles were mourning as their captors jeered
(Psalm 137). He promises' that soon the hills will "yield your
fruit to my people Israel." We do not know the date when this
prophecy was composed. We suppose it was months or years
after Jerusalem's fall, when the first exiles had been joined by
the bedraggled remnant from the homeland. Ezekiel is secure
in his position as spokesman for God. And finally he is able to
proclaim a message where God's will coincides with the human
will of the exiles. God has not changed during this time. The
exiles have begun to change. They have taken to heart the message of repentance that underlies the prophet's many warnings.
We know, from sources other than Ezekiel, that Hebrew faith,
instead of flickering out during the exile, reached its greatest
intensity of light.

To the hills the Lord says, "Behold, I am for you." This contrasts with the warning, "behold I am against you, Mount
36:9 Seir" (35:3). Since the Lord made both the hills of Edom and
those of Judah, He does not distinguish between them in their
capacity as hills. He is concerned rather with the people who
live, or will live, on these respective hills. One group has proved
obdurately blind. The others are beginning to see the light to
which long they have shut their eyes. When man is in right
spiritual relationship with God, man takes proper care of the
good earth, and God blesses the land.

Looking far into the future, Ezekiel sees the day when the
desolation will be rebuilt. God's people will dwell on the hills
36:10 and in the valleys. Flocks and herds will multiply, and the
people will know more of God's bounty than ever before. Eze-
36:11 kiel apparently did not share the disdain for material goods
that some Christians have adopted from the Manichaeans. He
believed that the bounty of the earth is a blessing from God.
He has warned often enough that man can turn a blessing into
a curse by worshiping it rather than the Giver.

The war-torn land has been so barren and unproductive that
other nations have said, "you bereave your nation of children."
36:13 (See Numbers 13:32.) No longer will this reproach be made.
36:15 No longer will the land "bear the disgrace of the peoples." And,
conversely, when the people are living in the light of their faith,
no longer will the land "cause your nation to stumble." Famine

and pestilence are "stumbling blocks" in spiritual life. We, who can see the mechanism behind famine and pestilence more clearly than our fathers could, recognize that man invites these disasters when he abuses the soil. But Ezekiel looks beyond agricultural malpractice to man's total relationship with God. He foresees a time when the land will be rid of false deities, when men will hold right thoughts about God, and express these thoughts in right actions. Thus the farmer will farm his faith. He will care for the God given soil, the land will be productive, and cities can stand secure and well-governed. This is not to say that agriculture is the base of life. Faith is.

3. The Cleansing and the Increase of Israel, 36:16-38.

No other passage in the Old Testament approaches so closely the doctrinal message in the Epistle to the Romans as does the section now before us. The same basic ideas occur in the same order: sin, forgiveness, rebirth, a new heart, the Spirit of God as the ruling power in life, moral living as an expression of the new life, and finally, corresponding with Romans 11, God's revelation of Himself in history. Underlying both doctrinal passages is the same belief. Ezekiel expresses it by saying that God acts, "not for your sake . . . but for the sake of my holy Name." In another epistle St. Paul expresses almost exactly the same thought (implicit throughout Romans), "By grace you have been saved through faith; and this is not your own doing, it is the gift of God" (Ephesians 2:8). This emphasis, in both of these inspired authors, is thoroughly consistent with the doctrine of individual responsibility, which both of them stress heavily.

To the Babylonians—and to many in Israel—the fall of Jerusalem was proof that God had failed. Ezekiel is responsible to show that Israel's suffering is evidence of God's righteousness, not His weakness. Ezekiel has compared Israel with an adulterous wife (e.g., Chap. 16). Here he employs a different metaphor, describing Israel as "a woman in her impurity." Today we consider a woman's period as a complex biological function and no more. To the Hebrews in ancient time it was a genuine ceremonial "impurity." Whoever would touch a woman during this period, or would touch her bed or her chair, would himself be "unclean" (Leviticus 15:19-24). During this time, although a woman's husband would not touch her, his love for her would remain constant. This is Ezekiel's message, that God has acted in love.

God has been harsh in His dealings with Israel, yet His love has never wavered. Israel's impurity has been expressed in
36:18   idolatry and bloodshed, that is, in false religious practice that leads inevitably to immoral life (e.g. 22:4). Ezekiel lays a heavier stress upon ceremony than we do, but he does not separate religion and morality. His emphasis is always upon a righteous faith. In this regard Israel's failure has brought divine retribution. Understandably, God's justice has been misunderstood as
36:20   weakness. The "nations" among whom the Hebrews are scattered openly scoff at the God who was unable to prevent the exile of His own people. Ezekiel has contended that God's action is just. Now, as he looks forward to the return, he is
36:22   concerned still for God's justice. There is little in the present spiritual condition of the Hebrews to justify God's returning them from exile. God will do this for the sake of His holy name.
36:23   Through the very people who have defiled and profaned His name, He will "vindicate" His holiness before the eyes of the nations. The restoration will be outward evidence of God's
36:24   power. But for God to perform this act without some spiritual change among the Hebrews would be a denial of His justice. The idea that God must exercise a moral rule, even over His own people, was unheard of among the "nations." Among the Hebrews only a few had grasped the thought. Yet this unpopular idea is the burden of Ezekiel's message.

The land will not remain clean if filthy people dwell in it; therefore God Himself will cleanse His people. Ezekiel uses the
36:25   language of ritual to describe an inward and spiritual cleansing. He does not refer to any particular ceremony such as that in Exodus 30:17-21, but to the general idea of cleansing from ritual and moral impurity. The important matter is not the figure of speech, but the one who does the cleansing. In the ritual lustration mentioned above, "Aaron and his sons" would wash their hands and feet; and similarly in any other act of ritual, some human agent would perform the ceremonial act of cleansing. But in the washing of Israel, God will act. Rabbi Akibah wrote, "Happy are ye, Israel. Before whom do you cleanse yourselves, and who cleanses you? Your Father who is in heaven, as it is written, 'I will sprinkle, etc.' " (Babylonian Talmud, *Yoma* 9,6).

In earlier passages Ezekiel has said that his people have a
stubborn, rebellious heart, here described as a "heart of stone"
6:26 (e.g. 2:4; 3:7). God Himself will give "a new heart" and "a new
spirit" to those who have demonstrated their flinty obstinacy
in the past. He will replace the "heart of stone" with "a heart
of flesh." Ezekiel's use of "flesh" differs materially from Paul's.
To Paul "flesh," as contrasted with "spirit," means human
nature in alienation from God (e.g. Galatians 5:13-24). Ezekiel
is contrasting "flesh" with "stone." He means that the redeemed
"heart" will be soft and impressionable, responsive to God's
will. As for Ezekiel's distinction between "heart" and "spirit":

> "Spirit" expresses the ruling principle in the mind, the force
> that gives direction and motion to the current of thought and
> conduct, or that prevailing current itself. The heart is more
> passive and receptive and but responds to influences, the spirit
> is active and regulative.   —A. B. Davidson

Ezekiel sees man, God's creation, standing in right relationship with his Creator. The verse restates the message of 11:19,
but there it was followed by a threat, while here it is expanded
and developed as a benediction. In the following verses and
chapter, Ezekiel brings the idea of the "spirit" to its greatest
heights in the OT.

Both in 11:19 and here the Lord promises "a new spirit."
Now comes a significant addition that creates an understandable
6:27 confusion. The Lord promises "I will put my spirit within
you." Is "my spirit" a supplement to the renewed human spirit
or is "my spirit" identified with the "new spirit?" The selfsame
confusion runs through the NT discussions of the Holy Spirit
(e.g., Romans 8:9-11). Confusion in general is deplorable, but in
this matter it is simply unavoidable; for the only way man can
know God is at the point of interaction between the human
spirit and the Holy Spirit. In the nature of the case this interaction is not susceptible to introspective analysis.

The prophets did not understand the Holy Spirit as Christians do. Even so, there is a continual, logical progression of
belief in the Holy Spirit from the days of the prophets until
the Christian developments as described in the Acts of the
Apostles. Some Christians and some Jews have been distressed
to find the idea of the Holy Spirit expressed in the so-called
Dead Sea Scrolls. They are distressed because a "Christian"

doctrine was held among Jewish people before Jesus was born. Christian orthodoxy has always claimed that the faith is the fulfillment of what had already been revealed. Ezekiel and others planted the seeds of faith in the Holy Spirit. These seeds grew and developed among the Hebrew people. Before Jesus was born, an unknown psalmist wrote:

> From my youth thou has appeared to me in thy just wisdom,
>   and with firm truth thou hast sustained me.
> With thy Holy Spirit thou dost delight me,
>   and to this day thou dost lead me.
>   —Thanksgiving Psalm ix, 31-32, Millar Burrows,
>   *The Dead Sea Scrolls,* p. 412

Jesus amplified and developed the earlier teachings, but it was not until the time of Pentecost that the Church became fully aware of the Holy Spirit's meaning in human life. Even so, Ezekiel's terse catalogue of the "fruit of the Spirit" in 36:27-31 merits comparison with Paul's in Galatians 5:22-23.

The first blessing Ezekiel names for the redeemed nation is morality. The Lord promises that the people with a new heart will "walk in my statutes." This does not mean mere external observance of a code. Ezekiel has already stressed that regeneration must take place in the heart. The statutes of God are expressions of His Spirit. The NT condemns the abuse of a moral code. This has led some Christians to the ridiculous conclusion that there is no proper right use for God's statutes.

The second blessing is security. This blessing is expressed in both "material" and "spiritual" terms. The redeemed people

36:28 will "dwell in the land," and, more important, "you shall be my people and I will be your God."

The third blessing is purity, deliverance "from all your uncleannesses." This is not deliverance from the consequences of

36:29 evil, but from evil itself. The "new spirit" will keep the people from the frequent lapses into sin that Ezekiel has so colorfully described in Israel's past.

The fourth blessing is material plenty. There is a rough correlation between godliness and material success. He who has

36:30 dedicated his whole life to God will do his daily work as unto the Lord. He who considers his toil sacred will work diligently. When a nation is filled with men who place God ahead of success, the agriculture and commerce of that nation will flourish.

The fifth blessing is repentance, a continuous re-examination of self in the light of God, who acts for His own name's sake, not to reward Israel for his meritorious deeds.

6:31

The exiles to whom Ezekiel sang his song were few and miserable. By every earthly calculation their continued existence as a people was doomed. Their homeland was ruin and desolation. Yet Ezekiel speaks of the homeland both as geographic fact and as symbol, predicting the day when men will say, "This land that was desolate has become like the Garden of Eden."

6:35

The last two verses in the chapter spell out the crowning blessing, children. Among the Hebrews the normal human hunger for children was intensified by a faith that thought in terms of an ongoing people, personified as Israel. The scanty evidence indicates that the exiles from the Northern Kingdom, which fell in 722 B.C., had been assimilated into the life and culture of Babylon. They had lost their identity as "Israel." Ezekiel's contemporaries were anticipating the same fate. They feared that their children, born in Babylon, would come to consider Palestine a foreign land, the Hebrew tongue a strange speech, and the God of Abraham a pathetic fantasy of the dying generation. Against this background of despair, Ezekiel makes his bold prediction that God will "let the house of Israel ask me" for sons. (See 14:3; 20:3; 31.) He will respond to His people's cry. The "waste cities" will be filled with men as innumerable as the "flock for sacrifices" that once poured into Jerusalem for the high feasts. This is not a mere increase in numbers and political power. The comparison suggests that the increase will be in the number of those who are dedicated to the Lord.

6:37

6:38

4. The Return from Death to Life, 37:1-28.

This most familiar portion of Ezekiel, and one of the few beloved parts of the prophecy, completes the vision of national restoration. The chapter concerns the return of Israel to the Promised Land. It does not directly concern the Christian belief in eternal life. There is a close connection between the vision and the Christian belief in the individual resurrection, but the connection lies in the nature of God, not in the nature of the resurrection body. Ezekiel's essential message to the exiles is that God's gracious purpose cannot be broken even by the total destruction of the Hebrew nation. Similarly, Christians base

their belief in eternal life, not upon the immortality of the soul,
but upon the gracious purpose of God. Although the chapter
deals with Israel's revival as a nation, Christians, immersed in
any kind of despair, are justified in finding strength and courage
through Ezekiel's eerie vision.

What appeared a fantasy was fulfilled in history. Israel returned to the Promised Land. This impossible thing happened
because Ezekiel and men like him clung to the faith through
days and years of blackness and horror. In Chapter 1, Ezekiel
faced the black storm cloud, and saw the light. Here again he
faces the horror of the present darkness in faith, and God employs him as an agent to change the dry bones into living men.

a. The Valley of Dry Bones, 37:1-14.

The opening verse descriptive of the vision invites comparison with 3:22, where "the hand of the Lord" led the prophet
37:1 to the valley-plain. At that time the Lord delivered to the
prophet a message of doom. The doom has been fulfilled to the
utmost. Now, apparently in the same visionary valley-plain, the
prophet receives an oracle of hope.

The oracle is an extended, untranslatable play upon the
various meanings of the word *ruach* (breath, wind, spirit). John
3:5-8 is a remarkably similar play upon the meanings of the
equivalent Greek word *pneuma. Ruach* refers alike to the movement of air (e.g. Genesis 8:1), and the physical act of breathing
(e.g. Job 9:18). Job 17:1 reads "my spirit [*ruach*] is broken,"
where the meaning is "courage." In Judges 8:3 the word is
translated "anger." In Judges 15:19 the same word means "vital-
ity." *Ruach* means the rational mind (e.g. Genesis 41:8). It also
means the mind as seat of the senses, affections, and emotions
(e.g. Proverbs 25:28). From the meanings above, we gather that
ruach is "the force that gives direction and motion to the current of thought and conduct" (A. B. Davidson) or, as we would
say in modern English, "personality." Beyond all these earthly
meanings, *ruach* refers to the Spirit of God, the divine power
which, like the wind and the breath, cannot be seen, but by
which all the world is filled and governed, and by which men
are enabled to live righteously (Psalm 51:11-13; 139:1-24).

The English word "spirit" is derived from the Latin *spiritus,*
which had much the same bewildering variety of meanings as
ruach. In contemporary English, "spirit" rarely means "wind"
and almost never "breath." But otherwise its rich connotation

is practically unchanged. Usually the context makes the meaning completely clear. Ezekiel's contemporaries had no more difficulty with the precise meaning of *ruach* than we have with "spirit." But in the oracle one finds a confusion of meanings that is completely inseparable from the phenomenon being described, the interaction of the Holy Spirit with human spirits that are, for all purposes, dead.

37:2 The *ruach* of the Lord set Ezekiel down (in a vision) in the midst of the valley-plain, which was reminiscent of a battlefield after the buzzards had finished their work and bones had long bleached in the sun. The symbolism is unavoidably clear. Israel is dead. The nation of the future will be a creation of God's grace. When the Lord asks Ezekiel if these bones can live, com-
37:3 mon sense answers "No." Reverence forbids such a response.

The Lord directs His servant, "Prophesy to these bones." The verse is perhaps the keenest analysis ever made of the preacher's
37:4 work and his feelings about that work. The preacher sees the sheer, brutal hopelessness of the task spread before him, to preach the gospel to unhearing ears. When he realizes his complete inadequacy to the task, then he recalls that he is to proclaim "the word of the Lord," not his own message. The "word" comes from God, not from the preacher. Ezekiel has already explored the depths of hopelessness. He teaches us here, as in so many places, to open our eyes to the light of God whatever the surrounding darkness.

Addressing the bones the Lord says, "I will cause *ruach* to enter you, and you shall live." What is *ruach*? Horses and dogs
37:5 have *ruach* in the sense of "breath." Yet, if there is to be "spiritual" life on earth, there must be "physical" life. So here, as
37:6 Ezekiel speaks of "sinews" and "flesh" and "skin," *ruach* probably means "breath."

When the prophet spoke in obedience to the divine command, there was a "rattling." The word is usually translated
37:7 "earthquake." This is another indication that the restoration
37:8 is God's work alone, not that of the exiles. With incredible vividness, the prophet pictures the bones uniting and being clothed with flesh and skin. The dry bones become hulks with the form of men but lacking *ruach*, clearly, in this instance, "breath."

Once more the Lord commands, "Prophesy to the *ruach*." RSV translates "breath," but indicates by a footnote that "wind"

37:9 or "spirit" are possible meanings. To prophesy is to speak a word. A word implies both a speaker and a hearer. A current of air cannot hear. So, while the meaning includes "wind" and "breath," it likewise includes the Power who created man and "breathed into his nostrils the breath [a different Hebrew word] of life" (Genesis 2:7).

The Lord commands the prophet to call the *ruach* from the "four winds" (*ruchoth,* the plural of *ruach*). This is an idiomatic expression that means simply, from "every direction." Perhaps, as some commentators say, the idiom was so common that Ezekiel used it without thinking that it involved different senses for the same word in one sentence. More probably, it is a subtle suggestion that the Spirit of God is not localized in Palestine. The prophet is to call the *ruach* to "breathe upon these slain." (The verb "breathe" is the same that was used in

37:10 Genesis 2:7.) The prophet obeys the divine voice, the *ruach* enters the corpses, and they rise, a mighty army.

In explaining the oracle, Ezekiel quotes another cynical expression that circulated among the exiles. (See 18:2; 33:17.)

37:11 The reasons for discouragement were obvious enough. To most of the exiles it was Ezekiel's reason for hope that was so obscure. The exiles were spiritually dead, and they knew it. Their nation had been divided into two kingdoms, and each kingdom had been destroyed. There were fragments of what had been the Hebrew people in Babylon, Egypt, and doubtless in other countries, but the faith and hope embodied in Israel were dead. Ezekiel, as the prophet of God, is not called upon to conduct the funeral service, but to be the agent through whom the divine transformation will take place.

The figure of speech changes. In 37:2 the bones lay unburied on a battlefield. Here the Lord promises to raise His people

37:12 from their graves. There is no contradiction. In both cases Ezekiel is using figurative language for the spiritual, political death of a nation. The graves suggest the various lands in which the remnant was scattered.

"I will put my *ruach* within you." What does the word mean this time? What can it mean, but the Holy Spirit?

37:14 Israel's restoration lies beyond human power, but not beyond the power of God. Notice the sequence of promised events. First, "you shall live." Before the physical restoration can take place, there must be a renewal of faith. Second, "I will place you in your own land." The physical restoration will take place. And third, "You shall know that I, the Lord, have spoken, and I have done it." In 36:31 Ezekiel shows the returned exiles in bitter repentance as they think upon the past. Here he shows them lost in reverence as they acknowledge the power and the unshakable moral purpose of God.

b. The Reunion of the Two Kingdoms, 37:15-28.

Following the vision of national resurrection is a dramatic parable concerning the eventual unity of Israel. The cleavage within the Twelve Tribes extended back to times before the entrance to the Promised Land. Under Rehoboam's disastrous rule the nation that David had solidified fell apart (I Kings 12). Two tribes, Judah and Benjamin, became the so-called Southern Kingdom, while the other ten became the Kingdom of Israel, with the capital city in Samaria. The latter was sometimes called Ephraim because its first king, Jeroboam, came from that tribe. The two kingdoms shared a language and a faith from which, as Ezekiel has said, both often departed.

In 722 B.C. Samaria fell. Fragments of "Israel" survived in Palestine and clung tenaciously to the lost cause. In Jesus' time the hostility between Jew and Samaritan was bitter. The two groups held essentially the same faith, but the common inheritance, instead of uniting, divided them. Jesus transcended the hostility, a fact that doubtless contributed to His unpopularity with the Jewish leaders.

Ezekiel has referred to the entire community of faith as "Israel." Here he describes the fragmented Northern Kingdom as "Joseph" or "Ephraim." A stick is, symbolically, a scepter. The prophet joins two sticks, representing the two kingdoms, and holds them in his hand so that they appear to be one. The over-all symbolism is transparent. When God's "Hand" (or "Spirit") is regnant, His people will be united. (See Zechariah 11:7.)

Ezekiel does not raise the essential problem of church unity, which is that an organized community tends to become fat and sluggish, its rulers content to leave well enough alone. Israel needs an occasional Amos or Luther to jar people from their complacency and to call them back to first principles. The burning question before Christians in our era is how to ensure the splendid strength of Protestant dissent without the hideous weakness of Protestant fragmentation. The passage offers no help with the organizational difficulties involved, but it makes abundantly clear that the present broken state of Christ's body is not the will of our Heavenly Father, who wills rather that His people be "one fold and one Shepherd" (John 10:16 AV).

37:21
37:22
37:23
37:24
At the time of the prophecy, "Judah" and "Israel" were scattered to the four winds. It sounded ridiculous even to talk of their union, when there seemed to be no hope for their survival. But in faith the prophet looks forward to the day when the remnants will return to "the mountains of Israel." The people will be cleansed from their idolatry and their transgressions. The ancient covenant will be renewed. The restored kingdom will be united under the reign of "my servant David," who will be both "king" or political ruler and "shepherd" or spiritual ruler. (See 34:23f.)

37:25
37:26
37:27
So ends the prophecy of hope. Ezekiel has sounded the depths of doom and despair. Now, when those around him are still despairing, he looks to the distant scene and sees the Promised Land filled with a godly, united people. The concluding thought is one of permanence. Words like "everlasting" and "for evermore" ring out. God's sanctuary will stand in the midst of His people, and the nations will know that He sanctifies Israel.

Christians have not been loathe to adapt this passage to their own uses. Sometimes they have read into it allegorical meanings that the author never intended. Yet, with the warning in mind, Christians still can see foreshadowed here the reign of the Messiah over "Israel." In the NT, the Church is called "Israel," *not* "the new Israel." The Church is heir to God's promises. (See Romans 9:8; Galatians 4:31.) Here God promises that "Israel" will finally be united.

III. GOG'S CAMPAIGN, A PROVIDENTIAL ACT, 38:1— 39:29.

After the vision of Israel restored to his homeland comes a new element in Ezekiel. Ostensibly this is yet another prediction of invasion comparable with that in Chapter 21. But the difference between the two is almost complete. The former is prophecy, both in its major sense of speaking for the Lord, and in its minor sense of prediction. The latter is called "apocalypse," a Greek term that means "taking away a veil" or "revelation." In the former Ezekiel uses many ideas to symbolize Nebuchadrezzar's predicted invasion. Here the exact opposite is the case. The predicted invasion is the symbol. The thing being symbolized is an idea.

An apocalypse is a kind of writing in which ideas are embodied in pictured events, "splashed on a ten-league canvas with brushes of comets' hair." Most of the characters are painted much larger-than-life size. There is a vagueness and lack of historical fact that contrasts sharply with Ezekiel's usual clarity and precision. From the amount of apocalyptic literature that has survived, we gather that there must have been a great volume of it in post-exilic and early Christian times. Some of it was work of great depth, much of it tedious rubbish. The invasion of Gog is the earliest appearance of apocalyptic writing in the OT. For this reason Ezekiel is called "the father of apocalypse." His outstanding student, by far, is John who wrote *The Apocalypse,* or *The Revelation,* while exiled on Patmos.

If the above analysis be taken seriously, it eliminates altogether a question that has troubled many: who is Gog? The chief candidate is Gyges, King of Lydia in Asia Minor from 690-657 B.C., who was known as Gugu in the records of Ashurbanipal. Some think that Gog is a symbol for the Babylonian monarch, whose destruction is graphically portrayed. Alexander the Great (356-323 B.C.) has been suggested. Residents in Palestine had excellent reason to dread him. But if the passage is apocalyptic, the identity of Gog becomes meaningless. He represents every force of evil that is marshalled against God. It is immaterial whether or not Ezekiel had in mind a historical prototype.

The Interpreter's Bible proposes that we think of Gog in terms of the barbarian within the soul, the forces of unreason and brutality that try to overthrow what has been built in the name of reason and humanity. These forces cannot finally succeed. Even while human passions work to destroy society, God is stronger than all the powers of darkness.

Many have doubted that Ezekiel wrote the apocalypse. For example, if Alexander the Great were really the prototype of Gog, then Ezekiel could not well have described him. There are parallels (38:2-4; 39:1-2) that suggest to some two different visions, combined by an editor into one. Some have found alleged contradictions, as in 38:4 the Lord brings Gog forth while in 38:10 Gog himself devises the plan of conquest. In 38:18-22 Gog is overthrown by earthquake and storm, while in 39:1-2 he and his army are still violently active. In 39:4 Gog and his host are devoured by birds and animals, in 39: 11-16 their bodies are buried, and in 39:17-20 they are devoured once more. The incongruities are undeniable; however, "they are just what we find in other apocalyptic writings; the final catastrophe is looked at from various angles, without any attempt to trace a logical order in the sequence of events" (G. A. Cooke).

If the chapters be considered apocalyptic, then the obscurities and the incongruities become of little importance. The predicted invasion, instead of contradicting the final message of Chapter 37, reinforces the message. The preceding chapter ended with a thought of permanence—God's people are secure in the land. The invasion threatens their security, but cannot destroy it. Gog's attack is directed, not against Israel, but against the Lord Himself. It is God, not Israel, who crushes the power of Gog. Historians who seek to identify Gog with some ancient tyrant, and modern students who seek here specific predictions of some contemporary tyranny (they usually select Russia) are equally wide of the mark. The apocalypse deals with every threat to faith in every time and every nation.

A. Gog's Campaign, 38:1-17.

38:2 "The land of Magog" has aroused almost as much discussion as has the name "Gog." The discussion has been about equally productive of spiritual benefit. Here Magog is clearly the name of a country, somewhere back of the beyond. In Genesis 10:2 Magog, Meshech and Tubal are listed among the tribes descended from Japheth. Josephus identified the people of Magog with the Scythians (*Antiquities* 1, 6, 1). In Rabbinic literature, Magog is an individual who, with Gog, leads a hostile army against Israel before or during the Messianic age. In Revelation 20:8, John describes Gog and Magog as "the nations which are at the four corners of the earth"; words that, one would think, should have ended controversy among Christians. Both names, in the Revelation, are symbolic of every evil force, and so we should understand both in Ezekiel.

Meshech and Tubal have been mentioned previously (27: 13; 32:26). A few centuries before Ezekiel's time these savage peoples lived in the mountains north of Assyria, then gradually they were driven north toward the Black Sea. Like the other peoples to be mentioned in the following verses, they had little or no historical contact with the Hebrews. They were tribes or nations on the outer fringes of the world as known to Ezekiel and his people, more remote by far than the Hottentots or the Bushmen are remote from a dweller in Kansas.

The expression "chief prince" is somewhat unusual. The word "chief" is *rosh*. The natural translation of the phrase would be "prince of Rosh." Today we are aware of no land or people called Rosh in Ezekiel's time. Some have decided that the word refers to Russia and then have invested all the ensuing details with allegorical significance applicable only in the twentieth century. Although this interpretation must be rejected, it contains a considerable element of truth. At the moment of my writing, Russia is ruled by a powerful clique hostile to God who are doing everything in their power to destroy faith. The message of Ezekiel is clear, that the rulers of Russia or any other country may attempt to destroy the Church of Christ, but in the long run their efforts must fail. Wherever faith is threatened, from whatever source, Ezekiel's vision of Gog brings courage and strength to resist.

When men bring their puny strength to bear against the Church of Christ, they do not realize that they are acting as instruments of divine Providence. With painful vividness, Ezekiel describes Gog and his forces dragged to the conquest by hooks in the jaws. Prisoners of war sometimes thus were cruelly led off to their doom (19:4, 9; 29:4), but these are soldiers advancing confidently to the attack. Ezekiel means that divine Providence can work even through hellish agents. The picturesque details about the heavily armed cavalry and the ethnic composition of the invading host matter little. (See 27:10, 14. Gomer may have been located in Armenia or in south Persia.) Ezekiel's message is that any power fighting against God is His unwitting and unwilling instrument. The clearest illustration of divine Providence operating through God's enemies is the cross of Jesus Christ. Ezekiel, like the writers of the NT, teaches us to see that the hand of God is at work when events in the world seem—in our eyes—to be crushing and defeating Him.

The invading host will descend upon the people who have been through much tribulation and at last are dwelling se-
38:8 curely in their own land "in the latter years." One often finds such formulae in apocalyptic writing. Here Ezekiel clearly means the Messianic age. Beyond this, the date is intentionally obscure. "The allusion is vague, in keeping with the air of mystery which invests the great peril of the future" (G. A. Cooke). At an unspecified time, when Israel is dwelling se-
38:9 curely under the rule of the Messiah, Gog and his hosts will advance "like a storm . . . like a cloud covering the land." Thus quietly the author reminds us of the first chapter of his prophecy, where the threatening storm did not destroy, but instead revealed the light.

Some have sought to find a contradiction between verses 4 and 10. In the former, the Lord drags Gog, willy-nilly, to the battle. In the latter, Gog himself devises the evil scheme. Quite possibly several oracles were fused together to form this chapter, a possibility that makes no difference whatsoever to its meaning today. There is no contradiction; Ezekiel points to the nature of human responsibility in a world where God is sovereign, making the same contrast that one finds in Exodus 8:32, and 9:12.

The horror of Gog's invasion is heightened by the picture of simple, inoffensive people, quietly carrying out their sev-
38:11 eral tasks under the guidance of the Messiah, in their un-
38:12 walled cities at the "center [lit: "navel"] of the earth." If one must insist that Ezekiel was naive, then it is true that Palestine stood at the geographic center of the world known to him, however distant it was from the economic and political center of world affairs. But if one admits that Ezekiel was a thinker with depth of spiritual understanding, then one finds his description of Palestine to be, not the pathetic jingoism of a frustrated exile, but a sober statement of fact. Where the Messiah reigns over people who love Him and try to live in charity with their neighbors, there is the center of everything that is spiritually important on earth. Yet even while the
38:13 Messiah reigns, some people hate and despise Him. Ezekiel pictures nations afar off (see 27:12, 20, 22) cackling gleefully at the thought of Gog's invasion, with its promise of oppor-

tunity to profit from human misery. Invading soldiers would
acquire immense quantities of booty, which they would sell
cheaply to merchants who then would distribute it through
normal channels of trade.

Again Ezekiel develops the theme that God works amid
what man calls disaster, operating in and through the agency
3:14 of men who are indifferent or antagonistic to His will. Again
3:16 the prophet draws the contrast, "you will bestir yourself"—"I
will bring you against my land." Again he likens disaster to a
"cloud covering the land." And now he makes explicit the divine purpose in permitting a greedy ruler to attack an inof-
3:17 fensive people, that the nations may know the Lord, when He
vindicates His holiness through Gog. The passage is tied in with
the mainstream of prophetic thought. "You are he of whom
I spoke in former days by my servants the prophets in Israel."
(RSV treats this as a question.) Ezekiel may be referring to
Jeremiah 4-6, to Zephaniah 1:14ff.; 3:8, or to other prophetic
utterances that are no longer preserved.

B. The Defeat of Gog's Army, 38:18-23.

The defeat of the hostile invading force is described in the
full gory detail that contributes so much to the popular
3:19 neglect of Ezekiel today. The Lord speaks "in my jealousy
and in my blazing wrath," words that are susceptible to gross
misrepresentation. The meaning is not that God suffers from
human frailty and passion, but that when man violates the
3:20 moral law, God enforces it. His vindication is described as
a "shaking" at which all created sentient beings will "quake"
and the very mountains will topple. The imagery and the
3:23 language became part of the apocalyptic outlook, as did the
conclusion, "So I will show my greatness and my holiness and
make myself known in the eyes of many nations. Then they
will know that I am the Lord."

C. Another Oracle of Gog's Invasion and Defeat, 39:1-20.

The "name" is God's essence, not, as we understand the term
today, merely the label by which we refer to Him. The invader,
39:7 who defies all principles of morality to attack an innocent people, is profaning God's "name." Ezekiel has made abundantly
clear that Israel, under the Messiah, will lack human resources
for defense against so powerful an aggressor. When this in-

vader is defeated, then the "nations" will know that God has done it, and thus will know that the Lord is disclosing His nature and His purpose through His chosen people, Israel.

The size of the invading host, hence the extent of the Lord's victory, may be judged from the fantastic accumulation of

39:9 weapons left behind, sufficient to supply Israel with fuel for seven years. The location of Gog's graveyard raises a ques-

39:11 tion of no great spiritual importance. It is clearly marked "in Israel," yet the site indicated is beyond Ezekiel's geographical boundaries of Israel (47:18), "east of the sea." "Travelers" was the designation for the area northeast of the Dead Sea. Apparently one major valley was so named, possibly because it served as a main artery for traffic from east to west. This valley will be blocked by the vast accumulation of bones. (AV follows Rabbi Kimchi with the hideous "it shall stop the noses of the passengers.")

Since the land of Israel is holy it must be cleansed of all pollution, though it take a full seven months to complete

39:12 the labor. At the end of this time special inspectors will be designated to tour the countryside, seeking isolated bones for

39:14 the burial parties to convey to the Valley of Hammon-gog (multitude of Gog). This is not, as we would understand it, a sanitary measure, but a cleansing from the defilement of ceremonial pollution (36:18; Numbers 31:19f). The city Hamonah

39:16 (multitude), like so many other references in Ezekiel, is a symbol rather than a projected memorial city to be constructed near the burial ground.

Time sequence has been of little import in the apocalypse. In the preceding verses the dried bones have been carried off

39:17 to the valley. Here, immediately following the victory, scavenging birds and beasts gather together for their grisly feast on "the mountains of Israel." The "princes of the earth" are

39:18 described as sacrificial animals. At a Hebrew sacrifice, the

39:19 blood and the fat were not eaten but were offered to the Lord (Leviticus 3:7-17). At this gruesome "sacrifice" these sacred parts are not offered to God, but are devoured by buzzards and hyenas. Ezekiel's meaning is almost concealed from us by his nauseating symbolism. He speaks of Gog and his princes, not as individual men, but as symbols of evil. In the final victory of righteousness, the blood and the fat, that is, the basic life-force of evil, are utterly destroyed.

D. The Meaning of the Apocalypse, 39:21-22.

The meaning of the apocalypse is expressed cryptically. The essential words in the explanation are "glory," "judgment," and "hand." As the "nations" survey the grim results of God's "judgment," they will recognize that the "hand," which can smite with such devastating fury, is the "hand" that can encourage and guide and strengthen. Thus they will learn to see God's "glory" through His dealings with Israel. Is there, perhaps, a touch of irony in the following sentence? Ezekiel intimates that finally Israel will recognize that God is the Lord, but only after He has smashed the invasion. Israel is the agent through whom the "nations" will learn who is the true God. In the end, even the agent of truth will become convinced.

E. Final Reassurance of God's Righteousness, 39:23-29.

The concluding section bears little logical connection with the preceding apocalypse. It is rather a summary of Ezekiel's message to the exiles. The point of view is not that of the far distant future, but that of Babylon where Hebrews are dreaming hopelessly about the restoration. Ezekiel emphasizes again that the exile was not a failure on God's part, but a disclosure of His essential nature, righteousness. Again Ezekiel stresses that the punishment demanded by righteousness is not God's final work; for He will have mercy upon Israel. Again he stresses that this mercy is not earned by Israel's good works, but that it proceeds from the nature of God Himself. Again he repeats the promise of restoration, not only in a geographical sense, but a spiritual restoration of those who have fled from God and have been brought back into the warmth of His love. Again the Lord promises that Israel's experience will be a message, both to Israel, and to the "nations" that God is almighty, and that He calls all people to respond to His holiness. Again we see the basic message of the book, that we should open our eyes to God's light amid the storm clouds. "They shall know that I am the Lord their God *because* I sent them into exile." The section concludes with a repetition of the Lord's promise, "I will . . . pour out my Spirit upon the house of Israel."

IV. THE REDEEMED COMMUNITY, 40:1—48:35.

The concluding section of the prophecy is divided into four parts that deal with the Temple, the ritual, the "river," and the redeemed people who dwell in the land. The vision is dated twelve years after the last dated occurrence (33:21), and thus the section forms the last part of the book chronologically, except for the brief fragment in 29:17-21. No dates are given, either for Gog's invasion or for the construction of the Temple, but one has the feeling that the invasion is far distant, while the new Temple is to rise in the fairly near future. The literary style lacks the moments of exaltation that we have seen, but, happily, it is free from the sanguinary horrors that have filled the earlier pages.

The concluding section can easily be separated from the remainder of the prophecy without destroying the meaning of either; so it is quite possible that Ezekiel composed two books, which his editor compiled into one. Josephus said Ezekiel "left behind him in writing two books concerning these events" (*Antiquities,* 10, 5, 1). "These events" means the chain of circumstance leading up to the exile. If the first book is what we now call Chapters 1-39, and the second is 40-48, then the description loosely fits the first and does not fit the second at all. We must do what we often previously have done, admit our ignorance even while we are finding light upon our present darkness from the pages of the prophecy.

The concluding section bristles with difficulties, more so, even, than the preceding chapters. There are outright contradictions of the code of laws in the Pentateuch, a burden that Christians can bear with fortitude, but a grave strain to the faith of our Jewish forebears. There are words found nowhere else, hence of dubious meaning. The text has suffered many things from the hands of many copyists; so today it is in woeful condition. The literary style is prosaic to the point of aridity. Much of the symbolism is difficult to grasp. The Rabbis said that Elijah, when he came, would be able to explain such difficulties (Babylonian Talmud, *Menahoth* 45a). Like us, they had to leave unsolved many problems of interpretation.

More serious than any of the above difficulties, to the Christian reader, is the oft-repeated charge that in this concluding

section Ezekiel ignores the moral demands of faith and concentrates exclusively upon the ceremonial. Ezekiel has nothing
to say in this section about civil and criminal law, or about the
secular duties of the prince. The prophecy hitherto has dealt
with such matters. If, in the concluding section, the prophet
emphasizes one thing, it does not mean that he is unconcerned
about other important things. Ezekiel's thoughts are God-
centered, not man-centered, in sharp contrast to the prevalent
humanism today, when many believe that concern for human
need is all that matters in religious faith. Ezekiel believes that
the political, economic, and social restoration of Israel depends
upon the spiritual restoration. It is all-important that the
glory of the Lord return to Jerusalem and *dwell* there. In
the concluding section, Ezekiel is stressing the right worship
that must underlie right living. He does not think of worship
as a substitute for righteousness, but as a necessary prelude
to righteousness.

A. The New Temple, 40:1—43:27.

The ensuing section is not, the reader must often remind
himself, an exercise in architectural drawing. It is intended
to help troubled people to think magnificently about God.
Ezekiel has told how God is working out His purpose, revealing Himself to the "nations" through the very tribula-
tions of Israel. He has described God's grace in restoring His
people, who now are living in the light of God's glory. Through
the elaborate imagery of the Temple, the prophet shows a
people saved by God whose worship serves two purposes: to
praise the Savior, and to keep themselves in the light of God
by making "diligent use of the means of grace." Unrighteousness forced the glory of the Lord to forsake the Temple. Now,
as the glory returns to the Temple, the people will live in
righteousness. Today we draw a facile distinction between
"moral law" and "ceremonial law." To Ezekiel they are one.
Ceremony divorced from righteousness is a perversion of ceremony. If Ezekiel does not stress here the importance of justice
and mercy, it is because such moral conduct is implicit in the
ceremony he is discussing.

1. Introduction, 40:1-4.

The twenty-fifth year of the exile was 573 B.C. Probably

the unnamed month was Tishri, in the early autumn. The
40:1 tenth of Tishri was the Day of Atonement. This date marked
the beginning of a Jubilee year (Leviticus 25:9). So a date
that, to us, is a mere mark on a calendar, may have been to
our fathers a glowing symbol of hope. The "very high moun-
40:2 tain" to which the seer was transported in his vision was
Mount Zion. Its height is spiritual rather than geographical.
(Even the Mount of Olives, not far distant, is some three
hundred feet higher than Mount Zion. See Psalm 48:2; Isaiah
2:2; Micah 4:1; Zechariah 14:10.) The "structure like a city"
was, of course, the Temple. As will be seen, the Temple consisted of many buildings surrounded by a gigantic wall, hence
40:3 the Temple area would roughly suggest a city. "He"—the
Lord—brought Ezekiel to the Temple, where in the gateway
was waiting "a man" whose radiance showed that he was
more than mortal. He was a messenger of God. (The reader
will recall that the much abused word "angel" is Greek for
40:4 "messenger." See Zechariah 1:9-14; Revelation 21:15.) The
man, who carried in his hand simple measuring instruments,
charged the prophet to observe carefully, and to report what
he saw to the "house of Israel."

2. The Courts of the Temple, 40:5-47.

a. The Outer Court and Its Gateways, 40:5-27.

Surrounding all the courts and buildings of the Temple
area was a massive wall, pierced on three sides by mighty
40:5 gates, enclosing an area five hundred cubits square. The
length of the measuring reed is obscure. A traditional Jewish
explanation is: "The standard cubit of the Temple premises
was six, that of the vessels five hand-breadths" (Mishnah
Kelim 17, 10). A handbreadth is about three and one-half
inches; so the short cubit would be about seventeen and one-
half inches, while the Temple cubit would be about twenty-
one, hence the reed would measure about ten and one-half
feet. It was not uncommon in the ancient east for a country to
have two sets of measurements, of which the longer was "royal."
The use of a royal cubit for the Temple measurements may be
a suggestion that the new community will be founded not
upon human specifications but upon divine.

A cross-section of the wall formed a perfect square. The
wall was relatively low, thus allowing the people of the city

to see the altar and the Temple constantly. The almost incredible thickness of the wall is a symbol of the barrier between the sacred and the secular. (See 42:20.)

The Temple itself lay on an east-west axis, hence the main gate was that to the east. The seer describes this gate—really **40:6** a series of gate-houses—in considerable detail, since the south and the north gates were built upon the same floor plan. Seven steps led up to the other gates. LXX likewise gives this number for the eastern entrance. So the gateway and the entire court were on a level above that of the city round about. The threshold was the thickness of the massive wall, thirteen cubits wide and apparently provided with two pairs of heavy gates.

After crossing the threshold, the seer entered a corridor twenty-eight cubits in length, on either side of which were **40:7** guardrooms, each measuring one square reed. Each was separated from the next by a masonry jamb five cubits thick, pierced with a splayed opening that served as a window. Beyond the corridor lay an inner threshold, of the same dimen-**40:9** sions as the outer. The inner threshold widened into a porch, eight cubits in breadth, which was marked by massive "jambs," two cubits thick. These must have been projecting wall ends to which gates were attached.

Archaeologists have made extensive surveys of Megiddo, a military and administrative center of Solomon. In the wall of the palace-fortress they have discovered a gateway remarkably similar to that described by Ezekiel, even to the three guardrooms on the side. G. Ernest Wright describes this:

The architectural details of the entranceway are, in places, quite obscure, thanks chiefly to 40:14, but the overall symbolism is clear and glorious. The entrance is, symbolically, the gateway to a fort, with impediment after impediment to the

As one came up the ramp from the outside, he first entered a double outer gateway, undoubtedly covered to ensure easier protection. Passing through it and making a sharp turn to the left, he entered the main gate, likewise covered. Tremendous double doors of wood were standing open, though in times of danger they could be closed and barred. Behind them were three additional entries, each with its guardroom on either side, for further protection of the doors.   —*Biblical Archaeology, p. 132*

invading enemy. Even the splayed window openings might
serve as defenses. If the outer gate were smashed through, defenders could wedge protective logs across the corridor into
the openings while others attacked the invader from above.
The gates, the guardrooms, the windows, the heavy walls,
every architectural feature spoke the same word to the worshiper who entered the Temple.

> He who dwells in the shelter of the Most High,
>   who abides in the shadow of the Almighty,
> Will say to the Lord, "My refuge and my fortress;
>   my God in whom I trust."
> For He will deliver you . . .
>
>   —Psalm 91:1-2a

The gate-house was fifty cubits in over-all length, and
twenty-five cubits in breadth. Thus it was half the size of the
40:13   Temple itself. If it was roofed over, as seems probable, then
with its majestic walls and its paucity of windows, it must
have been quite dark. From the semi-obscurity of the porch-
40:14   way, the worshiper would step into the dazzling light of the outer
court, where the essential symbols are light, space, simplicity,
40:16   symmetry, separation and elevation. In contrast to the lavish
ornamentation of the Babylonian and Egyptian temples is
the stern, austere simplicity of Ezekiel's, kept from monotony
by occasional carved "palm trees."

A pavement, fifty cubits wide, upon which were thirty
chambers, bordered the court. The size and arrangement of
40:17   the chambers are not given. Some have inferred from 42:6
that these chambers were pillared structures three stories high.
While one cannot be dogmatic, such structures would block
the view of the altar and Temple, and would seriously interfere with the visual symbolism. Most students today believe
that there were ten one-story chambers on the south, east, and
north sides, adjacent to the outer wall, divided on each side
by the gateways into banks of five. They would be used for
private acts of devotion (Jeremiah 35:2ff.). In the corners
were large kitchens (46:21-24), where the Levites would prepare the peace offerings for the people.

The south and the north gateways were identical with that
to the east, which Ezekiel has so carefully described. The
visual foci for the worshiper standing in the outer courtyard
would be the great altar and the Temple. The next most im-

pressive feature would be the three massive gate-houses.
Ezekiel did not intend to symbolize the Holy Trinity. Yet it
is almost impossible for a Christian to read his description
thoughtfully without considering the divine unity whom
man must approach in three different ways.

b. The Inner Court and Its Gateways, 40:28-47.

In his tour of the outer court Ezekiel entered by the east
gate, then examined in turn the north and the south gates;
hence it would be natural for him to enter the inner court
from the south. The gateways to the inner court were replicas
of the outer gateways, except that the positions of the porches
were reversed. In each case the porch led to the outer court.
(40:30 is omitted in LXX and in many Hebrew manuscripts.
The measurements given cannot be applied to any architectural feature that has been mentioned.)

A flight of eight steps led to the gateways. Thus the inner
court was elevated above the outer, which in its turn was
elevated above the surrounding city. Since today we find it
almost impossible to discuss ethical matters without using
such terms as "higher" and "lower," we need not impute to
Ezekiel any crude geographical concept that God is "up
above." The symbolism of the steps is glorious and meaningful.

A room, the location of which is not clear, was set aside
for washing the legs and intestines of the sacrificial animal
(Leviticus 1:9). Modern scholars generally believe that it was
in or near the east gate. Rabbis Kimchi and Rashi both
thought that it was located within the north gate, since the
sacrificial animal was traditionally slaughtered at the north
side of the altar (Leviticus 1:11). However, Ezekiel does not
employ the usual verb for washing in the sacrificial ordinances. LXX interprets the verse: "Its chambers and its door-
ways and its porches at the second gate served as a drain."

Three types of offering are named. The peace offering is not
mentioned here. The actual killing of the sacrificial animal
probably would not be done on a table, but the meat would
be prepared for the altar upon one of the tables dedicated
to the purpose. The location, and even the exact number, of
the various tables is unclear. The "hooks" are likewise quite
debatable. This is the traditional Jewish rendering of the Targum. LXX gives a completely different translation: "They

shall have within a border of hewn stone round about of a span broad, and over the tables above screens for covering them from the rain and from the heat." If this be the correct reading, then the border was to prevent the sacred flesh from falling to the ground. And the screens overhead can mean only that the tables were located in the open, not in one of the gates, a sanitary precaution that would occur to any sane architect today.

40:44 Apparently two separate buildings stood near the north and south gates, within the inner court, for the use of two classes of priests. (RSV here follows LXX. AV follows the Targum, which gives a meaningless verse. JPS translates, "Without the inner gate were chambers for the guard in the inner court.") Near the north gate was a chamber facing south,

40:45
40:46 which was for the administrative priests, while that near the south gate, facing north, was for the Zadokite priests who alone might serve the altar. The distinction between the two classes of priests will be discussed in connection with 44:15-31.

40:47 The inner court was a square, one hundred cubits on each side. And at its center, at the geometrical center of the entire Temple area, stood a massive structure rising by three terraces to a height of twelve cubits, the altar.

The over-all symbolism of the inner court is obscure to us, until we refer to history. Solomon's Temple was surrounded by a great courtyard in which were located the royal palace and other buildings. In theory the holiness of the Temple embraced the palace. But in practice harem intrigues and political knavery from the palace defiled the Temple. (See 8:3.) Ezekiel's plan doubly protected the sanctity of altar and Temple.

Many Protestants today are carefully ignoring God's message to us through Ezekiel's placement of the altar. To Ezekiel the sacrifice was the central act of worship. To the Christian today, the Sacrament of Holy Communion is the central act of worship. Ezekiel placed the central act in the central place. In many of the beautiful Protestant churches that are being built today, the table of Holy Communion is crowded back against the wall at the greatest possible distance from the congregation, as was the medieval Roman Catholic custom. But today in the beautiful new Roman Catholic churches that are being constructed the sacramental table is brought away from the wall; so that the congregation, insofar as it is physically possible, surrounds the table. Ezekiel certainly is telling us that church architecture should be an expression of theology. Yet many Protestant building committees today seem perfectly willing to ignore the theological implications of what they are doing, and to settle for something that is merely pretty.

3. The Temple and Its Side Chambers, 40:48—41:26.

Directly to the west of the altar lay the Temple, a structure quite similar to the gate-houses but twice the size. Ezekiel has
0:49 previously spoken of God's exaltation by the symbolism of wings (1:6). Here he speaks of the same exaltation by means of steps. Seven steps lead to the outer gates, eight steps lead to the inner court, and ten steps lead to the Temple itself. The closer man draws to God, the more he is aware that God is exalted. Before or within the entrance stood two unnamed pillars reminiscent of those at the vestibule of Solomon's Temple (I Kings 7:15-22). We do not know whether these were free standing pillars or supports for the architrave.

The interior of the Temple consisted of three rooms, each twenty cubits in width. The first was the vestibule, twelve
41:2 cubits deep. Then came the nave (the word is sometimes
41:3 translated "palace"), forty cubits. And beyond this was "the
41:4 Most Holy Place," an exact square, twenty by twenty cubits. In Hebrew the superlative degree is expressed by a construction difficult to translate directly into English, whereby the "song of songs" might be translated, "the most beautiful song"; and "the Most Holy Place" is, literally, "the Holy of Holies," as it is called in LXX and in Hebrews 9:3. Despite Ezekiel's being a priest, he was not permitted within this sacred room. According to the Law, only the High Priest might enter the innermost sanctuary, and he only on the Day of Atonement (Leviticus 16). The celestial guide entered alone and made his measurements.

The width of the three Temple entrances has its own significance. The outer entrance was fourteen cubits, that to the
41:5 nave was ten cubits, and that to the Most Holy Place six cubits. The progressively narrower entrances and the incredibly heavy masonry walls alike speak the same message. In contemporary terms, God is "absolutely other." In ancient Hebrew, God is "holy," *quadosh*. Holiness is that unspeakable quality which permeates all true religious faith, before which,

as St. Augustine says, the soul is "both a-shudder and a-glow."
There is no contradiction between the central placement of
the altar and the utter isolation of the Most Holy Place. Worship is a human activity. But God, whom man worships, is
exalted beyond all human comprehension. He is holy.

The only windows in the Temple were covered. The only interior light was a lamp in the nave. So within, the Most Holy
Place must have been almost dark. In Ezekiel's prophecy
symbolism is rife, often to the point of confusion. But in the
Most Holy Place, where one would expect a symbol to signify
God Himself, there is nothing. The Ark, presumably, was
destroyed in 586 B.C. Ezekiel makes no attempt to reconstruct
it, or to place any other symbol within the Most Holy Place.
There is no tawdry statue carved by human hands, no sound of
man or nature, not even the light which God created; for
nothing can adequately represent God. He is holy.

Surrounding the Temple are three tiers of small "side
chambers," thirty in each tier. The purpose of these ninety
41:6 side chambers would be well known to Ezekiel's fellow-exiles.
We can but conjecture that they were used as the Temple
treasury (I Kings 14:26), and for storing equipment used in
the sacrificial ritual. The forest of footnotes in RSV evidences
a text so confused that we can follow the seer's meaning only
at a considerable distance. The description of the similar side
chambers in Solomon's Temple is much more intelligible:

> He made side chambers all around. The lowest story was five
> cubits broad, and the middle one was six cubits broad, and the
> third was seven cubits broad; for around the outside of the house
> he made offsets on the wall in order that the supporting beams
> should not be inserted into the walls of the house. . . . The
> entrance for the lowest story was on the south side of the house;
> and one went up by stairs to the middle story, and from the
> middle story to the third.   —I Kings 6:6, 8

Ezekiel is following a quite similar plan, with a slight re-
duction in the size of the chambers. In designing a heavy
masonry wall the architect today may employ offsets to provide a firm base for a superstructure that, relatively, is lighter.
The description of Solomon's Temple explains how the architect made symbolic use of these mechanical devices. The offsets served as bases for the floor and roof timbers of the side

chambers. Hence there was no opening, even for a good and worthy purpose, in the wall of the Temple. God's holiness is not a thing to be locked in a vault, like a casket of jewels or a bar of gold. Yet the symbol of the impregnable wall speaks a message that still is needed.

As was mentioned above (40:49), ten steps led up from the inner court to the platform upon which the Temple stood.

41:8 Since the platform was six cubits, or about one hundred twenty-six inches high, each step would rise more than a foot, half again as high as an ordinary step, a silent reminder to the priest who entered the Temple that he was ascending no common stairway, but that he was approaching the Holy of

41:9 Hosts. The platform extended five cubits beyond the massive,
1:10 five-cubit walls of the side chambers. Surrounding the platform on the north, west, and south was a broad passageway, twenty cubits wide, separating it from the chambers of the priests. Many students believe that the positions of verses 10 and 11 should be tranposed, since the latter deals again with the platform, five cubits wide, from which led the only entrances to the ninety side chambers.

Directly to the west of the Temple lay a large structure, seventy by ninety cubits. This must have been an open court-
1:12 yard, since so great an area could not have been roofed without many interior pillars, which Ezekiel almost certainly would mention. It may correspond to the court where horses, dedicated to the sun, had defiled the Temple area (II Kings 23:11). Although the function is not named, a ritual demanding animal sacrifice would require a place very close to the Temple, perhaps within the Temple walls, where sacrificial animals could be kept. Since a comparable enclosure had once been used to stable horses, it is possible that this area was the holding place for the bullocks and other animals that were to be offered upon the altar.

It is painfully difficult to picture the interior of the Temple, because the text describing it is so utterly baffling. RSV has,
1:16 in general, followed LXX. MT is filled with confusing details that have given rise to many different architectural interpretations, of little discernible spiritual difference. According to RSV, the interior of the entire Temple was paneled with wood and dimly lighted with windows that must have been above

the height of the three-story chambers, and even these windows were covered with curtains or shutters.

Contrasting sharply with the colorful, sometimes grotesque, ornamentation of the pagan temples, is the subdued, repetitive motif of the palm tree and the cherub. The palm tree is almost certainly the date palm, *phoenix dactylifera*, a tall (60-80 foot), stately tree, which grows with a single stem of uniform thickness, crowned with a dense cluster of leaves and, in season, thick clusters of dates. This palm tree attains a great age. The leaves (popularly miscalled "branches") are useful for roofing, for fences, and for mats and baskets. The fruit is sweet and nourishing, in a land where sweetness is rare and nourishment is scanty. Even the seeds are ground and used for camel food. All of these attributes help to explain why the palm was a symbolic feature in Solomon's Temple and other sacred buildings (I Kings 6:29-35). In later ages the great leaves of the palm symbolized victory and peace (I Maccabees 13:51; John 12:13).

41:18

Between the palm trees were carved cherubim, the symbolic meaning of which has already been discussed (1:5-25; 10:1-22). The cherubim had but two faces, unlike those Ezekiel saw in his earlier visions. The lion suggests the divine majesty, and the face of the man the divine reason. In Solomon's Temple were carved gourds and open flowers, and there was a lavish profusion of gold overlay (I Kings 6:14-32). Ezekiel mentions none of these symbols.

41:19

The only piece of furniture pictured in the entire Temple is "something resembling an altar of wood." Probably this is the Table of Shewbread (Bread of the Presence), upon which were placed twelve loaves of bread, signifying the dependence of the twelve tribes upon the divine bounty. Each Sabbath the loaves were replaced, and the old loaves eaten by the priests in the Holy Place (Leviticus 24:5-9). The table looked somewhat like an altar. In I Kings 6:20 it is called an altar. According to Exodus 40:22 the table stood in the north side of the Holy Place, not directly before the entrance. A beautiful passage in the Talmud explains that this "altar" is called a "table" to signify that, even if the Temple is in ruins, the table in a man's house can serve as the altar for purposes of atonement (*Berakoth* 55a).

41:22

The double doors complete the symbolism. Every detail of

the architecture has suggested that God is exalted and unapproachable. While measurements are not given for the doors, they must have been massive to harmonize with the structure round about. A door can serve to let a person in as well as to keep him out. The doors to the nave and the Holy Place were hinged, not once but twice. Probably the doors would swing on posts set in stone sockets. Then each leaf of the doors was divided into two leaves; with the inner leaf swinging upon some sort of hinges. The doors symbolize that, although God is unapproachable, by His grace man can approach Him.

4. Other Structures, 42:1-20.

On the north and south sides of the inner court were buildings that served as robing rooms and refectories for the priests. (See 46:19.) The prophet gives a detailed description of the structures to the north, since those to the south were practically identical. Although the description is detailed, the text is so corrupted today that we cannot plot the ground-plan with any confidence. Possibly there were four buildings, those closer to the Temple measuring one hundred by twenty cubits, separated by passageways ten cubits wide from the other buildings, which were fifty by twenty cubits. Thus the inner buildings were the length of the Temple itself, while the outer ones were but half its length. The structures rose to a height of three stories. The upper story was recessed on each side, to allow for "galleries" (the meaning of the Hebrew is unknown). The outer walls of the fifty-cubit structures formed the wall between the inner and the outer courts. The remaining fifty cubits were shut off from the outer court by a wall (literally "fence"), fifty cubits in length. To the east of the shorter buildings were entrances from the outer court.

The purpose of the buildings, happily, is more clearly understood than is the ground-plan. The one hundred-cubit buildings comprised "holy chambers" where the priests were to eat the "most holy offering." (See 44:29; Leviticus 2:3, 10; 7:9f.) Other types of offerings might be taken home for the priest to share with his family (Leviticus 10:14), but the most holy things were to be consumed only by consecrated persons in a consecrated place. In the fifty-cubit structures the priests were to change from their street clothing into their sacrificial vestments. And upon leaving the Temple area, they were required to put away their holy garments before returning to the mundane affairs of life. When one sees a Protestant clergy-man shaking hands at the church door in vestments that belong only in the pulpit, one wishes that this symbolism of Ezekiel's were better known or better heeded.

The heavenly guide led the prophet back through the east gate, by which they had entered the Temple area, and meas-

42:15
42:16
ured the perimeter of the surrounding wall. It lay four square, five hundred cubits on each side. Thus (if a cubit is twenty-one inches), it enclosed an area approximately eight hundred and seventy-five feet square, or almost eighteen acres. The peculiar form of the Hebrew has led some commentators, in-cluding the great Rabbi Rashi, to believe that the wall was five hundred *reeds* long, hence the enclosure was three thou-sand cubits square. Most students today believe that the guide, using his reed, measured off five hundred cubits. A brief,

42:20
cryptic note, that seems almost an addendum to the descrip-tion, summarizes all that has been said by the preceding sym-bolism. "It had a wall around it . . . to make a separation between the holy and the common."

The land of Palestine was considered holy, set apart to the Lord. The city Jerusalem was holy. Yet the Temple must be set apart from the city and the rest of the land because of its special holiness. As we have seen, the Temple itself was di-vided into different areas, each more isolated than the other. In later ages the Hebrew Rabbis classified the entire land under ten degrees of holiness (Mishnah *Kelim* 1, 6-9). It must be repeated, Ezekiel did not naively believe that stones and mortar could entrap God's holiness and confine it to one area from which it would seep gradually through the walls. Ezekiel has told us bluntly that the divine holiness forsook the Most Holy Place because of unrighteous life in Israel. He has told us that holiness must pervade the farm and the market place and the political councils of the land. The massive walls and gateways and the heavy doors of the Temple are symbols that God is exalted above man's highest reach, and yet He is near. Wood and stone do not create this exaltation or nearness. But they can make vivid in the human mind the glory and the closeness of Him who is symbolized.

The reader has a natural curiosity about the elevation of the Temple. He has examined the ground-plan carefully.

What did the upper structure look like? This curiosity must remain unsatisfied. The prophecy of Ezekiel is about God, not about a building. In giving the ground-plan of the building (which never was built), Ezekiel has told us much about God. From what he has said we can make, with comparative safety, three conjectures about the elevation he dreamed of. There would be an absolute minimum of ornamentation, the symmetry would be almost complete, and the over-all impression of the viewer would be that of strength.

5. The Return of the Glory of the Lord, 43:1-12.

The climax of the prophecy is expressed, not in words of thunder, but in the still small voice. Years earlier, Ezekiel 43:1 watched in a vision as the glory of the Lord departed from the Temple by the east gate (10:19). In a vision he had beheld the glory of the Lord in Babylon, far to the east of Jerusalem (1:28). 43:2 Now in a vision the prophet stands at the east gate as the glory of the Lord returns. Describing this climactic vision, Ezekiel does not enter into the lavish profusion of detail of the earlier accounts. He merely hints at the chariot and the cherubim, by saying that "the sound of his coming was like the sound of many waters" (1:24; Revelation 1:15).

In an apparent parenthesis, Ezekiel sums up his entire prophecy, "the vision I saw was like the vision I had seen when he 43:3 came to destroy the city, and like the vision which I had seen by the river Chebar." This has been the central message of the book. As the reader has been wading through rivers of blood up to the horses' bridles, he may have forgotten what Ezekiel is saying. It is God who judges. The judgments of God are harsh. But His judgments are redemptive, not destructive. During all the anguish of the exile, even while the beloved city was being gutted, Ezekiel was proclaiming through his tears, "God is in charge of history. Commit your life to Him here, now, in the valley of the shadow. He alone can turn darkness into light."

The glory of the Lord enters the hallowed area through the stately eastern gate. (See 44:1.) The Spirit carries the prophet 43:4 to the inner court, where he sees that after the anguished years of desolation, once more "the glory of the Lord filled the 43:5 temple." In a usage that is almost peculiar to this prophecy, the noun "glory" is construed with verbs of action, as if it were a person (3:23; 9:3; 10:4; 18; 11:23; 44:4; Isaiah 58:8). This usage

we may accept as a vivid figure of speech, so bold that most of
the sacred writers were unwilling to employ it. Ezekiel uses the
glowing metaphor, not so that we can solemnly chalk up
another grammatical peculiarity, but so that we will see and
be guided by the glory of the Lord when we are standing beside
the river Chebar. A charming passage from ancient rabbinic
writing vividly portrays the return of the divine presence
(*shekinah*) to the Temple:

> The Shekinah may be likened to a king who left his palace in
> anger. After going out he came back and embraced and kissed
> the walls of the palace and its pillars, weeping and exclaiming,
> "O the peace of my palace, O the peace of my royal residence,
> O the peace of my beloved house! O peace, from now onward
> let there be peace."
> —Midrash, *Rabbah on Lamentations,* Proem 25

The prophet expresses his reverence obliquely. While the
celestial guide stands beside him Ezekiel hears a voice speaking
43:6   from the Temple. The speaker is not identified, but certainly
He is the Lord, since He cannot be the messenger. The re-
flexive verb form means speaking to one's self. Thus the prophet
suggests that God is exalted immeasurably beyond man's highest
comprehension, yet God speaks, and man, if he will, can listen.
(See Numbers 7:89 where the same grammatical form describes
the Lord's communication with Moses.)

The Lord calls the Temple "the place of my throne and the
place of the soles of my feet." The unusual Hebrew construction
43:7   emphasizes the idea of "place." Ezekiel has told us, with every
symbolic device he could command, that God is not bound to
this place. He could agree with the thoughts expressed in
Isaiah 66:1:

> Heaven is my throne
> and the earth is my footstool.

And he could echo the spirit of Solomon's prayer (I Kings
8:27). Yet, in a particular place, a hilltop in Jerusalem, man is
uniquely conscious of God's universal presence. In the Temple
area structures of wood and stone sing aloud the message that
the Lord who is sovereign over all the world has chosen Israel
to be His redemptive agent on earth.

Ezekiel has followed tradition closely. His ground plan of the

Temple area has agreed in many important aspects with that of Solomon's Temple. But Ezekiel is no slave to tradition. Here he makes a bold break with the past. In earlier times the Temple was, in effect, the royal chapel. A weak or indifferent king would permit hideous abuses within the Temple area. "Harlotry" probably refers to the actual practice described in, e.g. I Kings 14:24, rather than to the symbolic usage in Chapters 16 and 23. Ezekiel has expressed often enough his belief that the presence of a corpse was a ceremonial defilement. Hence the burial even of kings within the Temple area was an abomination that could not again be tolerated (II Kings 21:18, 26).

43:8   Solomon's magnificent palace stood in the same great courtyard with the Temple, separated only by a wall (I Kings 7:1-12). Ezekiel draws a clear line of demarcation between "church" and "state." The Temple is to be independent of the "prince," whose palace is excluded from the Temple area. (Some believe that "thresholds" and "doorposts" should be translated as royal mausoleums in the vicinity of the Temple.) Let the Temple be

43:9   kept pure from defilement, and the Lord promises, "I will dwell in their midst forever."

     Now Ezekiel describes the meaning of the intricate symbolism in the two preceding chapters. God sent the vision of the

3:10   Temple in order that Israel might repent. The Temple as described represents both continuity with the good in the past and a divorce from the weakness and evil in the past. Because of Israel's sin the former Temple was destroyed. Because of God's grace (Ezekiel does not use the term), the new Temple will

3.11   rise after Israel has repented. The repentant people, restored to their fatherland and to their Temple, will require ordinances and laws for their spiritual government. The essence of the law governing the Temple is that "the whole territory

3:12   round about upon the top of the mountain shall be most holy."

     During the bitter years of exile the Hebrew faith reached its most glorious growth and development. In days when it was not possible to worship God in the Temple, our fathers explored in depth the meaning of their faith and their worship. And when a major political change made it possible for the exiles to return to Jerusalem, they carried back a revitalized faith and a purified worship. They had given serious heed to Ezekiel's vision.

6. The Measurements of the Altar, 43:13-17.

In 40:47 the heavenly guide showed Ezekiel the altar at the geometrical center of the Temple area. Perhaps, in the first draft of the manuscript, the ensuing description followed immediately, among the dimensions given by the guide. In the prophecy as it stands today, the passage serves to introduce the ordinances that concern the altar and the Temple. It is difficult for us to picture the altar, because we do not know the meaning of the technical terms that unquestionably conveyed a clear, precise picture to our fathers. To them, each minute detail had a meaning that to us is almost completely lost. (See Josephus, *Wars,* 5, 5, for the symbolic interpretation of many architectural features in Herod's Temple.)

In Exodus 20:24-26, the altar is to be of earth or of uncut stone, and the worshiper is not to approach it by steps. In Solomon's Temple the great altar was of bronze (I Kings 8:64). King Ahaz substituted for this a new altar (probably of stone), patterned after that at Damascus (II Kings 16:10-16). When the exiles returned, before they laid the foundations of the new Temple, they built an altar and "offered the daily burnt offerings by number according to the ordinance" (Ezra 3:4). The post-exilic altars were built of uncut stone (I Maccabees 4:47; Mishnah *Middoth* 3:4).

We may picture a large square masonry structure of uncut stone, rising by terraces to the great hearth. Since the hearth 43:13 was twelve cubits square, and each lower section projected beyond the upper by a ledge one cubit in width, the base, one cubit high, must have been a square eighteen cubits. The rim was a span either in height or width. The base was not con- 43:14 sidered a part of the altar, which rose two cubits to a ledge, then four cubits to another ledge, with a surrounding rim, and 43:15 then another four cubits to the hearth. Possibly there is significance in the two spellings of the word translated "hearth." The first time it is spelled *harel* (mountain of God), and the second time *ariel* (lion of God). These forms apparently were popular etymologies of a similar word that is derived from a verb meaning "burn." LXX makes no distinction between the two terms. From the corners of the hearth projected four horns, each one cubit high. Possibly these horns symbolized those on the oxen that were to be sacrificed. In the course of the sacrifice, the blood of the victim was dashed upon the horns (Leviticus 4:7).

If the dimensions above are correct, then the altar rose to a total height of twelve cubits, including the base and the horns.

3:16 The height, coupled with the twelve cubit square dimensions of the hearth, may have symbolized the twelve tribes of Israel.

The commandment in Exodus 20:26 is quite explicit, "you shall not go up by steps [*ma'aloth*] to my altar." *Ma'aloth* can

3:17 mean any sort of ascent. In the plural it usually means "steps." According to Josephus (*Wars* 5, 5), the *Letter of Aristas* 87, and the Mishnah (*Middoth* 3, 3b) the altar in Herod's Temple was approached by a gradual slope.

7. The Consecration of the Altar, 43:18-27.

In Exodus 29:36-46, a sacrifice, extending for seven days, is commanded, to "make atonement for the altar." The Exodus legislation and that in Leviticus 8 lay heavy stress upon the consecration of the priests, which Ezekiel does not mention. When Solomon's Temple was dedicated, the detailed account does not speak of atoning for the altar (I Kings 8). Here, cleansing the altar serves as the dedicatory act for the entire Temple. In this solemn ritual a thing of stones and mortar is set apart for the special service of God. It is lifted above the necessary trafficking of agriculture and commerce, immeasurably above the degradation and corruption that once defiled the land. It is cleansed from all taint of sin.

The speaker, probably, is God, who in verse 24 refers to Himself in the third person. He states the two purposes of the altar:

3:18 it is for burnt offering, a token of complete surrender to God, and for "throwing blood against it." Modern man, who thinks of blood physiologically, has difficulty understanding the meaning of the sacrificial ritual. In the Old Testament "the blood is the life" (Deuteronomy 12:23). It was permissible for a Hebrew to eat the flesh of certain animals, but under no circumstances could he consume the blood (Genesis 9:3ff.). Under the Law, the blood of an animal killed in the chase or slaughtered in the shambles was poured out and covered with earth, because God had withheld it from man's consumption, and kept it for purposes of atonement (Leviticus 17:1-14). In the gory practice of sacrifice, life was given vicariously.

Ezekiel is directed to conduct the atoning sacrifice, but this

43:19 probably is a convention meaning "Moses," or the officiating priest, as in the Exodus legislation. Ezekiel as an individual did not expect to see the rebuilt Temple. But he dedicated his life to the task of convincing others that Israel would see it. The faith would survive. The flames of devotion would rise once more from the altar of God, kindled by an unknown successor to Moses.

The reason why the Zadokite priests were chosen for service at the altar will be discussed in connection with the next chapter.

The officiating priest was ordered to give a bull to the Zadokites, who would slaughter it. The priest would fill a bowl with
43:20 blood from the victim and dash it upon the four horns of the altar, the corners of the ledge and the rim. (This differs slightly from the legislation in Exodus 29:12.) Thus everything within the space enclosed by the rim would be made holy. The sacrificial carcass would be taken to an undesignated spot within the Temple area, but outside the inner court, and there it would be completely burned. The priests received the flesh from private sin-offering or guilt-offering, but this sacrifice, for the atonement of the altar itself, must be totally consumed. In Exodus 29 and Leviticus 8, certain parts of the bullock were to be burned on the altar. This is not mentioned in Ezekiel,
43:22 who, however, adds the sacrifice of a he-goat that is not included in the other legislation. The cleansing sin-offering continues with the burning of sacrifices. Although the remaining part of the cleansing ritual is not completely clear, much of the
43:23 symbolism is. The bull or ram offered is to be "without blem-
43:24 ish." Only man's best is to be presented to God. The salt sprinkled upon the sacrifices is not mentioned elsewhere in the OT. (Leviticus 2:13 concerns a cereal offering.) From Mark 9:49 we gather that salt was customary in NT times. The salt was a sign of the covenant, originating possibly with the sacredness of oriental hospitality. "There is salt between us."

Over a period of seven days the ritual shall continue, to "make atonement for the altar and purify it, and so consecrate
43:26 it." The last verb is literally "fill its hands." It is used for the consecration of a priest, in the sense of imparting spiritual power and holiness to him, filling his hands with the responsibility of office (Judges 17:5). When the seven days are com-
43:27 pleted, then the regular,.ongoing ritual of sacrifice can begin,

"and I will accept you, says the Lord God." Ezekiel does not say, here or elsewhere, that God accepts His people upon the condition of their fulfilling the minutiae of the sacrificial ritual. He has made the point abundantly clear that ritual without righteousness is sin. He is looking forward to the day when a cleansed altar in a cleansed land will bear the sacrifices of a cleansed people. The ritual will serve as the focal point for the people's righteousness, and the means by which man may know the divine glory.

B.   The Worship of God in the Temple, 44:1—46:24.

Ezekiel has told us that the reality of worship takes place where a human heart recognizes the glory of God, even though it be beside the river Chebar. The ongoing ritual is the outward and visible symbol of worship. Sacrifice is to take place in the Temple, where of necessity it will be carried on by human hands. The following section deals with men who have the perilous duty of ministering to the Lord. Ezekiel outlines the spiritual qualifications of those who may serve at the altar, and he provides for their daily bread as they devote their time and energy to God's service in His house. While doing so, Ezekiel quietly smashes many centuries of religious and political tradition.

1.   The Closed East Gate and the Prince, 44:1-3.

In a dry, brief, almost parenthetical section Ezekiel announces a complete break with Israel's past. The Temple will stand independent of the "prince," who will be, not the master over his people, but their representative. Within the Temple area he will be accorded special recognition, as is the due of one who bears special responsibility, but he will be among the people who come to worship, not one who dictates the policies that govern the altar.

All of the above is expressed in a brief revisit to the east gate. Upon returning with the guide, Ezekiel finds the gate 44:1   shut. The guide explains that the gate must remain closed because the Lord has entered the Temple through it (43:4), 44:2   thereby forbidding it forever even to the passage of a cleansed people. The gate's being shut is an indication that the Lord will not again leave His holy place. In 8:16 Ezekiel spoke scathingly of the sun-worship that once defiled the Temple. Possibly it had been the custom to open the eastern gate at the time of the spring and the fall equinox, to let the morning sun shine through. Such a practice could be symbolic of faith; it could likewise be destructive to faith. Even the light of the sun may not pass through the gate henceforth; for God has entered. (The verse has likewise been interpreted mystically, to support belief in the perpetual virginity of Mary.)

The "vestibule of the gate" opens to the outer court. The prince may enter by this vestibule to partake of the sacrificial **44:3** meal within the eastern gatehouse. In this brief sentence Ezekiel is telling us two important things about the civil ruler. First, he has a sacred function, sharply divided from that of the priest. The prince is a minister of God. He who bears the lonely burden of government is accorded a unique honor, in being allowed to enter a holy place where others may not tread. While the priests and the people of the nation are partaking of the sacred meal that follows the peace offering, the prince, as representative of the nation, eats in the hallowed gateway alone. The long history of clericalism shows the wisdom of this provision. Yet, in the same sentence that announces the prince's freedom from priestcraft, the opposite principle is likewise stated. The prince is stripped of all the priestly functions and prerogatives that the kings of Israel had known (I Kings 8:22, 54, 62ff.; 9:25; II Kings 16:12f.; II Chronicles 26:16). His function is recognized as sacred, but he is excluded from the altar. Modern history is replete with examples demonstrating the wisdom of this provision likewise.

2. Qualifications for Service in the Temple, 44:4-14.

A priest is one who serves as a bridge between man and God. The Protestant, who holds to the priesthood of all believers, is not so far from Ezekiel as one might think. The Protestant agrees that certain priests should be set apart by ordination to perform certain duties within the church for which most of the other priests are not qualified. The layman-priest gives moral and financial support to these ordained priests, in order that they may give their full time and strength to the work of the organized church. He believes that his own work, be it ditch digger or bank president, is holy. It is a large part of his reasonable service to God. Much of the meaning in worship lies in renewed realization that the common task is holy. In sacrament and prayer the Protestant learns to see the holiness in washing dishes and plowing a furrow. Allowing for the differences in Christian terminology, these are exactly the principles that Ezekiel upholds. He does not picture a nation given over to worldly pursuits, with the priests going through an elaborate hocus-pocus to spread a film of holiness over the savage competition in the market place. Rather he pictures the consecrated nation expressing its worship of God through the ministry of selected priests. The prophet's thought is close to that expressed centuries later: "You are a chosen race, a royal priesthood, a holy nation, God's own people" (I Peter 2:9).

In one respect, Christians today must depart completely from Ezekiel's philosophy of worship. The idea of hereditary priesthood is repugnant. As will be seen, Ezekiel gives special prominence to the Zadokite priests, because of their loyalty in previous years. The Christian today would say, "The former loyalty is important. But this particular Zadokite might be a person of low moral character, a disgrace to his ancestors. And this particular person, whose ancestors sinned, might be a person of exemplary character, far more worthy to engage in the work of sacrifice than the Zadokite." Modern thought has so enthusiastically embraced Ezekiel's doctrine of individuality that we sometimes forget the complementary truth. Man is a member of society.

a. Foreigners, 44:4-9.

The consuming passion in Ezekiel's life is the glory of God. He has seen the glory by the banks of the Chebar. He has 44:4 taught us the lesson—which we are so unwilling to learn —that God's harsh judgments are designed to strip the blinders from the eyes of men and nations; so that we too may behold the glory. As, in the vision, Ezekiel approaches the Temple, he is once more overwhelmed by the glory of the Lord. The Christian today might well evaluate some expressions of modern piety in the light of Ezekiel's vision. Consider, for example, the ultimate blasphemy yet achieved under Protestant auspices in the alleged hymn, "Oh that will be glory for me."

The Lord commands Ezekiel to give his best thought to the question who may be admitted to the Temple and who shall 44:5 be excluded from it. This is not to keep any from the worship of God, but to see that the great sacrificial acts are conducted 44:6 by qualified persons. First named among the qualifications is

the will to put aside the ancient habit of rebellion, a term that
occurs frequently in the early pages of the prophecy, but only
rarely after Chapter 12. In the earlier chapters Ezekiel stressed
other aspects of this rebellion. Here he mentions one that, at
first glance, seems harsh to the contemporary Christian. "For-
44:7   eigners" are forbidden to participate in the Temple service.
One can appreciate that the sacrificial ritual demanded a great
deal of filthy drudgery. There was wood to chop and stack and
carry to the altar. There was the frequent task of cleaning
away the ashes. Someone must lug about the heavy sides of beef.
It was but natural to seek menials to perform such tasks. The
Babylonians used temple slaves. It appears that the Hebrews
followed the custom from the time of their entrance to the
Promised Land (Joshua 9:23, 27). In later years there was a
class of hereditary *nethinim,* or men given to the sanctuary, who
carried out the drudgery and were likewise assigned to administrative duties. The ancestral *nethinim* may have been "foreigners," prisoners of war assigned to work in the Temple, or hire-
lings. They definitely were not priests. Their service was a job,
rather than a keeping of the covenant (I Chronicles 9:2, etc.).
The objection is not that these people were of lesser clay—Ezekiel surely knew the story of Ruth—but that they were "uncircumcised in heart." God's covenant was with Israel, and Israel
alone must perform the covenant acts of sacrifice. Ezekiel considers it a profanation for a slave or hireling, who is not a sharer
in the covenant relationship, to take even a menial part in the
44:8   Temple ritual much less to keep "charge of my holy things."
Protestant performance in employing janitors, secretaries, or-
ganists, and others might well be scrutinized in the light of
Ezekiel's prophecy.
    Ezekiel is battling with one of the persistent dilemmas of
Hebrew thought. On the one hand, God is Lord of the entire
44:9   earth, who created both the "foreigners" and Israel. On the
other hand, it is absolutely necessary to keep pure the worship
of God. Most of the "abominations" to which Ezekiel has referred were introduced by "foreigners." The prophecy of Jonah
shows that God's love includes even the people of Nineveh. Yet
post-exilic regulations are so exclusive that they seem to ignore
the claims of compassion for an alien (Ezra 4:3, Nehemiah 13:
1-3, 30). In Herod's Temple was a wall beyond which no Gentile
was allowed to pass, upon pain of death (Josephus, *Antiquities,*

15, 11). To us, this seems tragically exclusive. To the Hebrew of
the time, it was inclusive. The Gentile was welcome to come
and worship, but he was not allowed to participate physically
in the sacrificial acts. Christian history in this regard has not
been so brilliant that we can afford to throw stones at any.

b. Levites, 44:10-14.

All the work that once was done by "foreigners" is assigned
to the Levites, who are stripped of their former prerogatives as
44:10 a punishment. The Levites were the hereditary priests of Israel
(Deuteronomy 18:1, etc). They did not have a tribal inheritance; their income was derived from their priestly duties. During the long years when the local sanctuaries were being progressively defiled by foreign customs, the Levites continued to
serve at the shrines, but, as Ezekiel had said, their service became
idolatry. When Josiah closed the high places, he executed some
of the priests (probably those whose abuse had been most flagrant), and attempted unsuccessfully to bring the rest to Jerusalem, to serve God at the central altar (II Kings 23:8f, 15, 19f).
This plan is supported by the legislation in Deuteronomy 12
and the subsequent chapters. But the plan broke down, quite
possibly because the Zadokite priests in Jerusalem were unwilling to admit a large number of newcomers to the service, and
revenue, of the central altar. So, before the time of Ezekiel,
there was a cleavage between the priests in Jerusalem and those
in the countryside. Ezekiel sharpens this cleavage. Because the
44:11 Levites had succumbed to idolatry, he assigns them to work as
44:12 gate keepers, butchers, and table servers. The Levites had been
44:13 unfaithful to their heavy responsibilities, therefore they must
"bear their shame."

If the reader will examine Ezra 2, he will discover that among
the forty thousand exiles who returned were more than four
thousand priests, but only seventy-four Levites. This would be
far in excess of the necessary number of priests, but far below
the necessary number of Levites. It was necessary to call to
service the *nethinim*, or hereditary Temple servants (Ezra 8:15-
20). One must conclude that most of the Levites were unwilling
to leave their comfortable homes in Babylon to go back to Jerusalem as menials. Yet, across the centuries, we must pay a silent
tribute to the seventy-four whose love for God led them to
return. They sought not the rewards but the privilege of serving
God. They lived their faith:

I would rather be a doorkeeper in the house of my God
than dwell in the tents of wickedness.   —Psalm 84:10.

c. The Zadokites, 44:15-31.

44:15 Zadok (just, righteous) was a young warrior who helped win
the kingdom of Saul for David (I Chronicles 12:28), and who
served as a priest during David's reign (II Samuel 15:24-
35). When a plot arose to dethrone David, Zadok remained
loyal to the King, while his colleague Abiathar supported the
usurper. When David learned of the plot, he instructed Zadok
and Nathan the prophet to anoint Solomon as king (I Kings
1:5-45). Solomon expelled Abiathar from the priesthood, leaving Zadok as the sole occupant of the high office (I Kings
2:26f.; 4:4). Thereafter the sons of Zadok were considered the
only legitimate priests in the Jerusalem Temple. Hence in the
Messianic age they alone may carry out the central sacred acts
44:16 of sacrifice and "approach my table," or eat the sacrificial flesh.

Josiah's reforms disclosed many abuses in Jerusalem, which
abuses Ezekiel has roundly castigated. The Zadokite priests were
chiefly responsible for instigating the reforms. Undoubtedly
there had been corruption in the Zadokite ranks (Jeremiah 8:
1-10, etc.), but on a comparative scale much less than among the
country priests, or, as Ezekiel calls them, the "Levites." The
reason for choosing the Zadokite priests, like that for rejecting
the Levites, is moral. Spiritual leadership must be entrusted to
those who have demonstrated their willingness to stand firm for
God. The Christian can accept the goal, even while rejecting
the hereditary method of attaining it.

The requirements that follow should be understood in their
deeper meaning. The ceremonial cleanliness of the priest sym-
44:17 bolizes the moral cleanliness of the people. He who engaged in
the sacred acts of sacrifice stood as representative of the faithful
throughout the nation. Linen was considered more clean than
44:18 wool, in part because it produces less sweat. Only that which
is clean may be worn in the inner court.

The prohibition against wearing ceremonial garments beyond
the inner court is expressed in a thought form baffling to the
44:19 Christian mind, as if holiness were a form of contagion that
could be transmitted by physical contact. And yet the baffled
Christian would, quite rightly, consider it a desecration to use
the table of Holy Communion for a writing desk or as a dinner

table. There is nothing wrong with writing or with eating, but the table, like the linen vestment, is set apart for a special purpose. Through the right use of dedicated objects, we are enabled to see that every act in life is, or ought to be, directed to the glory of God. Symbols of divine holiness should be treated respectfully. The garment, or the table, is not harmed by the common touch, but the person who treats it disrespectfully is harmed. In ancient time a person who touched a "holy" thing, except in the line of duty, must go through a ritual of purification. Rather than calling this a primitive superstition, we should re-examine our own practice of handling or mishandling sacred objects. (See Haggai 2:11ff.)

Shaving the head and letting the hair hang long and disheveled were both signs of mourning (Deuteronomy 14:1), but

44:20 here the ban is probably a reaction against some pagan custom
44:21 (Leviticus 21:5). The reason for prohibiting the use of wine is,
44:22 unfortunately, obvious (Leviticus 10:9). Ezekiel is more strict in regulating the marriage of priests than is the Torah (Leviticus 21:7), but far less strict than the post-exilic legislation, where not only priests, but all Israelites were forbidden to marry foreigners (Nehemiah 10:30; 13:23-30). The modern application is clear. The person who is engaged in the Lord's work needs a life partner who is committed to the Lord.

The priest's duties, apart from offering the sacrifices, are briefly mentioned. First, the priest is a teacher, charged with
44:23 responsibility to help the people discriminate "between the holy and the common" (Deuteronomy 33:10). The priest is a judge
44:24 who applies the principles of divine law in specific cases (Deuteronomy 17:9; 19:17). Thus Ezekiel makes explicit what has throughout been implied, that righteousness is to bind the redeemed nation together, not mere ceremonial correctness. Ceremony is the means by which righteousness is symbolized, by which the people are kept constantly reminded of the Lord's moral demands, and by which they are strengthened to do justly, to love mercy, and to walk humbly with God. Hence the priest is likewise guardian of the ritual observances.

Beyond the duties that directly affect the people, the priest must keep himself clean. The whole idea of defilement by con-
44:25 tact with a corpse is simply incomprehensible to us, but it was intensely real to our fathers (Numbers 19:11-19). Only for the closest of blood ties may the priest allow his natural human

affection to interrupt his ceremonial cleanliness. (See Leviticus 21:11.)

After defilement by contact with death, the priest must cleanse himself. Here RSV has followed the Syriac version. MT reads,
44:26 "After he is cleansed, they shall reckon unto him seven days." The normal period of cleansing was a week (Numbers 19:14). Thus, if MT be correct, the priest must wait an additional week before returning to his hallowed duties, and the other priests
44:27 are responsible to enforce this wait. The idea of a "sin offering" in expiation of the "defilement" caused by a natural display of affection is, like the rest of the passage, incomprehensible to the Christian today. In priestly language, any ritual defilement was a sin, and must properly be atoned for. The Christian today may discern, through the thought forms of another generation, that the spiritual leader must demand of himself and of his fellow leaders the highest standards of cleanliness from all that defiles.

In a culture where a man's place in society depends largely upon the size and location of his inheritance, the priests are
44:28 to have none, for God will be their inheritance (Deuteronomy 10:9). Even so, there must be provision for those who spend their time in the economically unproductive work of the Temple. The rough and ready procedures detailed in I Samuel
44:29 2:12-17 are bad, both for the spiritual welfare of priest and people. All must clearly recognize the portion that is rightly due the priest.

The "first" can be translated likewise as the "best." Offering one's best to God is good for the donor, though it carries grave
44:30 dangers for the human recipient. The practice of offering the first-fruits to the Lord extends back to the earliest days of the Hebrew people (Exodus 34:26). The cryptic phrase "from all your offerings" refers probably to the priest's part of the heave-offering (Numbers 18:19). According to the Mishnah, at every baking a private person was expected to give one twenty-fourth and a public baker one forty-eighth of the dough to the priests (*Halla* 2, 7).

The prohibition against eating anything that has died or been torn is puzzling; for this applied to all of Israel (Exodus
44:31 22:31). The Rabbis claimed, with more ingenuity than plausibility, that since the priests were permitted to eat some things forbidden to the rest of the people (Leviticus 5:8), they received

a special warning in all other respects to abide by the dietary law (Babylonian Talmud, *Menahoth,* 45a).

The injunctions above are quite general. They presuppose a long, clearly understood tradition that is to be carried on in the Messianic kingdom. Ezekiel has proposed—and will propose— breaks with past custom. But he envisions in the days to come the continuity of faith. Despite all failure in years bygone, despite the fall of Jerusalem and the razing of the Temple, God will carry out His covenant made with Abraham.

3. The Temple Area and Its Surroundings, 45:1-8.

After seeing the glory of the Lord in the Temple and hearing the responsibilities of those who minister there, the prophet receives a mandate concerning the division of the land among the several tribes. Here the subject is introduced, to be developed more fully in 47:13—48:35. Inevitably the reader will ask how much of what follows is symbol and how much was intended to be put into effect. The prophet's passion for symmetry as a symbol for divine holiness overrides mere considerations of geography, that most unsymmetrical science. The proposed division is, to put it mildly, not practical. It was never even attempted when the exiles returned. They understood the division as a symbol of the equal justice for which they must strive.

The Temple stands in, yet above, a holy land. The spacing of the buildings and the massive walls with their fortress-gates 45:1 symbolize the fact that God is separate, holy. Now the prophet adds that the Temple is to be within a large area "set apart . . . as a holy district." AV's "offer an oblation" is both more colorful and more faithful to the spirit of the passage. The Hebrew is *tarimu terumah,* "offer an offering." The basic meaning of the verb is "to lift up." Hence the noun suggests exaltation, something "lifted up" from the whole. It is used often in connection with sacrifices. The same noun denotes an offering to the prince (45:13, 16) or to the priests (44:30). The "oblation" is indubitably a "district," but it is more. It is the joyous sacrificial offering that a grateful nation returns to the Giver of every gift.

We do not know the exact size of the oblation. RSV probably is correct in following LXX rather than MT, since "twenty" fits with the following figures and "ten" does not. RSV translates "cubits" where the Hebrew does not give the unit of

measurement. AV gives "reeds," which would make the area described of truly colossal proportions. If "cubits" is correct, the oblation is a giant square, a bit more than eight miles on a side. At the exact center of the district, immediately surround-
45:2 ing the Temple, is a clearing fifty cubits wide, a further sug-gestion that the Lord is holy, set apart from the world, and yet at the very heart of the world.

The district is divided into three major sections. The first, enclosing the Temple, is a large rectangle ten thousand by
45:3 twenty-five thousand cubits, the holy portion for the priests. In an area of this size the priests would be able to provide for
45:4 many of their physical needs by practicing agriculture. Indeed, slight emendation will make the text read, "a place for houses
45:5 and for pasture lands and for cattle." Adjacent to the priests' estate is a similar area for the Levites. The forty-eight cities in which the Levites formerly dwelt were scattered about the land
45:6 (Numbers 35:1-8). The city Jerusalem is about three miles south of the Temple where it occupies an area only half that of the priests' estate or the Levites' estate, or one-fifth of the holy district. The whole house of Israel will be represented in the city. That is, any Hebrew may dwell there without tribal distinction.

It is easy to lose sight of Ezekiel's message in wondering about the real estate problems involved. Ezekiel is saying, symbolically, that man's central business is the worship of God, and that the city is an integral part of divine worship. Within the city the basic decisions of commerce, finance, and government are made. These activities are holy when God is the focal point of life.

Ezekiel has expressed his passionate hatred for tyranny in language so strong that he seems, at times, to deny the need for
45:7 secular authority. Here the prophet quietly demonstrates that the nation must provide the prince (not the Messianic King) with revenue sufficient for him to carry out his heavy responsi-bilities. He is assigned a tract twenty-five thousand cubits in width, extending westward from the holy district to the Medi-terranean and eastward to the Jordan. This tract is almost half the width of the area allotted in Chapter 48 to any one of the tribes.

In the austere prophecy we are considering, tenderness is conspicuous by its rarity, but here the Lord, speaking of the
45:8 civil rulers, calls them "my princes." (The expression is so

unusual that some believe it is a textual corruption.) Civil authority is from God. Only its abuse is evil. The prince has been limited in his activities within the Temple. But he has likewise a large area of responsibility where the priest may not interfere. In the Messianic age, when the religious leaders and the civil leaders are alike carrying out their duties, God will delight to call the rulers "my princes." With adequate revenue to support his office, the prince will not oppress the people. Rather, each in his own capacity, prince, priest, Levite, and commoner, will fulfill his part in the life of a nation that is dedicated to the worship of God.

4. Regulations Governing Temple and Community, 45:9–46:24.

Two chapters are given over to regulations, most of which deal with sacrifice. Without straining to squeeze the last drop of allegorical significance from each minute particular, we see the entire Hebrew sacrificial system as a preparation for the sacrifice of Christ upon His cross. We find in that system, not a religious gloss over business-as-usual, but the profound wrestling of dedicated pre-Christian souls with the issues of sin, forgiveness, and righteousness. Much of what Ezekiel says here is dated, but much of his message has a terrifying ring of modernity.

Ezekiel has scourged with scorpions the rulers who practiced "violence and oppression." In the Messianic age he enjoins the

45:9 princes to turn from the former abuses to the right. No one could quarrel with such a noble principle. But Ezekiel implements his injunction with a specific illustration that jarringly brings him to the twentieth century. "Cease your evictions of my people." In a large city in the United States poor people were evicted by the thousand from their ramshackle, dangerous homes. The slums were torn down. Bright, attractive new apartments rose on the land where there had been squalor. Rich people moved into the new apartments. The slum dwellers still are living in degradation, in other parts of the city.

The principle of integrity in commerce sounds strangely out of tune today, when business men openly encourage "planned

45:10 obsolescence." (The seller, not the buyer, does the planning.) The phrase means making and selling equipment so constructed that it will break down in a predictable period, and thus force

45:12 the purchaser to buy a new model. The shekel is a unit of

weight, not a coin. Even so, the managers of today's fiscal policy
might well consider the stern injunction "five shekels shall be
five shekels." "Creeping inflation" produces an illusion of prosperity, always at the expense of the poor. A pound of bread, or
steel, or almost any other necessity, costs far more today than it
did fifty years ago. The poor man finds that five pounds is three
pounds, or less.

45:13
The families of Israel, as well as the prince, will give their
substance to support public worship in the Temple. We have
no record of a Temple tax in pre-exilic days, though unquestionably some such arrangement must have existed. The ephah,
homer, and cor are as out-dated as the bushel and the gallon
will be in another twenty-five centuries, but the principle of
giving will continue to apply as long as people dwell on earth.
Ezekiel asks men in a simple agrarian economy to give propor-
tionately, each as he has been blessed. Today a farmer computes
his tithe upon the basis of his profits from farming. Ezekiel

45:14
rather directs the farmer to give one-sixtieth (1⅔%) of his
45:15
total grain harvest, 1% of his oil, and ½% of his flock "to make
atonement." The seer does not think of the Messianic age as a
time when sin will be impossible, though he does foresee the
end of Israel's passionate rebellion against God. Through "error
or ignorance" (45:20) people will sin, and the ongoing ritual
of sacrifice will be required to forgive them of past sins and to

45:16
guard them against future sins. The people will deliver the
Temple tax in kind to the secular authority, who will supply
45:17
the materials necessary for the several kinds of sacrifice on
various holy days.

The cleansed sanctuary must constantly be recleansed; for
even a renewed people will continue to be subject to human

45:18
frailty. Thus at the beginning of the year the priest must "make
atonement for the temple." Many students believe that the
atoning sacrifice was repeated at midyear. LXX reads, "in the

45:20
seventh month, on the first day of the month," which is inher-
ently more probable than the obscure reading of MT that RSV
follows. Ezekiel divides the year into equal parts—once more
symmetry as a symbol of holiness. Each part begins with a Day

45:23
of Atonement (if LXX is correct), then, after two weeks there
45:25
is a sacred feast lasting seven days, the Passover in the spring-
time, and the Tabernacles (*succoth*), in the fall. There are
serious discrepancies between Ezekiel's mandate and the basic

Hebrew law regarding feasts, as laid down in Deuteronomy 16 and many other places. Most surprising to us is the complete omission of The Feast of Weeks in the summer. Not at all surprising, though, is the tenor of the feasts as Ezekiel foresees them. No longer are they periods of rejoicing for divine deliverance and bounty; instead the focus of attention is upon sin and its forgiveness.

We have seen that the outer east gate was to be closed perpetually (44:1f.). The inner east gate was one of three that led
46:1 from the outer court where the people assembled to the inner court within which were located the altar and the Temple. This inner gate likewise was kept closed on working days, but on the Sabbath and the day of the new moon it was opened. The prince would enter the gate from the outer courtyard, and would go
46:2 through it to the threshold, from which point he could witness the sacrifice and worship the Lord, but he could not set foot within the inner court nor in any way participate physically in the sacrificial act. In this way Ezekiel recognizes the dignity and spiritual importance of the prince's office, while drastically curtailing his ancestral prerogatives (I Kings 8:22, etc.). The prince provides the materials for sacrifice from the revenues the people have given him and from the revenues of his own vast estate.
46:3 Thus he is considered the representative of the worshiping people who stand beyond the gateway.

More detailed regulations follow that again differ materially from those in the Torah (Numbers 28:9; 15). The worshiping
46:4 crowds are required to go straight through the Temple court-
46:9 yard; that is, he who enters by the north gate shall leave by the
46:10 south, and vice versa. The rule holds for prince and peasant alike. Perhaps we can see here more than wise traffic management. In the opening vision, Ezekiel emphasizes and re-emphasizes that the divine chariot-throne goes "straight forward" (1: 12). Perhaps he is suggesting here that the worshiper should not deviate nor turn back in the central business of his life.

Day after day, year in and year out, the solemn ritual proceeded. Every day a yearling lamb, without spot and without
46:13 blemish, was sacrificed. The materialistic critic today is prone to bewail the destruction of food in the name of religion. The complaint is almost without substance. Only a small part of the lamb's flesh was burned, the rest was eaten. Somewhat less than
46:14 a quart of grain, saturated in about two quarts of oil, was con-

sumed each day upon the sacrificial fire. This was a small price to pay for the sacred ritual that was the focal point of the life of a nation. To the Christian the sad part is that the sacrifice must be repeated endlessly. The Christian looks to a sacrificial act that has taken place once and for all time. The best Ezekiel could foresee was a daily succession of sacrifices, with a much larger sacrifice each Sabbath, even larger sacrifices on the feast days, and a semiannual recleansing of the Temple (Hebrews 10:1-10).

The Protestant today needs Ezekiel's emphasis upon the order and dignity and continuity of worship. But he must remember always the complementary truth that Ezekiel has emphasized in other places: physical acts of worship, by themselves, are not enough. "The sacrifices of God are a broken spirit; a broken and a contrite heart, O God, thou wilt not despise" (Psalm 51:17, AV).

Among the bewildering sacrificial technicalities is another evidence of Ezekiel's concern that faith and economics are in-
46:16 separable. If he does not foresee every possible financial abuse that could arise in history, still he sees and corrects an abuse with which Israel was painfully familiar. He allows the prince full possession of his estate with the right to bestow it upon whom he will, but not the right permanently to alienate it from
46:17 the royal family. In the year of liberty all property that has been given to courtiers shall revert to the royal estate (Leviticus 25:10). Since the royal family always will be provided for, the temptation will be less for a king to evict his people from their lands. Ahab's villainous act was clearly remembered, centuries later (I Kings 21:1-16). But other prophets than Ezekiel make clear that land seizure was still practiced in later pre-exilic times (Micah 2:9).

Two brief paragraphs seem to us out of place. The first logically follows the description of the priests' chambers (42:1-14).
46:19 At the western end of these chambers was a kitchen where the
46:20 priests were to prepare the food that they alone might eat. The other paragraph logically follows 44:10-14, where the Levites' duties are described. One of these duties is preparing the sacri-
46:21 ficial meals for the people. In each corner of the great outer
46:22 court is a smaller courtyard, the walls of which contain hearths
46:23 with openings on top for the cooking vessels. Thus, the sacrifice is slain at the altar in the precise center of the Temple area.

The flesh is then carried to the extremest parts of the Temple, where the Levites prepare it. Then it is distributed to the people, who eat it in the many rooms provided for the purpose. In this manner the priests conduct the central sacrificial act, and the entire nation participates in the sacrifice.

C. The River That Flows from the Temple, 47:1-12.

The preceding chapters have been a strange mixture of symbolism and legislation, where in many instances the student must admit that he cannot tell what is mandate, and what is symbol, expressed in terms of geography, architecture, or law. The reader recognizes instantly that the river flowing from the Temple is the stream of grace (the NT term that has no exact OT equivalent).

Water supply in Jerusalem has always been precarious, though apparently there was less shortage in biblical times than today. Some ancient writers mention a spring within the Temple area (*Letter of Aristeas* 4b, Tacitus *History,* 5,12). But no confirming archeological evidence has ever been discovered. "More probably Ezekiel's stream was suggested by the water-system *outside* the temple, which was connected with the Virgin's Spring near the N.E. of the present area; its water once flowed on the surface down the Kidron valley, until it was diverted, as it is now, through the tunnel under Ophel to the pool of Siloam" (G. A. Cooke. See also G. Ernest Wright, *Biblical Archeology,* Chapter 10).

The Temple faced toward the east. Before the Temple stood the altar and the seldom used inner gateway. Beyond this lay the outer gateway, closed always to human traffic. Beyond the gateway lay the Valley of Kidron and the Mount of Olives. Between the Mount of Olives and the Dead Sea is the Arabah, some of the most inhospitable, barren, desolate land to be found anywhere in the world. This is a gigantic geological fault, at the bottom of which lies the Dead Sea (the Salt Sea in the Bible), 1292 feet below the level of the Mediterranean, the lowest known spot on the surface of the earth. To one familiar with its rugged contours, the land east of the Temple is a symbol, as vivid as the Valley of Dry Bones (37:1-3), of man's spiritual failure.

One would expect, from the infinite care Ezekiel has given to express his vision of the Temple, that the stream would be at

47:2   its greatest depth and width in or very near the sacred area. Not so. Ezekiel is concerned with the holiness of the nation, at the heart of which he believes must be the Temple, with its stately ritual and elaborate ceremonial. However, the faith is lived not in the Temple but out in the redeemed land. A small spring, at the south of the Temple threshold, ripples through the courtyards and beneath the outer wall, just south of the eastern gate. The rare Hebrew verb translated "coming out" is related to the noun "flask." It suggests that, immediately beyond the Temple wall, the stream is comparable to what one could pour from a bottle. JPS translates "trickled forth."

As usual, Ezekiel's symbol of the divine goes "straight forward." At a distance of about a quarter-mile to the east, the

47:3   guide leads the prophet through the small stream, which is "ankle deep." The Hebrew is "water of the extremities" (*aphesim*). Perhaps it would be more accurate to understand water so shallow that it could but wet the soles of the feet, though most of the versions translate "ankles." However, the Greek translators, in despair of an accurate interpretation, transliterated the word, giving *apheseos*, or "redemption." Hence the early Church fathers referred to this passage in speaking about the waters of baptism. In the largest sense they were correct; for Ezekiel is describing the stream of grace, of which baptismal water is an expression.

Successive measurements reveal progressively greater depths until, about a mile and a third from the Temple, the stream

47:5   is a vast river, too deep by far for wading. Turn back and re-
47:6   read Chapter 8 for the full impact of the angel's question. There an angelic guide shows the prophet the abomination that fills Jerusalem, and asks repeatedly, "Have you seen this, O son of man?" Now the question no longer is an accusation, but a cry of victory.

Like Moses, who was forbidden to enter the Promised Land (Deuteronomy 34:1-4), Ezekiel is not taken the full length of

47:7   the stream, even in his vision. He sees the transforming power of the river along a short part of its miraculous course, but the

47:8   celestial guide must describe to him the farther shores, as the river flows across the Mount of Olives and down into the desolate Arabah. The Dead Sea, at the depth of the Arabah, is dead because it has no outlet. The natural salts of central Palestine are carried to the Sea by the Jordan and a few other tributaries.

The water evaporates and the salt remains in a concentration at which almost no life can survive, except in the brackish areas near the inlets. Today we would say that only a miracle could sweeten the waters of the Dead Sea. Ezekiel is talking about such a miracle, to be wrought in stagnant and lifeless human hearts by the healing grace of God.

Where the waters of the river flow there will be life. Engedi is a settlement surrounding a hot spring, about 612 feet above the Dead Sea level, on the west shore, at about the midpoint of the Sea's length. Eneglaim is perhaps a village now called Ain-el-feshkah at the northwest end of the Sea. A caravan route led down the western shore between the barren cliffs and the barren waters, across the salt flats and through the tortuous canyons. Here, where the camels can with difficulty find their way, will be a scene of useful, productive work; for the once-dead sea will abound with fish, like the Mediterranean, and fishermen will sail its waters and dry their nets along the shore.

Many critics believe that the verse concerning salt marshes is an insertion by a late editor or scribe. However, this thought is in keeping with the rest of Ezekiel's vision; for he is ever intent upon preserving the best of the past, while destroying the evil. The Dead Sea then, as today, provided an inexhaustible supply of that vitally needed mineral, salt. In the Messianic age, when much will be added, this good will not be taken away.

Out in the redeemed land, through which flows the stream of grace, will be endless fertility and health. Christians are familiar with this verse in its NT setting (Revelation 22:1f.), where John makes the significant addition, "the leaves of the tree were for the healing of the nations." Though Ezekiel has told us that Samaria and even Sodom will be redeemed (16: 53-63), his emphasis here is upon Israel's redemption and security in ages to come. Others than Ezekiel were to emphasize the message that Israel's true mission is not so much to be saved as to be the bearer of divine salvation to the nations.

D. The Boundaries and Allotment of the Land, 47:13—48:35.

Many critics believe that the original prophecy ended where the celestial guide described to Ezekiel the miraculous stream of grace. But the canonical Book of Ezekiel continues the lengthy discussion of territorial allotment begun in 37:15-28 and developed in 47:13-23. There are marked similarities and marked

differences between Ezekiel's allotment and the others recorded
in the Bible. Ezekiel ignores the grandeur envisioned in the
extension of the land from the Nile to the Euphrates (Genesis
15:18, etc.). The territory west of the Jordan was lost to Israel
when the Northern Kingdom fell. Ezekiel does not attempt to
recover it, even in an idealized vision; hence his allotment differs materially from that in Numbers 34:1-15, and Joshua 15:
1-4. However, he accepts the tradition that the Mediterranean
is the western border of the Holy Land, which did not become
historical fact until the second century B.C. More significant,
Ezekiel emphasizes the concentration of Israel, not the world-
wide rule of the Messianic King (cf. Isaiah 40:5; Zechariah 9:10;
Psalm 72:8; 80:11; 89:25, etc.).

From a practical viewpoint, Ezekiel's division of the land
would have been almost impossible to implement. It ignores
mountains and fertile plains, rivers and caravan trails, the geographical facts with which civilization must cope. The returning exiles made no attempt to carry out this portion of the
prophecy. Should we then conclude that these final words are
meaningless for the reader today? By no means. Here Ezekiel
expresses an ideal in geographical terms. To the community of
faith the prophecy says as clearly as it can be said, "Put yourself
in the hands of God. Let Him set up boundaries and jurisdic-
tions. Forget your ancient rights and jealousies." As the fragmented Church of Christ is talking today about union, Ezekiel's
message is sorely needed.

The Christian may disagree, at first, with Ezekiel's strategy
for achieving the rule of God in the hearts of men. Jesus said,
"Go therefore and make disciples of all nations" (Matthew 28:
19). The other Son of Man directs Israel to stay at home, to
develop spiritual life there to the utmost, and to resist manfully
all alien defilement of the faith. The Christian who shrugs off
Ezekiel's strategy might well look at recent urban Protestant
history. In laudable zeal to reach the suburbs, Protestants have
all too often allowed their work in the city to suffer and sometimes to die. Ezekiel's strategy is just as much part of God's plan
for the church as the global strategy of Isaiah and Jesus. If the
church is not spiritually strong at home, the world-wide reach
will be futile.

Of the twelve tribes, Levi would receive no portion, since the
Levites were provided for in the sacred area (45:5). However,

47:13 the tribe of Joseph was divided into two great families, Ephraim and Manasseh, each of which was considered a tribe. Thus the land divinely promised as an inheritance to Israel—apart
47:14 from the sacred area and the princely domain—is divided into twelve similar parts. The allotment in Numbers 26:54 is far more realistic, in that the size of the tribe determines the size of the territory. The ideal of equal justice, which Ezekiel here is expressing, has always been extremely difficult to approach, and has seldom been reached in history.

The idealized northern boundary begins at an undesignated spot on the Mediterranean, and is traced with a precision that
47:15 we may well admire, even though the confusion of the text and our ignorance of the places named make it impossible to reconstruct the line today. Hamath was the northern extent of Solomon's conquest (II Chronicles 8:3f.). This was a Hittite stronghold about 120 miles north of Damascus. The "entrance" probably was the valley between the Lebanon and the Anti-Lebanon mountain ranges, through which the road led to Hamath. The "entrance" was the traditional northern limit of the Holy Land
47:17 (Numbers 13:21; I Kings 8:65). The northeastern point of the boundary was Hazar-enon (Numbers 34:10), a border village
47:18 between Damascus and Hauran, possibly to be identified with the modern Kirystein. From this settlement the boundary runs
47:19 southward, down through the Jordan valley to the Dead Sea. Trans-Jordan is not included in the redeemed land. Tamar is a place south of the Dead Sea. The Romans had a garrison in a village named Thamara on the caravan trail to Elath. Possibly this is Tamar, the traditional southeastern corner of the Holy Land. The southern boundary is described more fully in Numbers 34: 3-5, and Joshua 15:1-4, where the term Kadesh-Barnea is used for the border village. The name suggests a spring at which a controversy was settled. A sweet water spring, now called Ain Kadis, about fifty-one miles south of Beer-sheba has been suggested as the location. The Brook of Egypt is now called the Wadi el Arish. This is a dry river most of the time that swells suddenly and dangerously when the rains fall on the Sinai Peninsula. The valley runs northward, and opens into the
47:20 Mediterranean about fifty miles south of Gaza. The western boundary of the land is, of course, the Mediterranean Sea. The land enclosed within these boundaries is roughly a trapezoid, perhaps one hundred seventy-five miles in length, almost one

hundred miles on the southern edge and less than thirty miles on the northern. Among the nations of the earth it is insignificant in size, wealth, or power. Yet this tiny land has exerted an influence upon history that never can be measured. In historic fact—not only in Ezekiel's grand visions—God has revealed Himself through persons and events in the land of which the prophet speaks.

47:22   Ezekiel's lack of world-wide sympathy has often been condemned. Yet in the sensitive matter of territorial allotment he goes far beyond the finest tradition of his people. The legal code enjoined high standards of hospitality, liberality, and charity in dealings between Hebrew and resident alien (Deuteronomy 10:18, etc.). But it stopped short of considering the non-Hebrew a full citizen of the land. Ezekiel allows the resident

47:23   alien who settles and raises a family to receive an allotment of the Holy Land on the same terms as a native son of Israel.

The division of the land among the tribes is a symbol of equality, not a politically or economically feasible design. The

48:2-7,   trapezoid, north and south of the sacred oblation, is divided
23, 29   into twelve strips, apparently of equal width. Reading from north to south, the allotments run: Dan, Asher, Naphtali, Manasseh, Ephraim, Reuben, Judah, the Oblation, Benjamin, Simon, Issachar, Zebulun, and Gad. Some of the tribes are not in the same positions that they occupied in pre-exilic times (Joshua 14-19). We cannot always see the reasons for the change.

Apparently the guiding principle in the arrangement is the maternal descent of the twelve tribes. (See Numbers 2.) The descendants of Israel's two wives, Rachel and Leah, are placed closest to the sacred area, while the descendants of the concubines, Bilhah and Zilpah, are placed at the farthest extremeties of the land. (See Genesis 29-30.) Since there were five "Leah" tribes (excluding Levi) and three "Rachel" tribes, and since the sacred area lies in the southern part of the Holy Land, a completely symmetrical division would be impossible. The allotment is a symbol of distributive justice and not a working blueprint; so probably it is but coincidence that Manasseh and Ephraim, the descendants of Joseph, are in a fertile area, while Zebulun and Gad are in a bleak desert.

The earlier description of the sacred area (45:1-8) is apparently a condensed version of that given here. And this version

48:8   contains its fair share of difficulties. For example, the word

48:9
8:14
"portion" (*terumah*) in verses 8 and 9 is used in quite different senses. Here is made explicit what was implied in the earlier description, that the Levites' estate may not be sold or exchanged or in any way alienated from the Lord's service.

The layout of the city was but suggested in 45:6. Here a more detailed description is given. Before the exile, Jerusalem

8:15
lay to the south and west of the Temple. In Ezekiel's bold vision, the city is moved about three miles to the south, while the priests' domain encompasses the area that once was Jerusalem. In the vast sacred area, twenty-five thousand cubits on each side, the southern rectangle, five thousand by twenty-five thousand cubits, is the city's. The city itself is to lie in the middle of the

8:17
8:18
8:19
rectangle, surrounded by an open park. The rest of the rectangle is given over to gardens, which the "workers" of the city shall "work." (The same word is used, once in its noun form and once in its verbal form. Ezekiel foresees no laziness in the Messianic Kingdom to come [I Thessalonians 4:9-12].)

The city is laid out as a square, each side of which is about a mile and a quarter in length, or a total circumference of about

8:30
five miles. Josephus reports that the outer walls of Jerusalem in his day totaled thirty-three stadia, or about four miles (*Wars of the Jews*, 5, 4, 3). Josephus likewise reports the irregular shape of the city, necessitated by the steep hills and valleys in southern Palestine. In other words, we have here the last glorious symbol in Ezekiel, not the practical design of a city planner. The visionary city represents order, stability, and security in the age to come. The twelve gates imply walls behind which the faithful will live in peace. Through the gates they will pass to the surrounding parkland, to the nearby gardens and fields, to the Temple, and to the remainder of the Promised Land.

The city is a symbol for all Israel, as expressed by naming each gate for one of the twelve tribes. On the north and the

1,33
south sides are the gates named for the tribes descended from Leah, including Levi. Ezekiel has dealt harshly with the past sins of the Levites, but in his final symbol of the redeemed people dwelling safely behind the fortress walls of the redeemed

8:32
city, all of Israel is represented. On the east side, possibly the place of greatest honor, are the descendants of Rachel. The two tribes Ephraim and Manasseh are represented jointly at the

8:34
"Joseph" gate. Dan was the son of Bilhah, Rachel's handmaid. On the west side are the descendants of Bilhah's other son,

Naphtali, and the descendants of Leah's handmaid, Zilpah. Since the city symbolizes each of the twelve tribes, it symbolizes the nation. The glory of the Lord fills the Temple. But the stream of grace flows *from* the House to transform the entire land. Ezekiel's final concern is not with the stately ritual at the altar, but with the lives of people as they go about their daily tasks. And so the last symbol in the prophecy is the new name given to the redeemed city. The name tells us that the people of Israel are purged of the rebellion that once filled their hearts, the Spirit has breathed upon the dry bones, and the stream of grace has done its transforming work; for "the name of the city henceforth shall be, The Lord is there."